PRINCESS
MARGARET

PRINCESS MARGARET

A Life Unfulfilled

NIGEL DEMPSTER

MACMILLAN PUBLISHING CO., INC.

New York

Macmillan Publishing Co., Inc.
866 Third Avenue, New York, N.Y. 10022
Collier Macmillan Canada, Inc.

Library of Congress Cataloging in Publication Data
Dempster, Nigel.
Princess Margaret, a life unfulfilled.
1. Margaret, Princess, Countess of Snowden,
1930–   2. Great Britain—Princes and
princesses—Biography.   I. Title.
DA585.A5M3323   1982   941.085′092′4   [B]   81–20854
ISBN 0-02-530800-9   AACR2

10 9 8 7 6 5 4 3 2 1
Designed by Jack Meserole
Printed in the United States of America

For CAMILLA, LOUISA
and EMILY

ACKNOWLEDGEMENTS

I would like to thank Peter Townsend for his help in checking facts and for his permission to quote from his autobiography *Time and Chance*; Colin Tennant for his unstinting hospitality in the Caribbean and for his considerable aid; Jocelyn Stevens for introducing me to Princess Margaret in 1970 and for his courtesy in assisting my researches; Jon Bradshaw for bringing me to Mustique and without whom this book would never have been started; Roddy Llewellyn for the loan of personal material and, especially, Dr. Anne Smith for her enthusiasm in editing my manuscript.

For Princess Margaret, who has never sought to impede my possibly unwelcome project, I have only praise and admiration.

FOREWORD

By blood almost a Queen, by nature not quite a Princess, Margaret Rose of York, as she was born on August 21, 1930, would dearly have loved to sit on the ancient Throne of England. But that unique and intimidating destiny awaited her elder sister and, despite childhood cries of "I'm heir apparent to the heir presumptive," Margaret's role in relationship to the Monarchy was one of ever-decreasing importance. The realization served to erode her innate sense of royal responsibility, fating her to a wilful course which led ineluctably to an emotional and physical solitude for which, like a terminal condition, there are no cures and the remissions are temporary.

To assuage the nascent feelings of a child who was being educated to be second best, Margaret was spoiled by her parents who, not fully appreciative of her needs, indulged her urges. While Elizabeth was tutored in the history of the Constitution and the innermost mechanics of State, Margaret learned to sing, to dance and to play the piano, discovering a talent to please and developing a performer's ego to match it.

As virginal as her eponymous ancestor, the elder sister chose to marry her first love, sowing seeds of envy in the younger which were to be reaped in bitterness: the burgeoning happiness of one reflected in the growing anguish of the other.

With her breeding, wit, and unusual beauty, Margaret soon attracted the attentions of the blue-blooded bucks of her generation and became the cynosure of every warm-blooded romantic seeking dreams to color the monotony of post war Britain. She was the unchallengeable superstar of her era and she revelled in her position. Her actions and attitudes were copied in the sureness that her style was faultless, and when she began to smoke in public places, she liberated a million ordinary women who had been condemned for doing the same. By carousing in night clubs, she demonstrated that there was no guilt in pursuing self-gratification, even if ration books were the passports of the day. High society justifies its existence, and perpetuates itself, as a guardian of excellence and a patron of achievement and, for a while, Margaret was its symbol.

Hearing only praise and receiving only flattery, Margaret came to believe there was nothing beyond her grasp, but when that belief was put to the test, she found herself thwarted. It came as a cruel shock, and those who conspired to administer it were never forgiven. Margaret salvaged her *amour propre*, but learned that no matter how high you are, the Constitution and the Law are above you.

Half her life now has been spent with three men. Group Captain Peter Townsend, the wartime fighter ace whose nerve, ironically, deserted him at the critical juncture of their affair; Antony Armstrong-Jones, 1st Earl of Snowdon, who aspired to regal estate only to reject its constraints at last, and Roderic Llewellyn, seventeen years her junior and of precarious means, whom she described simply as her "companion," but who was not welcome in any of her sister's homes. For several years it seemed that Llewellyn was the man Margaret had chosen to see out her days with, but in March of 1981, while on holiday in Mustique, he surprised her by announcing that he had fallen in love with a woman of his own age and they intended to wed. Alone again, and while her contemporaries are securely ensconced in the mellow middle years of married life, Margaret in any case has been living with the conviction that she must face the future without a husband. "I don't see myself ever marrying again," she has always answered queries on the subject. "As a member of the Royal Family one is used as a figurehead and, being the sister of you-know-who, it would put her in a difficult position. Anyway, it would probably be too much of a bore!"

If her beloved father, King of Great Britain, Northern Ireland, and the British Dominions beyond the Seas, Defender of the Faith, Emperor of India, had lived longer, she would have married a duke and never have been tainted by divorce. Her two children almost grown-up, Margaret claims she has no ambitions and lives in solitary splendor in Kensington Palace, rebuilt in 1690 by Sir Christopher Wren, busying herself with a dwindling number of official engagements concerned with the charities she heads, like Barnardo's and the N.S.P.C.C., the two regiments of which she is Colonel-in-Chief, and, closer to her heart, her presidencies of the Girl Guides Association, among whose ranks she and her sister spent many carefree childhood days, and the Royal Ballet, a compensation for failing to fulfil her fantasy of becoming a dancer. She is aware that many of her duties will be taken over when the young members of the Royal Family come to involve themselves in public life and says "Old Auntie won't be needed then."

On any other level, Margaret's life would be deemed to have been one of qualified success. Her tragedy is that, judged against the exemplar of her sister's achievements, it is seen to have been a studied failure.

PRINCESS
MARGARET

THE DEE VALLEY HAD NEVER SEEMED SO TRAN-
quil or beautiful as Princess Margaret looked out from the
bedroom she had known since childhood, on the morning of
her fiftieth birthday. Beyond the still green cap of firs, the
beeches fused into heather-clad hills teeming with grouse.
The bright blue skyline was dominated by "the hill," as the
Royal Family call Lochnagar, a rugged peak which had inspired Prince Charles to write a boyhood fairy tale for his
younger brothers. Here, Margaret's first innocent flirtations
with Peter Townsend, her father's Equerry, had taken place
under the benevolent eye of the King and here, too, that
hopeless love had finally died when, eight years later, she
had accepted the marriage proposal of Antony Armstrong-
Jones.

Since the War, Margaret had spent all but a handful of
her birthdays at Balmoral, the Aberdeenshire estate described as "dear Paradise" by Queen Victoria. It had been
bought by Prince Albert in 1852 out of the Sovereign's
£385,000 annual Civil List allowance, to be rebuilt as a cas-
tellated mansion in the Scottish baronial style, in white gran-
ite, now faded to a dour gray. Victoria had established a
calendar which took the Royal Family to Sandringham for
Christmas, Windsor for Easter and Balmoral in August; King
George V had rigidly maintained the schedule, and to the
Duke of Windsor the migration was "as regular, as unchange-
able, as permanent as the revolution of a planet in orbit."
Queen Elizabeth has not altered it.

The day followed a routine set by the late King. The guns, mostly attired in the gray-green tweed of the royal estate, would leave at 9:30 A.M. for the butts on the hill over which the plump young *Lagopus scoticus*, the only game bird indigenous to the British Isles, would be driven by beaters for a day's sport. Shortly afterwards a group of riders, led by the Queen or Princess Margaret on polished mounts, would set off for two hours along the endless trails and paths. Occasionally, Prince Charles would join his grandmother, Queen Elizabeth the Queen Mother, by the swift-flowing Dee to fish its well-stocked waters. The day's bag of grouse and succulent salmon would supply the Balmoral dining table and in the late King's day, grouse would be on the menu every night from the Glorious Twelfth, the opening day of the season.

At noon the ladies would join the guns at the butts for a picnic lunch, and in the early evening, before changing for dinner, the party would congregate in the bow-windowed drawing room, with its view of the hills and its tartan-covered walls with their Landseer engravings, to chat about the day's activities, enjoy a drink or play cards. For dinner the men with Scottish connections would dress in kilts, jabot and jacket while the others wore black tie, and the meal would end with the Queen's pipers deafeningly blowing their way round the table playing traditional airs like "Scotland the Brave," one of Margaret's favorites. The ladies would then retire to the drawing room—where a fire was always made up ready to be lit should the temperature drop —leaving the men, temporarily, to their port and cigars. When the men rejoined them, they would play party games like charades, and later, sipping a whiskey and water, Margaret would sing to her own accompaniment at the piano, drawing on her extensive repertoire of evergreens and theatrical hits of three decades.

On this particular day, Margaret, who was with her children David and Sarah, had received congratulations from their father as well as a telephone call from Roddy, who was in London working on a gardening commission. One of the points of discussion that evening, before Margaret and her sister went alone to a knoll in the woods to light a bonfire to mark the occasion, was the arresting quality of the official photographs taken for the occasion by Norman Parkinson, which all the newspapers had published to mark the half-centenary, accompanied by unusually sympathetic captions.

Balmoral was her bedrock, one constant in an uneven life, and Margaret, as she went alone to bed, would have reflected that it did not matter that Roddy was not present to share her special day. To have invited him would have been a sign of official approval from the Queen for a still controversial relationship and in any case Roddy, with whom she would shortly celebrate an anniversary of their own at the Peeblesshire estate where they had met and fallen in love seven years previously, had no connection with the brooding beauty of Balmoral. Their love belonged elsewhere, among the bougainvillaea and humming birds of the West Indies, where tender moments had been shared under tropic nights, away from Parliament and the press which criticized and ridiculed her attachment. Looking back on half her lifetime, she may well have thought, "If I had been allowed to marry Peter, I am sure we would have been happy. And who knows? It might have lasted."

The first member of the Royal Family to have been born in Scotland for more than three hundred years, Margaret had come into the world at twenty-two minutes past nine in the evening at Glamis, the gloomy scene of Duncan's murder in *Macbeth*, and, by legend, haunted: the heir to an Earl of Strathmore had been produced so hideously deformed that he had been locked away for a lifetime in a secret chamber.

That night was one of the wildest weather: driving rain, rolling thunder, and flashing lightning which far outshone the Glamis beacon when it was lit the following evening as the estate workers toasted the new arrival from barrels of beer provided by the Laird. With dark hair and dark blue eyes, the infant was said to take after her father, Bertie, the Duke of York, who had married Lady Elizabeth Bowes-Lyon, daughter of the 14th Earl of Strathmore and King-horne, on April 26, 1923. She was christened by Dr. Cosmo Lang, the Archbishop of Canterbury, who sprinkled water from the river Jordan on her head over the lily-shaped font in the Buckingham Palace Chapel on October 30. Her god-parents were her uncle David, the Prince of Wales (who was absent), the Princess Victoria, Princess Ingrid of Sweden, Lady Rose Leveson-Gower, sister of the Earl of Strathmore, and the Hon. David Bowes-Lyon, her mother's brother.

Four years and four months younger than her sister Eliza-beth, Margaret took over the green-and-white decorated nursery on the top floor of 145 Piccadilly, her parents' official London home which was a short stroll across Green Park from Buckingham Palace, where the girls' grandfather, George V, King Emperor over five hundred million subjects, lived in austere magnificence. Soon after the age of one, Margaret was saying "mama" and "papa" and, to the evident satisfaction of Elizabeth, "sis." The Princesses had a Scottish governess, Marion Crawford, to see to their upbringing and a nurse and two nursery maids to take over at 6 P.M. The family's holidays were taken at Birkhall, a small estate in Aberdeenshire given to the Duke of York by his father in 1931, at family gatherings at Windsor Castle, or at Sandring-ham in East Anglia.

Near to the Throne but not groomed for power, the easy-going Yorks had no intimation of the momentous events to come when the King died at Sandringham on January 20, 1936 and the Prince of Wales became King Edward VIII. Although they were aware that the problem of Mrs. Wallis Simpson loomed ever larger, the York household never conceived that David's infatuation would create a crisis so cataclysmic that it would lead to his abdication. But on December 11, 1936, the King, who was never crowned, renounced his Throne, broadcasting the stunning decision to the nation from the study of Fort Belvedere, his old home near Ascot, which he shared with the twice-divorced Mrs. Simpson, whom he was to marry the following June in France. Accepting the heavy burden, Bertie became King George VI and moved his family within hours to Buckingham Palace, where for Princess Elizabeth, the grooming to be Queen one day began in earnest: prayers were offered up for her in church services and both daughters learned to curtsey to their parents in public. In private Princess Margaret was heard to moan: "Now that Papa is King, I am nothing."

When Bertie was married, his father wrote to him: "You have always been so sensible and easy to work with and you have always been ready to listen to my advice and agree with my opinions about people and things that I feel we have always got on well together. Very different to dear David." So it was with father and elder daughter. Elizabeth was the King's pride, his heir, and she quickly learned to play her part with the same sense of duty and devotion that had been instilled in him. Margaret, however, entranced her father with her vivacity, her pranks and her sense of comedy. She appealed to the lighter side of his nature and was able to both soothe and entertain him after stuffy, tedious days of Court procedure by playing and singing. He encouraged her gift of mimicry, for he enjoyed fun at others' expense, and the courtiers, who were the closest and therefore the butts of her take-offs, were glad that she was the younger.

With the King closeted with Elizabeth for long periods to initiate her into her future role, Margaret spent more time with her mother, who regretted that circumstances had prevented an ordinary upbringing for the children. Scots mother and Scots-born daughter shared many characteristics. Margaret was taught thrift from an early age (the Bowes-Lyons were not among the wealthiest aristocrats), and had impressed upon her the sort of manners which would ensure that she treated her inferiors, especially servants, with courtesy. Under her mother's benevolent eye she developed a more extrovert personality than her sister, and was not reproved for being less conscientious or dutiful.

It was to instil "ordinariness" into the sisters that the Buckingham Palace Girl Guide pack was formed. Because of her age, Margaret began as a Brownie. There were weekly meetings in the gardens of the Palace—the size of a London park with its own boating lake—of thirty-four girls drawn from the children of Court officials and employees. Guiding activities were a welcome relief from the sequestered existence, and fostered in Margaret a lifelong attachment to the movement.

The sisters called each other Lilibet and Margaret, as they do to this day, and, according to the legendary "Crawfie," Margaret was difficult to discipline, although neither of the girls was above a fight: shrill cries of "brute" and "beast" would emanate from the nursery to the sounds of thwacks, at the end of which Elizabeth would invariably be scarred with teethmarks. "Margaret," she used to complain, "always wants what I want." Rather chubby as a child, Margaret used to be teased by her sister: during swimming lessons in the Buckingham Palace pool when she was practicing breast stroke movements on a bench, Elizabeth remarked, "You look like an aeroplane about to conk out!"

By her fourth birthday, Margaret was taking music lessons, and when she was seven, she commenced singing classes with the Countess of Cavan. It was a family joke that Margaret was so musically inclined that she had been able to hum the "Merry Widow Waltz" before she could talk. Both children delighted in dressing up and playing charades, and Margaret revealed an imaginative streak by inventing a "Cousin Halifax," on whom she was able to heap the blame for being late, not attending to her lessons and forgetting things. Crawfie noted that while Lilibet favored *Lamb's Tales from Shakespeare* and *Black Beauty* for reading, Margaret immersed herself in penny comics redolent with blood, thunder and piratical escapades.

For a Hanoverian, Margaret's was an almost Semitic beauty, with a lucite complexion, eyes that were more purple at times than blue, and a figure, when it had shed its puppy fat, that was petite yet voluptuous. Like her mother she was small—the King himself was only of medium height —but she joined in the robust pursuits of her sturdier sister, and became a Sea Ranger as well as a Guide. Crawfie observed that her tongue, witty but sometimes too sharp, seemed to frighten the older men in the Household, who worried that they might suffer the brunt of her satire without the opportunity of retort.

Subjected to the precise timetable of Monarchy, and quartered in the vastness of the Palace, a gray, square edifice built around a central courtyard, life for the girls had altered dramatically from the halcyon days in No. 145. It was to change again, equally dramatically, when the announcement of the outbreak of war interrupted the Royal Family's Balmoral holiday in the autumn of 1939. "Who is this Hitler, spoiling everything?" asked Margaret, adding when she heard the Prime Minister's broadcast to the nation, "Do you think the Germans will come and get us?"

That first Christmas was spent at Sandringham, before the big house was closed for the duration of hostilities, then the family went to Royal Lodge, Windsor, which Bertie had acquired at the same time as Birkhall. There they saw the first enemy aircraft scything through the Berkshire skies. With the threat of a bombing raid they were moved to Windsor Castle, where the dungeons served as shelters, for a weekend—and stayed for five years. On February 3, 1940, the first German bomber (a Heinkel) to be brought down on British soil since World War One crashed near Whitby in North Yorkshire. The King was informed that the plane, with its crew of four, had been shot out of the sky by Squadron-Leader Peter Townsend of No. 43 Squadron (known as Kate Meyrick's Own: Mrs. Meyrick was famous for running the Forty-Three, one of London's most fashionable clubs).

Elizabeth made her first broadcast from Windsor, addressing the young of the nation, and allowed Margaret to chime in "Goodnight children" at the end. Past puberty, many of her thoughts were devoted to the handsome Dartmouth cadet, Prince Philip of Greece, whom she had met shortly before the outbreak of war when the sisters had visited the Royal Naval College with their parents on July 22, 1939. A second cousin of the King, and nephew of Lord Louis Mountbatten, Philip had not a drop of Greek blood in his veins, and Crawfie was right to compare him to a Viking, with his ash-blond hair and sculptured features, for he was essentially a Dane of the royal house which had been invited to take over the Greek Throne in 1863. He was five years older than Elizabeth who, according to Crawfie, never took her eyes off him the whole time of that first encounter.

Crawfie found him good-looking but offhand in his manner, although he knelt beside Elizabeth as she played with a clockwork train-set in the house of the officer-in-charge of the College, Admiral Sir Frederick Dalrymple-Hamilton. "He soon got bored with that," Crawfie wrote later. "We had ginger crackers and lemonade in which he joined and then he said, 'Let's go to the tennis courts and have some real fun jumping the nets.' At the tennis courts I thought he showed off a great deal but the little girls were much impressed. Lilibet said, 'How good he is, Crawfie! How high he can jump!' He was quite polite with her, but did not pay her any special attention. He spent quite a lot of time teasing plump little Margaret."

The first Christmas at Windsor was enlivened by the pantomime *Cinderella* which the Princesses and their friends performed before an audience of six hundred, including servicemen, in the Waterloo Chamber of the castle. Margaret took the name part, dressed up in the most splendid amateur tradition in crinoline, white periwig, tights and beauty spot, but Elizabeth, for once, stole the show and Crawfie noted: "I have never known Lilibet more animated. There was a sparkle about her none of us had ever seen before. Many people remarked on it." The reason was in the front row—Prince Philip with whom, she confessed to her sister, she was in love.

As the war progressed, the gap between the sisters widened. Elizabeth, on reaching her sixteenth birthday, registered at the local labor exchange as required by law, and was later allocated her own sitting room at Windsor and a lady-in-waiting to assist with her growing correspondence—much of it, joked her parents, to Philip, whose photograph adorned her desk. At eighteen she joined the Auxiliary Territorial Service as a second subaltern, No. 230873, learning to drive a car, change its wheels and dismantle its engine. While Elizabeth was allowed to make regular forays to London, Margaret had to remain at Windsor. Crawfie saw Margaret then as "a girl at a most awkward age, neither child nor grownup, taking the interlude much harder than Lilibet."

The tide finally began to turn in Britain's favor and Peter Townsend, now a twenty-nine-year-old Wing Commander with a D.S.O., D.F.C. and Bar to show for his heroics, again came to the King's notice. On February 16, 1944 he was summoned to the Palace to be appointed Equerry to His Majesty for an initial period of three months. The King saw a slim-built man of his own height, and eyes that met his own from a square-cut face with high cheekbones, which had become more prominent through the fatigue of war.

Townsend had been recommended for the post by Air Chief Marshal Sir Charles "Peter" Portal, who had explained at a meeting a few days earlier at the Air Ministry in Whitehall that it had been decided that equerries, usually picked for regimental or family connections, were now being chosen for their fighting record. Desk-bound after a "crack-up" and resigned to see out hostilities in command of a flying training school—not the most glamorous of jobs—Townsend was delighted to accept the intriguing appointment. At the end of his interview with the King, he was being shown out by Sir Piers Legh, the Master of the Household, when the two Princesses came bounding down the corridor on a tip-off from their father that a dashing pilot was in their midst. They were introduced, and two weeks later Townsend started the ninety-day assignment which was to end nine years and four months later when he was banished to Brussels, taking the heart of one of those Princesses with him. Strangely, Margaret remembers their first meeting as taking place in the Great Hall of Windsor Castle with both her father and mother present, but Peter stands by his "photographic memory."

With a middle-class, colonial background—his father had been a Commissioner in Burma, one of a handful of Englishmen ruling over fifteen million inhabitants—Townsend was an oddity at Court, where the key posts were traditionally staffed by the aristocracy, well-qualified to smooth the Sovereign's path. As Equerry, Townsend received visitors and announced them into the King's presence. Margaret remembers: "My father became very fond of Peter. They both stammered and that was a bond. When he first appeared, I had a terrific crush on him, but there was no question of a romance until much later—he was a married man."

Educated at Haileybury, a private school with a services tradition, Townsend had decided on a flying career after visiting the R.A.F. base at Old Sarum near Salisbury at the age of thirteen and being taken up in the back cockpit of a Bristol Fighter, a World War One biplane. In 1933, approaching his nineteenth birthday, he enrolled at the Royal Air Force College, Cranwell, a diffident, painfully shy young man with dark, wavy hair and handsome, almost effeminate features. Flying was to be his life, but he was sent home during a posting to Singapore when doctors diagnosed a virulent nervous eczema and recommended a complete break from the cockpit. He was back in service in the summer of 1937, at R.A.F. Tangmere, near Chichester, when he fell in love for the first time. Her name was Bodil, she was Danish, and the romance, conducted at great expense when she returned home to Scandinavia, lasted until the war.

After twenty months of night and day combat, during which he was shot down twice, once being miraculously saved from the freezing North Sea by an off-course minesweeper, Townsend described himself as a "nerve-wracked, sleep-starved wreck" and confessed that the fight had gone out of him. He was grounded and put on barbiturates by doctors, given a staff job with the rank of Wing Commander,

Night Operations, and posted to Hunsdon in Hertfordshire in June 1941. At twenty-six he had confronted death so often and so casually that life seemed to have little relevance. Freed from combat, it was not surprising that he fell in love with the first woman he was able to relate to.

She was called Rosemary Pawle, her father was a Brigadier, and the family lived beside the airfield. "She was twenty, tall and lovely—never more so than that first evening we met at a local country house. I could not wait to make her my wife, for life in those dangerous days seemed a brief, precarious thing," Townsend writes. "So, true to that wartime phenomenon, the urge to reproduce, we rushed hand-in-hand to the altar. Exactly nine months later, our first child was born." But between marriage and fatherhood, Townsend had suffered the "inevitable" breakdown which had been threatening and had been hospitalized for three months. Rosemary found not a hero for a husband but a zombie. It was not an auspicious start.

When he recovered, he was sent to Drem, near Edinburgh, to command the station and 611 Squadron with its "sexy" Spitfires. There he reacquired his zest for flying, which took him back to operations as leader of 605 Night-Fighter Squadron defending the Channel coast. But piloting clapped-out, patched-up planes and losing baby-faced pilots by the handful, as much for mechanical reasons as from enemy aggression, Townsend soon experienced a new emotion, fear, and he could not shake it: "I knew in my bones that I should never again be the pilot I once had been. I had gone too far down the hill ever to get to the top again. In my thoughts and visions I saw myself crashing, over and over again, to a horrible death. I was convinced I was going to die—an abject state of mind, exactly the reverse to what I had felt during the heroic days of 1940, when I was convinced that I was going to live! The more I flew, and there could be no relenting, the more fear, stark degrading fear, possessed me. Each time I took off, I felt sure it would be the last."

In October 1942, he was transferred to Staff College and the following January given command of the fighter station at West Malling in Kent. When summer brought the opening of the second front, taking the war to Nazi-occupied Europe, Townsend suffered another breakdown and contracted septicaemia, a serious condition then because there were no antibiotics to treat it. Once more he was invalided to a ground job, this time with Training Command, and then posted to Montrose, in Scotland, for a flying instructor's course to prepare him for the training school. Montrose was a dreary backwater for a feted hero, and the summons from "Peter" Portal provided timely relief.

At Buckingham Palace Townsend worked two weeks on permanent call, with one month off when he would return to Rosemary and their son Giles. Their house was in that part of Kent known as "Bomb Alley" but they soon moved to Windsor to share a home with two newlyweds, Lord Rupert Nevill, brother of the Marquess of Abergavenny, and his wife Micky, daughter of the Earl of Portsmouth. It was cramped but convivial, and when the King learned in the spring of 1945 that the Townsends were expecting another baby, he offered them Adelaide Cottage, a grace-and-favor house beside the Thames in the Home Park of Windsor Castle, built in the early nineteenth century as a teahouse for Queen Adelaide. In June, six weeks after VE Day, a second son was born and christened Hugo in St. George's Chapel, Windsor, with the King as a godfather, cementing into permanency a relationship which began as a temporary appointment. "I'd have liked a boy like Peter," the King is reputed to have said.

The war had seen Elizabeth grow into a woman and for

her it ended as it had begun—in love with Prince Philip, whom, as she told her younger sister many times, she was determined to marry. But he was a Greek citizen, and naturalization—without which he would not be allowed a permanent commission in the Royal Navy—was held up, first by the Greek civil war and then by the ramifications of the March 1946 plebiscite, in which a majority of Hellenics voted for a monarchy. Because it was felt by the British Government that the restoration would not be helped by a member of the Greek Royal Family's immediately renouncing his nationality, Philip was ordered to wait. This did not deter him though from proposing to Elizabeth in the late summer, when he was granted a few week's leave and spent them at Balmoral.

Ignoring the situation, Elizabeth accepted. Her father only allowed the engagement on the understanding that it would be kept strictly secret: apart from the problems over Philip's nationality, such an announcement would be bound to interfere with the Royal Family's plans for a tour of South Africa early in 1947. This tour was being organized as a "thank you" from the King and Queen to the Dominion for overthrowing Prime Minister Hertzog in 1939, when he had advocated neutrality and sought to prevent his country from coming to Britain's aid.

IN ANTICIPATION OF THE TOUR, WHICH
would require them to be away for three months, the Princesses took lessons in Afrikaans from A.P. van der Post, a senior
Trade Commissioner at South Africa House in Trafalgar
Square. They left on February 1, on the *Vanguard*, and arrangements were made for Elizabeth to celebrate her coming-
of-age on April 21, in Cape Town. It was to be a thankless
time for Margaret, not yet seventeen and totally over-
shadowed by her sister, on whom most eyes focussed.

During the sixteen-day sea journey to the Cape, the Princesses only saw Townsend at meals, but they were giggling
spectators when he became one of the principal victims of
the King Neptune ceremony, to be ducked and tossed in a
blanket when the ship crossed the equator. Once the tour
proper began, however, they were thrown together, often in
confined spaces (thirty-five nights were spent on the white,
air-conditioned train in which the royal party toured), and
Margaret, never one to be upstaged, envious of her sister's
engagement, could have been forgiven for allowing her
crush on Townsend to develop into infatuation, of which he
was not immediately aware. For his part, he fell in love with
the country, and wrote enthusiastically to Rosemary that
their future lay in South Africa.

When Townsend returned to Adelaide Cottage in early
May, he found that his "ravings" about South Africa and a
new life in the sunshine had been received with hostility
by his wife, who had no wish to give up her position in

England for the uncertainties of a fresh start with two young children some 6,000 miles away. Reluctantly, Townsend gave up his new ambitions, but Rosemary's intransigence took them another step along the road which would end in divorce, five years later. Their marriage had anyway lasted longer than most which were forged in the heat of battle: in 1945 there were 15,600 divorces, the following year 33,000 and in 1947 some 52,000.

On July 10, the engagement of Princess Elizabeth to "Lieutenant Philip Mountbatten" was announced from Buckingham Palace. On naturalization, Philip had given up his title of Prince and changed his name from Schleswig-Holstein-Sonderburg-Glucksberg to the anglicization of his mother's name, Battenberg. The marriage took place on November 20. Margaret, in the meantime, was beginning to perform public duties on her own, and when she went to Belfast to launch the liner *Edinburgh Castle* in the autumn of 1947, Townsend was part of her entourage, a role he was to play more and more often as she fulfilled some of the tasks which had previously been left to her elder sister.

The King, not realizing the growing intensity of Margaret's feeling for Townsend, but sensing her loneliness since her sister's youthful marriage, encouraged her obvious pleasure in his company. Where Peter had once ridden the royal estates with both Princesses, he was now accompanied only by one, and no one remarked on it. Word of the breaking-up of the Townsend marriage was kept very firmly from the royal household, and to all outward appearances the couple seemed happy, given the constraints of service and the sometimes lengthy partings. But Margaret was falling irrevocably in love: the danger signs were there for all to observe when in the autumn of 1948, Townsend accompanied her to Amsterdam, along with the Duke of Beaufort and Princess Alice, Countess of Athlone, for the Investiture on September 6, of Crown Princess Juliana as Queen of the Netherlands. During the celebration ball, Margaret danced with him, her head on his chest, and the following day she was to be seen leaning on Peter and occasionally taking his arm as they were shown over the Rijksmuseum. Despite the splendor of the occasion, her looks during the trip were exclusively for Townsend, and only a naïve man would have misinterpreted them.

Townsend was by no means the only man Margaret met regularly, but he was the oldest—nearly sixteen years separated them—and with the war still a fresh memory, easily the most glamorous, although the potential suitors the King was gently pushing in her path were from the richest, most venerable families in the realm. At the Buckingham Palace dances, their names soon cropped up with such frequency that the press, robbed of gossip about Princess Elizabeth, were quick to latch on to "The Margaret Set."

It was led by the Earl of Dalkeith and the Marquess of Blandford. Dalkeith, seven years older than Margaret, was heir to two Scottish dukedoms and three massive estates, over which he shot and hunted with a passion. The Marquess of Blandford, son of the Duke of Marlborough, was the heir to Blenheim Palace and its 11,500 acres. "The Margaret Set" also included Lord Porchester, heir of the Earl of Carnarvon, who lived at Highclere Castle, set in a 6,000 acre Hampshire estate; the multimillionaire Earl of Dudley's younger son, the Hon. Peter Ward, who had fought for two years with the Royal Canadian Air Force and then joined the Fleet Air Arm; the Hon. Colin Tennant, the elder son of Lord Glenconner and heir to a 9,000 acre Scottish estate, who worked in the family City trading company; Lord Ogilvy, heir of the Earl of Airlie who owned two castles and a Scottish estate in Angus; ex-Coldstream Guards Major Simon Phipps, later to join the Church, whose naval-captain father was an old friend of the King; the Hon. Dominic Elliot, an Old Etonian who was attending Madrid University and was the younger son of the Earl of Minto, a Roxburghshire landowner; and other wealthy Old Etonians like Billy Wallace, who had inherited a fortune on the death of his father, a former Tory Minister.

But when he was on duty, it was Townsend that Margaret saw, often several times a day, and not without her contrivance. In June 1949, Margaret visited Italy and requested that Townsend meet her at London Airport on her return, which he did, although it was outside the scope of his position as King's Equerry. Later in the year, when Townsend flew in the annual King's Cup air race, it was in a Miles Whitney Straight entered by the Princess.

Indulged by her parents, Margaret led an increasingly spoiled life, discovering that there were few limits to what she could do or have. She had only to ask and the King, who greatly missed the company of his elder daughter even though she was a short distance down the Mall at Clarence House, was content to humor her, and resisted any inclination to encourage her to find a purpose in life. Her mother was similarly dilatory, since she felt sure that Margaret was but a year or two away from marriage to an eminently suitable aristocrat, after which she would of course devote herself to her husband's estate and to bringing up her children, only occasionally being called upon to perform royal duties. It was the fashion for women of rank to marry young rather than pursue a career, and the Queen saw no sense in curtailing Margaret's fun or restricting her youthful urges.

By Margaret's twentieth birthday, Elizabeth had given birth to both a son and a daughter, which ensured the succession but made Margaret feel more aimless than ever: while the elder sister settled into family life, the younger took to night life, quickly becoming an established patron of clubs like the 400 in Leicester Square, which demanded black tie and long dresses at all times, and Les Ambassadeurs at the foot of Park Lane, where bandleader Paul Adam became her favorite, especially as he encouraged her to join in on the piano.

As someone who lived in the most rarified strata of privilege, Margaret was sophisticated beyond her years, volatile by nature but generous in her praise and appreciation of others less fortunate. She gave friendship easily and asked for nothing more than loyalty in return. She was a born leader and innovator, but did not seek to impose her will on others—nor did she have need to, for her personality and charm were hard to resist. In her company, contemporaries of both sexes found it difficult sometimes to remember they were with the King's daughter, such was her lack of affectation and informality. Intimates were able to call her by her Christian name, whereas in later years when her role was tinged with regality "Ma'am" or at best "Ma'am darling" were the only greetings allowed, in public and in private.

She rode well, though not with the same style as her sister, and enjoyed racing to the extent of taking great pleasure in having her friends to stay at Windsor Castle for the Royal Ascot Meeting every June. Her favorite pastimes, however, were as they continued to be, playing the piano and singing, demonstrating her mastery of the latest dance steps, and amusing her circle with her mimicry. She was a comedienne at heart and her place, not just by birth but by achievement and talent, was center stage. Selfish though her existence appeared, Margaret liked to share her good fortune. She was noted for the generosity of her presents and for her meticulous memory of friends' birthdays and, later, anniversaries. If her own group found her irresistible, so did the Palace staff. They adored her for brightening the solemnity of their ceremonial tasks, for bringing gaiety and life into the grave Palace with its six hundred echoing rooms.

By night she would roister in the West End with Billy, "Sunny" Blandford or Johnny Dalkeith; by day she would seek out the company of Peter Townsend who, having been promoted to Deputy Master of the Household in August 1950, had a green-carpeted office on the south side of Buckingham Palace. The full-time job added to his estrangement from Rosemary, with whom he no longer had a physical relationship, and during their chats Margaret, without having to pry, learned that although Townsend was no longer in love with his wife, he was trying desperately, honorable man that he was, to hold the remnants of the marriage together for the sake of his children who were the inevitable sufferers from the discordant home life.

Townsend wrote about these days: "What ultimately made Princess Margaret so attractive and lovable was that behind the dazzling facade, the apparent self-assurance, you could find, if you looked for it, a rare softness and sincerity. She could make you bend double with laughing; she could also touch you deeply. I was but one among many to be so moved. There were dozens of others; their names were in the papers, which vied with each other, frantically and futilely, in their forecasts of the one whom she would marry. Yet I dare say that there was not one among them more touched by the Princess's *joie de vivre* than I, for, in my present marital predicament, it gave me what I most lacked—joy. More, it created a sympathy between us and I began to sense that, in her life too, there was something lacking."

When the King opened the Festival of Britain on May 3, 1951, it was obvious that he was very weary and in all probability ill. Later that month Margaret went to Balmoral for a short break with her parents, accompanied only by a lady-in-waiting and Townsend. The brief holiday in the Highlands did the King some good, but he needed months, not days, of rest and back in London he went down with "flu." He was treated with penicillin and after a slow recovery, convalesced during June and July, returning early in August to Balmoral, where he hoped he would recover his health completely. But the weather turned wet and cold and the King caught a chill, which somewhat subdued the celebrations for Margaret's twenty-first birthday.

She had invited Johnny Dalkeith and Billy Wallace to stay for these celebrations, giving rise to speculation in the press that an engagement to one of them was imminent. The Earl was the favorite, much to the delight of the King's Private Secretary, Sir Alan ("Tommy") Lascelles, who was related to Dalkeith's mother. He seemed convinced when he told Townsend one morning: "Dalkeith and the Princess were making sheep's eyes at each other last night."

When the weather was good, Townsend had another experience of Margaret's gentleness and recounts: "One day, after a picnic lunch with the guns, I stretched out in the heather to doze. Then, vaguely, I was aware that someone was covering me with a coat. I opened one eye—to see Princess Margaret's lovely face, very close, looking into mine. Then I opened the other eye, and saw, behind her, the King, leaning on his stick, with a certain look, typical of him: kind, half amused. I whispered, 'You know your father is watching us?' At which she laughed, straightened up and went to his side. Then she took his arm and walked him away, leaving me to my dreams."

It was the Queen who sent to London for the royal physicians when the King's condition showed no sign of improvement, and he was examined at Balmoral on September 1. In London two weeks later, he underwent a bronchoscopy and was told that he was suffering from a bronchial tube blockage which would necessitate the removal of his left lung and certain nerves in his larynx, which might permanently affect his speech. On September 23, Clement Price Thomas, the leading chest surgeon, performed the operation in the Buhl Room at Buckingham Palace and discovered that the King's other lung was also affected. In fact he had cancer, and his doctors doubted that he could live more than two years, but he was never told. Margaret was with him constantly during his convalescence, and although he lost twenty-one pounds and could only speak to her in a whisper, he surprised his family by his quick recovery, which allowed Princess Elizabeth and Philip to make a thirty-five-day tour of North America that had been temporarily postponed.

The King's apparent return to health was celebrated with a day of National Thanksgiving on Sunday December 2, in churches all over the country, and he spent his fifty-sixth birthday on December 14, quietly at Buckingham Palace with his family, travelling down to Sandringham with them a week later for Christmas. He had been invited by the Prime Minister of South Africa, Dr. Malan, to recuperate at his official residence near Durban in Natal in warm sunshine rather than suffer the British winter, and in mid-January Townsend was sent to inspect the house, which he found totally suitable. It was arranged that the King and Queen would leave England on March 10, and a tour of East Africa, Australia and New Zealand would be carried out on their behalf by Princess Elizabeth and Philip. On January 30, the eve of their departure, they went with the King and Queen to the Drury Lane Theatre to see *South Pacific*, with Townsend and Princess Margaret making up the party. Next day, hatless in a chilling wind, the King waved goodbye forever at London Airport to his elder daughter, and returned to Sandringham for a week's rough shooting.

On Tuesday February 5, a crisp, sunny day of blue skies,

the King's shooting party went after hares and bagged 280. After dinner Margaret played the piano for him while he struggled with a crossword, and at 10:30 P.M. he kissed her goodnight before going to his bedroom, where he read for an hour and a half after his valet brought him a cup of hot chocolate. In the early hours, with his heir sitting in the top of a tree 4,000 miles away in Kenya, he died of a coronary thrombosis, very peacefully. At his funeral his younger daughter's wreath bore the simple message: "Darling Papa, from his everloving Margaret."

3

"IF THE KING HAD LIVED," SAYS COLIN TEN-
nant, a tall, rakishly handsome figure on the fringes of The
Margaret Set at the time, "he would have made Princess
Margaret marry Johnny Dalkeith. With his houses and his
land, she would have had a virtual state of her own."

Following Margaret's coming-of-age at Balmoral, the
Royal Family began to expect great things of Dalkeith, son
of the Duke of Buccleuch and Queensberry, who was to
inherit three stately homes, 247,000 acres of Scotland and
England and an impressive art collection including the only
Leonardo da Vinci in private hands. A little too staid and
serious, perhaps, to appeal to the frivolous side of Margaret's
nature, he was not her first choice of husband. Although she
was strongly attracted to Townsend, it had never occurred
to Margaret that she would marry anyone but an aristocrat
approved by her parents. Before her twentieth birthday, she
had conducted an amorous flirtation with "Sunny" Blandford
and told her parents that she thought he would make an
ideal husband. But he fell in love with one of Margaret's girl
friends, Susan Hornby (whose father was vice-chairman of
W. H. Smith & Son) and by June 1951, a few months before
they married, the Princess's eye had moved on when she
invited the couple to Windsor Castle for the Royal Ascot
races.

Perhaps sensing a character he would never be able to
control, Dalkeith was equally unreliable, and within months
of the King's death began courting a shapely model, Jane

McNeill, an ex-debutante and daughter of a Q.C. [Queen's Counsel] who practiced in Hong Kong. Dalkeith was with Margaret for her twenty-second birthday, heightening the hopes of her family, but four days later he wrote to inform her that he was becoming engaged to Jane and they married in January 1953. Margaret, who had always expected to emulate her sister by marrying young, was beginning to feel that her options were running out. At the same time she was thrown into even closer contact with Peter Townsend, who had relinquished his post as Deputy Master of the Royal Household to become, at the request of the Queen Mother, the Comptroller of her Household which, after a period for redecoration, moved to Clarence House. When Margaret (with the Queen and Prince Philip), lunched with Townsend and Rosemary at Adelaide Cottage in June, she knew their marriage was in the process of dissolution. Six months later, shortly before Christmas, Townsend was awarded a decree *nisi* against his wife, with the legal custody of the two sons whom he left in the care of their mother. He cited John de Lazslo, son of the celebrated portrait painter Philip de Lazslo, whom Rosemary married two months later. The last few months of the marriage were deeply depressing for Townsend who, at one stage, found himself accused of having an affair with the Queen!

Destiny in the irresistible shape of Princess Margaret awaited Townsend when he found himself, in the New Year of 1953, on duty at Sandringham. Both he and Margaret were free of emotional involvements for the first time in the nine years they had known each other and, with an urgent need for love after the arid years of a marriage without physical contact, Townsend was amazed to discover that his awakening feelings for Margaret were reciprocated. In the red drawing room at Windsor Castle a few weeks later, alone with her after the rest of the Royal Family had gone to

London for a ceremony, Townsend declared his love for the Princess and she for him. It was to prove an impossible dream, so impossible that although the couple were able to spend hours in each other's company in Margaret's home or riding in Windsor Great Park or at Balmoral and Sandringham, the two people closest to the Princess—her mother and her sister—were totally unaware of the affair until she felt obliged to confide in them.

"We had known each other for nine years, during which time she had grown up from a schoolgirl into a young woman whose beauty, charm and talent had attracted scores of admiring and faithful personal friends. Yet among none of them had she found the man of her choice," writes Townsend "That—incredibly—was the lot that destiny had reserved for me."

Townsend informed "Tommy" Lascelles, who was to spend a year as private secretary to the Queen to show her the ropes, and was brusquely told, "You are either mad or bad." And from that moment Lascelles, out of a misguided sense of responsibility to his late master, did everything in his power to destroy any chances that the lovers had of lasting happiness, while outwardly he gave the impression of helping to smooth their path. "I shall curse him to the grave," says Princess Margaret who has been able to do so at all too close quarters—Lascelles, until his death in August 1981 at ninety-four, also had a grace-and-favor apartment at Kensington Palace.

Although privately very disturbed by the news, the Queen Mother, mindful no doubt of the lopsided fortunes of her two daughters, made no attempt to dissuade the couple and continued to indulge Margaret, as did the Queen, also beset with grave misgivings, who invited her sister and Townsend to the Palace for an evening. Prince Philip got on well with Townsend, whose eldest brother, Michael, had been the

Captain of the destroyer *Chequers* on which Philip had served. The two men had played squash and badminton at Buckingham Palace and Windsor, and during this fraught evening, Philip did his best to brighten the mood, making lighthearted remarks—not all welcome to Townsend and Margaret—about a situation which, had it been written as fiction, would have been met with incredulity.

Townsend immediately offered to resign but was told to stay put, while Lascelles advised the Queen that under the Royal Marriages Act of 1772, framed after a Hanoverian marriage scandal, Princess Margaret could not marry without her consent until she was twenty-five. After that she would be free of the Sovereign's veto, but would still need the consent of Parliament and all the parliaments of the Dominions as well. As titular head of the Church of England and Defender of the Faith, the Queen, because Townsend was divorced, could not in any case give her consent constitutionally unless advised otherwise by her Prime Minister. When the Queen did put the situation to Sir Winston Churchill, he told her bluntly that it would be disastrous for her to give her permission, especially with her Coronation due to take place on June 2, and felt it best for all parties if Margaret waited for her twenty-fifth birthday.

Behind the scenes, and unbeknownst to Townsend and Margaret, Lascelles was stirring it up with Churchill and insisting that the Prime Minister bring all his weight to bear to remove Townsend from his post and banish him abroad without delay. But the Queen refused to rob her sister of her new-found happiness, and Peter stayed on at Clarence House as the gossip began to permeate from the royal cloisters into the public domain. With Coronation Day approaching, the British Press made no mention of the delicate situation which was receiving headlines in America and on the Continent. Incredibly, no one told Townsend or Margaret that their secret—originally confided to the Queen, Prince Philip, the Queen Mother and Lascelles—was now on the lips of several hundred million people. So, on Coronation Day, when Margaret was chatting with Townsend in the Great Hall after the Westminster Abbey service and, without giving it a second thought, brushed a hair off his Group Captain's uniform, the intimate gesture was the sign the assembled press had been waiting for, and it received headlines the next day in New York. Still there was no mention in Fleet Street. That came in a Sunday newspaper on June 14 when the *People*, in age-old style, repeated the stories and then denounced them: "It is high time for the British public to be made aware of the fact that newspapers in Europe and America are openly asserting that the Princess is in love with a divorced man and that she wishes to marry him. The story is of course utterly untrue. It is quite unthinkable that a royal princess, third in line of succession to the throne, should even contemplate a marriage with a man who has been through the divorce courts."

With scandal looming on the Buckingham Palace doorstep, Lascelles advised the Queen on June 15, that Townsend should be removed from the scene as quickly as possible, to dampen press interest and comment. Churchill agreed, ordering Viscount De L'Isle, the Secretary of State for Air, to find the Group Captain an Air Attaché's job abroad. There were three vacancies, in Brussels, Johannesburg and Singapore, and Townsend chose the nearest to be close to his sons (aged eleven and eight). It was agreed that he would leave for Belgium after Princess Margaret returned on July 17, from her trip with the Queen Mother to South Rhodesia to attend the Rhodes Centenary Exhibition in Bulawayo. On June 29, in the privacy of Clarence House, he kissed her goodbye, confident that they would meet for a proper farewell in three weeks' time.

But the following day, while Townsend performed his final royal duty as Equerry-in-Waiting to the Queen on a visit to Northern Ireland, the Buckingham Palace Press Office imprudently released the news of his transfer. Cameramen in Ulster then were focussing more on the Equerry than the person he served, an embarrassing situation which brought Lascelles to confer yet again with Churchill. The result was that Townsend's departure was brought forward to July 15, a decision which he communicated to a tearful Margaret in Umtali. They were not to meet again in over a year.

"Horrid Churchill! We never did say a proper goodbye," says Princess Margaret. "We were given to believe by Lascelles that we would be able to marry. Peter went to Belgium and we were asked to wait a year. Then there was a muck-up and we were asked to wait another year. If Lascelles hadn't told me that marriage was possible, I would never have given it another thought. The relationship would have been out of the question and Peter could have gone off quite peacefully. Instead we waited for ages and then discovered it was quite hopeless. It seems frightfully stupid to have gone on all that time but it was wicked to have given us false hopes. When Peter was sent away, Prince Philip was marvellous, very comforting. He used to say: 'Don't worry, it will be all right.' He was on our side, a real chum."

In daily contact either by letter or telephone with Peter, Princess Margaret relied on her women friends for companionship. The closest of these were Lady Elizabeth Cavendish, sister of the Duke of Devonshire, and a newcomer to her circle, Judy Montagu, the wealthy granddaughter of the 1st Lord Swaythling, a prominent merchant banker and pillar of London's Jewish society. Judy was seven years older than Margaret, and made up in enthusiasm and character—she was a born leader—what she lacked in looks.

Usually with Judy was Colin Tennant, then twenty-six and working in the City for the family firm, which had been founded as East India merchants and had prospered. Given to outrageous sartorial extravagances—he had a suit made without any pockets—and a headlong pursuit of amusement, he made a welcome addition to Margaret's inner circle at a time when her spirits needed boosting most.

"Judy wasn't pretty but she was talented and amusing and a great organiser," says Tennant. "She made a beeline for society and soon displaced everyone as Princess Margaret's best friend and that was where I came in—Judy was my best friend. Townsend had been sent away and Princess Margaret went into purdah for a while, but that didn't mean she stopped enjoying herself and her situation could have changed at any time. Like many young people in those days I had met Princess Margaret casually and had been at Buckingham Palace dances since 1946. But I was really on the fringes and not one of what I would call the real nobs like Johnny, Sunny, Porchy or Peter Ward. They had socially prominent parents and mine were divorced, so I came rather lowish down on the list."

While the Townsend drama was dying down, there were theatricals of another kind for The Margaret Set, who put on a play for charity, Lord and Lady Algy, in the West End. Leading the cast were Porchester, Lord Plunket (the Queen's Equerry and soon to be Deputy Master of the Household) and Raine Legge, the daughter of romantic novelist Barbara Cartland. Margaret was pleased that it made a few thousand pounds—the production received press coverage quite out of proportion to its merits—and encouraged Judy with her plans to put on a larger, more lavish play the following year.

With the agony of separation receding, Margaret made the most of the 1954 Season. It was at this time that, in a spirit of defiance, she started smoking in public—fine for the factory bench but considered a *faux pas* in Society—and her extra-long tortoiseshell holder soon became her trademark. She was the center of attraction at debutante dances, cocktail parties and weekends in the great country houses of England. For escorts she would rely on old faithfuls like Billy Wallace and Peter Ward, and gallants like Colin Tennant and Henry Porchester. In keeping with her star status, she had a permanent table in London's best nightclubs, often dancing after parties until 4 A.M. But the greatest excitement of that summer was Judy's presentation at the Scala Theatre of *The Frog*, an obscure Edgar Wallace thriller, again in aid of charity. Colin was the Frog, Billy Wallace secured a bit part as a sergeant, and again Porchester, Plunket and Raine were prominent, along with Lord Brooke, the heir to the Earl of Warwick. Banned through protocol from appearing on stage, Margaret was given the title of Associate Director, which neatly placed her in the center of events.

There were three performances which raised a total of £13,000, and when the curtain came up for the first night, Margaret was brought on the stage to make a short, shy speech. "I remember telling everybody that they ought to give the cast a jolly good round of applause," she says. It was reported that among the company there were ten titles and as many sons of peers, and each night the cast with its supporters would adjourn to the nearby 400 nightclub to pass judgment on each other's 'performances—many lines were fluffed to accompanying hilarity on both sides of the footlights. At the 400, Rossi, the manager, would place a silver flower-vase on the Princess's table (an honor accorded only to royalty), and the group would spread out along the banquettes facing the band across the dance floor onto which Tennant, a graceful, natural mover, would be the first to lead Margaret. If she missed Townsend she did not show it, and the conversation never turned to that arcane part of her life that seemed locked away in a hidden compartment to which only two people had keys.

The London Season ended in July and, accompanied by Lady Elizabeth Cavendish, Margaret journeyed north at Tennant's invitation to stay at Glen, a 9,000-acre estate in Peeblesshire that Colin was to inherit from his father. Fleet Street was quickly on the scent and started predicting an engagement, as if Townsend had never existed. The reports appeared to gain validity when Tennant went on to Balmoral with Margaret, and they spent the first night there unchaperoned—the Queen and Prince Philip were temporarily away.

"Princess Margaret had had such a dizzying time culminating in *The Frog* that I asked her to Glen for a rest and then went on to stay with her at Balmoral for her birthday. There I was greeted at breakfast with headlines like 'Tennant to marry Margaret.' They had a curious effect and for a moment I almost believed them myself," says Colin. "But an engagement to Princess Margaret was never on. I fled afterwards to Venice to see Judy Montagu and then became involved with Lady Jeanne Campbell, and Dominic Elliot took over with Princess Margaret."

The flirtation with Tennant had been insurance, as much as reassurance, during a testing period when the two sides to Margaret's character were trying to assert themselves. On the one hand, there was the Princess cast in a tragic role, waiting for an uncertain length of time for her Crusader to return, and wondering whether her feelings would be the same. On the other, there was a wilful, attractive young woman who remained the greatest catch in Britain and wanted to live for the moment, experiencing as much and as quickly as possible. So, bolstered by the security of Townsend, who remained faithful across the seas, she attempted to walk an emotional tightrope, falling off occasionally, and being hurt.

Although Churchill had forbidden Townsend to break his exile (almost the last decision he made as Prime Minister before he suffered his stroke), Peter started to slip undetected across the Channel to meet the Princess for discreet weekends at the homes of understanding friends—one unlikely rendezvous began in the Harrods book department—and his occasional homecomings served to strengthen her resolve. It would after all, Margaret became convinced, end happily in marriage and through the summer of 1955, as her landmark twenty-fifth birthday approached, her thoughts and actions were directed solely to becoming Mrs. Peter Townsend. The newspapers had convinced themselves and their readers that Tennant and Elliot were red herrings, and that, finally, the dashing war ace was to be the one. Since early March, there had been a steady build-up of anticipation, all focussed on what was to happen at Balmoral after August 21.

Townsend had not pined listlessly away on the Continent; he had become an accomplished amateur jockey, competing in races in France, Austria, Germany, Italy, Switzerland, Belgium and Denmark, and winning a fair proportion of them. The new surge of publicity also brought attention from an unwelcome quarter—his life was threatened by the I.R.A. and the Brussels Police provided him with an armed bodyguard in the person of Commandant Etienne de Spot, a senior officer with sophisticated tastes which coincided with Townsend's. Continental life appealed to Peter, who had become a connoisseur of French wines and cuisine which made a delicious change from the simple fare of roasts and grills that were the staple meals of the royal households. He had also acquired a partiality for garlic-accented dishes, hitherto unsampled, which he was never to lose.

But in reality he was just marking time, and having set

into motion the process whereby she thought that a marriage to Peter would receive official backing as Lascelles had originally promised her, Margaret arranged to meet him in London on October 13. Her chances, if anything, seemed improved, for the new Prime Minister, Sir Anthony Eden, had himself been divorced in 1950, and had remarried two years later. He was invited to Balmoral on October 1 and with him he brought the feelings of the Cabinet.

On her birthday Margaret became free to give notice to the Privy Council and, in theory, become publicly betrothed to the man of her choice. But Eden was, uncomfortably, the bearer of bad tidings. As he sat in the drawing room, with its autumn view of the valley and hills, he explained that in practice nothing had altered since 1953. There were, he disclosed, urgent voices in the Cabinet, headed by the Marquess of Salisbury as Lord President of the Council and Leader of the House of Lords, who would resign rather than allow the Princess to marry a divorced man, even if Townsend were the innocent party. It would be out of the question that she could then remain in line of accession and receive the customary boost in her Civil List allowance from £6,000 a year to £15,000.

Margaret was aghast. She felt betrayed by the Establishment, but decided to do nothing until her meeting with Peter, at which she would acquaint him with the bitter news and gauge his reaction. It was still possible, but at what cost? Ominously for the Princess, the Cabinet's mood was echoed by the Queen Mother who, while increasingly concerned for her younger daughter's peace of mind, knew that the late King would never have tolerated the union. The Queen herself was open-minded on the question, refusing to influence her sister in either direction: she was very fond of Townsend, she respected him for the devotion and friendship with which he had served her father, and she had felt troubled about his banishment—if Margaret wanted Peter Townsend and could have him without promoting a constitutional crisis, then so be it.

On October 12, Townsend set off from Brussels in his green Renault. Margaret curtailed her stay at Balmoral and, wearing a biscuit-colored suit with a pleated skirt and a double string of pearls, boarded a train at Aberdeen, waving at the station to a small crowd of well-wishers. As the express steamed south, the rhythm of the rails might have spelled out to her the message: "I will marry, I will marry, I will marry. . . ."

After driving to Le Touquet, Townsend put the car on the air ferry to Lydd and took the copilot's position in the fourteen-seater craft as it crossed the skies he had defended so valiantly fifteen years before. On arrival in England he drove—with an attendant procession of reporters and cameramen in cars and on motor bicycles—to the Belgravia flat in Lowndes Square of the Marquess of Abergavenny, Lord Rupert Nevill's elder brother. He planned to spend the weekend at Allanbay Park, the Binfield, Berkshire, estate of tobacco millionaire Major John Lycett Wills, whose wife, Jean, was a niece of the Queen Mother. Early on the thirteenth, Margaret arrived back at Clarence House and called Townsend to arrange a meeting that evening there—her afternoon was occupied with a sitting for the painter Denis Fildes, who said that he had never seen the Princess looking more beautiful. After lunch with Townsend in the flat, Mrs. Willis drove him around town on some errands—he went to one custom tailor to order a suit and to another for a pair of riding breeches, then to a Chelsea cake shop en route to his 6:30 P.M. appointment at Clarence House. Outside Clarence House an expectant throng jostled one another in the hopes of catching the first glimpse of the couple. But Margaret took Peter into the privacy of her own sitting room and, as

(35)

they embraced, closed the door on the outside world and its importunate fascination with her private life.

When Townsend arrived at Allanbay Park, separately from Margaret, on Friday evening, he found the Wills's twenty-room Georgian residence and its fifty acres of grounds being patrolled by police-dog teams with no less than the Chief Constable of Berkshire, Mr. J. W. Waldron, personally directing a large force of patrol cars, motor-cyclists and foot officers equipped with walkie-talkies. The world's press had began its long siege: offers of up to £1,000 in cash in exchange for information were made to the Wills's household staff, but in vain, and nothing much of interest occurred. On Sunday, Princess Margaret was driven by Jean Wills to attend morning service at the Chapel Royal, she then went to see her mother and accompanied her on a forty-minute walk, while Townsend remained indoors at Allanbay with Major Wills, whose children were away at boarding school. On Monday morning, the couple returned to London, their minds still not made up, but with the knowledge that on the following day a Cabinet meeting would discuss the Princess's marriage, after which Eden would drive to Buckingham Palace for his weekly audience with the Queen. Somewhat ominously, this lasted an hour and a half instead of the usual thirty minutes.

Margaret showed composure beyond her years and perhaps secretly enjoyed being the focus of the world's attention. But whichever way she looked at the situation, it was as clear as the chimes of the St. James's Palace clock which nightly intruded on her fretful sleep, that marriage to Townsend meant forfeiture of her royal rights, her duties, and her income from the Civil List. On Wednesday, October 19, the couple did not meet for the first time in eight days, and Margaret dined with the rest of the Royal Family at Lambeth Palace, after the Archbishop of Canterbury, Dr. Fisher, had rededicated a war-damaged chapel. On Thursday there was another meeting of the Cabinet, at which a Bill of Renunciation was discussed. It would be brought before Parliament to free the Princess of her responsibilities under the Royal Marriages Act, and enable her to marry Townsend in a civil ceremony. That afternoon Hugh Gaitskell, the Leader of the Labour Party and by coincidence Townsend's first cousin, informed his colleagues in the Shadow Cabinet that the wedding was on. His Opposition party decided to make no objection.

Already faced with horrendous sacrifice if she wanted to marry the man she loved, the only one with whom she had been in love, Margaret was delivered a final, numbing blow: like her Uncle David, she would have to live abroad, possibly for as long as five years. The immediate future suddenly seemed cruel and bleak for the Princess, who had once said breathlessly: "I cannot imagine anything more wonderful than being who I am."

On October 24, the *Times*, always an ally of the Church and the Establishment, broke its thundering silence on the issue with a forthright editorial against the marriage, stating that the Queen and her family were a symbol for her subjects throughout the Commonwealth, and that the vast majority of these people would not recognize the marriage. At 4 P.M. that day, Margaret met Townsend at Clarence House. With him he brought a piece of paper on which he had written in pencil. The phrases jumped out at her moistening eyes as she read: "I have decided not to marry Group Captain Townsend . . . mindful of the Church's teaching . . . conscious of my duty to the Commonwealth. . . ."

As he handed it to her he said: "I have been thinking too much about us during the last two days, and I've written down my thoughts, for you to say if you wish to." They realized their joint sacrifices had been in vain, and their enforced separation a worthless trial of loneliness: they had reached the end of the road. After reading Townsend's writing a second time, Margaret looked at him and said barely above a whisper: "That's exactly how I feel."

Margaret wanted to release a statement clarifying her position as soon as possible, but vacillation by Buckingham Palace advisers caused another week to pass, during which the press became even surer of a happy outcome, while the two people involved wept silent tears. On Thursday the twenty-seventh, the Princess drove to Lambeth Palace and found the Archbishop, who had presumed her appointment was to consult him, with all the books of reference appertaining to her dilemma spread out around him. "Archbishop, you may put your books away. I have made up my mind already," she informed him, before going on to Buckingham Palace to receive her sister's commiserations.

Before the official announcement, Margaret and Townsend then spent one last weekend together in the country, with Rupert and Micky Nevill at their Sussex home on the outskirts of Uckfield. They returned separately to London on Monday, October 31. Around 6 P.M., Townsend made his final call on the Princess and was shown into her sitting room. They drank to their past and to their separate futures. There were, naturally, tears but no recriminations, and it was with a lighter heart than for many moons that Townsend made his way back to Uckfield as the statement was broadcast to the world at 7 P.M.:

I would like it to be known that I have decided not to marry Group Captain Peter Townsend. I have been aware that, subject to my renouncing my rights of succession, it might have been possible for me to contract a civil marriage. But, mindful of the Church's teaching that Christian marriage is indissoluble, and conscious of my duty to the Commonwealth, I have resolved to put these considerations before any others.

I have reached this decision entirely alone, and in doing so I have been strengthened by the unfailing support and devotion of Group Captain Townsend. I am deeply grateful for the concern of all those who have constantly prayed for my happiness.

(signed) Margaret

Monday, October 31, 1955.

The *Times* declared: "All the peoples of the Commonwealth will feel gratitude to her for taking the selfless, royal way which, in their hearts, they had expected of her."

Later that week, Townsend drove back to Brussels, two weeks before his forty-first birthday. The rest of his life had started, and he felt a curious elation now that he was no longer faced with making his future among the British Establishment, for many of whom, with reason, he had acquired an abiding distaste. The turning point for him had been, simply, the stark and humiliating consideration that he did not possess the finances to sustain a marriage and existence to which he and Margaret were being condemned: he was paying the major part of a minor income for the support and education of his two sons. Pride would not have allowed him to sponge off the Princess who, in turn, would have been forced to look to her family for support. When asked some years later why they had not gone through with it, Margaret replied in a small voice: "It was Peter who didn't want to."

With her daughter's anguish pervading every corner of Clarence House, the Queen Mother felt impotent to help beyond murmuring the usual consoling platitudes that time was a great healer and that in due course Margaret was bound to find someone else to fall in love with. She had suspected from the start that the affair would never be allowed to reach a truly happy conclusion, and her thoughts went·back to the days when she and the King had discussed suitors for Margaret, little realizing just how wide of the mark her eventual choice of husband would be. Although the Queen Mother, who had personally chosen him as Comptroller of her Household, to supervise its internal organization when she was widowed, loved Peter like a son, she had never been able to picture him as a son-in-law. He had been part of her life for eleven and a half years, helping her children out of adolescence into adulthood, and his final departure would leave an unfillable void. But she believed Margaret's decision to have been for the best, one which her late father would have approved of.

Margaret was able to take comfort in her religion, even though it had been a major stumbling block to her proposed marriage. "I try to lead a Christian life," she says now. In the early fifties there were rumors that she would convert to Roman Catholicism—officially denied by the Vatican—such was her dedication to worship and her preference for High Church services with their incense and greater regard for ceremony. With her sister she had visited the Pope for the first time in 1951, but there was never any question of her leaving the Church of England for Rome, a move which one Roman Catholic official said "would send Anglo-Saxons en masse back to the religion they abandoned four hundred years ago."

4

DELIVERED FROM A DAUNTING DESTINY AND
relatively unscarred by the cruel conclusion to her affair,
Princess Margaret faced another, though lesser dilemma.
The matrimonial cupboard, it had to be faced, looked decidedly bare. She told her friends that she felt "left on the
shelf." Blandford and Dalkeith, of course, were gone irrevocably and, by the end of 1955, Margaret found that
Tennant, Porchester and Ward were all spoken for. Of the
eligibles who had steered her through the heady days of The
Margaret Set, only Billy Wallace was around and available
to help her recover the tempo of her single life in London.

Billy Wallace was the youngest of five sons of Captain
Euan Wallace, a Scottish landowner and one-time Conservative Minister of Transport. When Captain Wallace died, his
wife Barbara, daughter of the distinguished architect Sir
Edwin Lutyens, married Herbert Agar, a wealthy American
who had been Special Assistant to the American Ambassador
in London. They lived in Beechwood, a country estate near
Petworth, where Margaret now became a regular weekend
guest. Billy, who was three years older than the Princess,
had become sole heir to a seven-figure family fortune on the
death during the war of two half-brothers (the Captain had
first married Lady Idina Sackville, daughter of the 8th Earl
De La Warr) and his own two brothers.

His father died in 1941, when his youngest son was still at
Eton. The Thames Valley had not agreed with Billy's health
(he had kidney problems among others), and he went to

Millfield, a pioneering coeducational school in Somerset. After he came down from University College, Oxford, Billy had carved a niche for himself in society and had quickly been welcomed into Margaret's inner circle. A man of wealth whose continuing uncertain health precluded him from pursuing a career—he had dabbled with the Stock Exchange and trained in merchant banking with Kleinwort, Benson, Lonsdale—he lived in some style in a South Street, Mayfair, house, attended, on the occasions when he gave parties, by uniformed flunkeys. In common with his moneyed contemporaries, he used to fly to Le Touquet for a weekend's gambling at the casino; attend fashionable race meetings at Newmarket, Epsom, Ascot and Goodwood; lunch and dine at his London clubs, White's and Pratt's in St. James's; and end his evenings in either the 400 or another nightclub where there was a floor show, like the Casanova.

"He was endlessly socially ambitious and must have asked Princess Margaret a thousand times to marry him," says Tennant. "All the grandees had gone, Peter Townsend had departed, we were otherwise occupied and so she was left with Billy, who took full advantage of the situation."

Wallace, a tall, slightly stooping figure with the languor of a P.G. Wodehouse hero, pressed his suit and Margaret was receptive. While her feelings for him did not approach the great passion that had been engendered by Townsend, she felt comfortable with him, and familiarity brought a dimension of its own to their meetings. Billy knew her life, understood it, aspired to it. It was not, she realized, the most brilliant match she might have made but, given the circumstances, it seemed right. As Peter Townsend prepared, then, to set off on a eighteen-month round-the-world odyssey to exorcise his demons, Margaret, probably to be rid of hers, provisionally accepted Billy's proposal.

The engagement was to remain unofficial until it was certain that there were no obstacles to marriage; Margaret did not want to repeat the embarrassment of the Townsend affair. Billy, however, felt secure enough in the knowledge that the betrothal would receive the Queen's approval to take himself off for a bachelor holiday in the Bahamas. He went to Lyford Cay near Nassau on New Providence Island, where Canadian brewer and industrialist E.P. Taylor had begun an exclusive development of villas, a club, golf course and yacht marina. There he joined up with friends: publishing millionaire Jocelyn Stevens, aviation heir Tommy Sopwith, and Hampshire landowner Andrew Craig-Harvey were there, taking the winter sun. Billy, now thirty, intended to celebrate the last of his bachelor days in roistering good style.

"Then he behaved stupidly. While at Lyford Cay he had a fling and, flushed with success, returned to London and didn't even bother to call Princess Margaret," says Colin Tennant. "She soon heard, obviously, that he was back and telephoned to ask him if he was doing anything that evening. He said nothing much so she asked him to Clarence House to have an egg or something for supper, and when he arrived he told her all about his fling. She was furious and threw him out and I don't think spoke to him for ages. He told me he was rather surprised by her attitude. He was very silly."

Eight years later, in 1965, Wallace married Elizabeth Hoyer Millar elder daughter of diplomat Lord Inchyra. Princess Margaret forgave him eventually, when she began to realize that she had had a lucky escape, but friends like Jocelyn Stevens remember that she "became very bitter about Billy after that." Wallace, who took up farming in Berkshire for the country air, died of cancer in 1977.

Margaret's feeling of isolation had grown during 1956, when four of her former escorts married—attending their weddings was a roll call of might-have-beens for her. In April she went with the Queen Mother to Holkham, the magnificent Palladian mansion of the Earl of Leicester, set in 29,000 acres close to Sandringham, for the marriage of his eldest daughter, Lady Anne Coke, to Colin Tennant. The bridegroom remembers Margaret looking "very cross" that day. Yet it did produce a bridge to the future, for Tennant had engaged the up-and-coming Antony Armstrong-Jones to take the official photographs. It was the first time Princess Margaret set eyes on Armstrong-Jones. He had taken some portraits of Tennant the year before, which Tennant thought rather good, and so the two struck up an acquaintance.

The previous year another loyal Margaret escort, Mark Bonham Carter, the grandson of Edward VII's Prime Minister, Asquith, had married. Shortly after Tennant wed, Henry Porchester (now the Queen's racing manager) married Jean Wallop, a niece of the Earl of Portsmouth, and Peter Ward married Claire Baring, a darkly pretty cousin of Lord Ashburton. Quite simply, with Wallace *persona non grata*, there was not a suitable man in sight, and any prospect of matrimony was dismissed from Margaret's mind. Only the women of her "gang" kept in close daily touch now. Tennant says: "She thought then that she would never marry and became quite reconciled to the fact. So she set off on a different tack, and started being mildly adventurous."

The mood of the late fifties coincided with hers—swing was giving way to jazz and the big band sounds of Duke Ellington, the foxtrot was being replaced by Latin American crazes like the cha-cha, and in 1956 jive had arrived with Bill Haley and the Comets. An avid record collector, Margaret built up a formidable collection of LPs and 45s in her "den" at Clarence House. There, although they had separate quarters, widowed mother and spinster daughter lunched or dined together practically every day, moving to Royal

Lodge in Windsor Great Park for weekends. Margaret saw Count Basie and his band twice in one day at the Royal Festival Hall, and when Louis Armstrong met the Princess after a concert, he was so impressed by her knowledge of his music that he declared to the press: "Your Princess Margaret is one hip chick." For the first time she touched mildly bohemian life, making friends with artists, among them Gerald Bridgeman, a cousin of the Earl of Bradford.

There were royal duties also to help Margaret take her mind off personal matters. She looked forward to them for they were an enjoyable and gentle introduction to the outside world. The King had brought her up to perform with the public in a manner that was dignified but not standoffish. She had been tutored in the royal art of putting the nervous at their ease with a personal, reassuring word, of mastering the small talk necessary when opening schools, lunching with provincial lord mayors, or taking tea with the Women's Institute. It was duty, but certainly at the beginning, it was pleasure as well. Margaret found that the "ordinary people" responded to her, the more so after the Townsend episode, as they were appreciative of her obvious sacrifice. Her life ahead seemed to be paved with handshakes, attendances at mundane functions, and participation in ceremonial, and she looked forward to it all. It made her feel useful, wanted.

During 1956, she undertook two official trips, the first with the Queen and Prince Philip to Stockholm for the equestrian events of the summer Olympic Games, and then, after spending her twenty-sixth birthday at Balmoral, she toured Kenya, Tanganyka, Zanzibar, and the Mauritius, by chance meeting Francis Townsend, Peter's youngest brother, who was the British District Commissioner in Arusha, Tanganyka. She won over stuffy Colonial officials with her knowledge, enthusiasm, and wish for informality, and once, when Sir Evelyn Baring, Governor of Kenya, took his leave of her with a bow, she told him: "See you later, alligator." An aide-de-camp was able to explain to a puzzled Sir Evelyn that the phrase came from the film *Rock Around The Clock* and that the correct response was: "In a while, crocodile!"

Returning from East Africa, with time on her hands, she agreed to have her portrait painted by Annigoni, for whom she sat fifteen times, first at Clarence House and then at his studio after he had complained about the light. Margaret made two small criticisms of the finished work, which the artist obligingly corrected before it was hung in the Royal Academy: a small bow on her dress and a strand of hair were out of place. In January 1957, the Princess—who was by now an expert at the jive, jitterbug and Charleston—became associated with the respectable end of the dance spectrum when she was made President of the newly formed Royal Ballet. At the same time, opinion was growing that her energies might be more useful employed in an appointment as Governor-General of the West Indies, a move which both the Queen and her Tory Cabinet thought inadvisable for a single woman. She was called to the Bar after dining with the benchers of Lincoln's Inn, and undertook an increasing number of official engagements.

Many of her public activities did not reflect her private interests. For instance, although she had only a cursory knowledge of nursing, she was made Commandant-in-Chief of the Ambulance and Nursing Cadets of the St. John Ambulance Brigade, and President of the Student Nurses Association. Then, following time-honored tradition, she was appointed Colonel-in-Chief of the Royal Highland Fusiliers and the 15th/19th King's Royal Hussars, but war games, inspections and regimental life have always bored her. Such appointments came either through death or retirement of older members of the royal family or public figures, and were accepted so that she might take a greater share of the royal work load, rather than to expand or approximate her own involvements. Within the confines of her situation, Margaret pronouned herself reasonably content. She was escorted to the theater and other social events by charming, attentive men, but she felt no physical attraction for them. Caged at Clarence House, while a couple of hundred yards away her sister reigned in an enviable tableau of handsome husband and two appealing children, her resentment was bound to spill over. Which it did, say friends, over the plans for the Queen's tenth wedding anniversary celebrations.

The event was to be commemorated with a ball at Buckingham Palace on November 20. On that evening Margaret chose to take a party, including Sir Eric Miéville, who had been her father's private secretary, to the Coliseum to see *The Bells Are Ringing*. Afterwards she dined at the Savoy, arriving at her sister's festivities around midnight, an hour and a half after dancing had begun, and stayed for less than an hour. Her apparent insouciance was noted by Fleet Street and a banner headline in a popular New York newspaper blared: "MEG AND QUEEN IN NEW BREAK?" Rumor had it that Margaret's attitude was: it's all right for my sister to celebrate ten years of marriage, but, thanks to her, I am still unmarried. Perhaps she was beginning to feel that a marriage to Townsend might have been possible without sacrifice, if the Queen had been firmer with Eden and persuaded Salisbury to withdraw his threat of resignation. Peter, who was nearing the end of his sixty-thousand mile, eighteen-month trek in a Land Rover, was still on her mind, especially in the dark hours of the early morning. . . .

In the last week of March, the Clarence House switchboard operator put through to Margaret the telephone call she had been waiting for: Townsend was back and he was ringing to request a meeting. He had much to tell her of his adventures and wanted to hear her news, but the Princess was due to leave for Germany on Friday, March 28, and, for the first fortnight in April, Townsend was taking his two sons to Spain to try to get to know them again after his long absence. A reunion was finally fixed for the twenty-sixth at Clarence House, with the Queen Mother's blessing. She could see no harm in giving her permission for the get-together which Margaret so obviously wanted: the affair was clearly dead and, besides, she herself wanted to see Peter again after so long. Having in their naivety failed to learn from past experience, Margaret and Townsend did not believe that their situation retained any piquancy for the public, or that it would attract any press attention. Next day, of course, it was front-page news all over again, relegating reports of the Queen's State Visit to Holland to inside pages. Margaret was accused of being "headstrong" and Townsend of gross discourtesy by "barging in behind the Queen's back." A second meeting, planned for the twenty-seventh, was sagely cancelled.

But Margaret was not done with Townsend yet—it appeared that she couldn't allow the memories to remain simply that. Even a successful tour of the Caribbean, where a colorful throng cheered her every move, failed to lay the ghost, and back in Britain in early May, she traced Townsend to his sister Stephanie's home in Somerset, inviting him to a lunch the Queen Mother was giving at Royal Lodge. Walking in the lovely gardens, which the late King had himself designed and laid out from scratch, that clear spring day, the couple were treading in old footprints, almost feeling the immediate presence of the man who had, unwittingly, brought them together fourteen years before. Caught up in that spirit of romantic nostalgia, they met again twice in the following week, at Clarence House. But before the romance could start all over again, Margaret and Townsend were brought down to earth. Marriage rumors, dormant for thirty-one months, were multiplying and, for the first time, Buckingham Palace issued a denial. Margaret took heed of advice—or it may have been an order—to "cool it." She and Townsend met once again, on May 20, to say adieu. It was their last meeting, but one final salvo, late the following year, was to have fateful consequences for the Princess who says now: "We tried to get along on the basis 'if you're here, drop in' but it didn't work."

MARGARET SEEMED LISTLESS, NOTICEABLY SO, as she performed her public duties and joined in the royal routine. This included the Epsom Derby on the first Wednesday in June, a stay at Windsor Castle for the four-day Royal Ascot race meeting later in the month and, at the beginning of August, the trek to the Highlands for her birthday at Balmoral and the Braemar Games. When she returned to London, Lady Elizabeth Cavendish gave a small dinner party at her Chelsea home to lighten the Princess's mood, inviting for her delectation one of the more outré members of London society. Since their last meeting, Antony Armstrong-Jones had graduated from taking party pictures for the glossy magazines like *Queen* and *Tatler* to specializing in theater photography. An ambitious man, he had made his mark with the publication of the official studies to commemorate the Duke of Kent's twenty-first birthday in October 1956, a commission he gained after writing a letter recommending himself to the Duke's mother, Princess Marina. Lady Elizabeth, who has herself never married because of a life-long devotion to the Poet Laureate, Sir John Betjeman, a married man disinclined to divorce, had known Tony Armstrong-Jones from his days as a house photographer for the John Cranko revue *Cranks*, in which she had a small investment, before it arrived in the West End in 1956.

Margaret had forgotten—if indeed she had ever remembered—their first meeting, when Tony had lined up the Tennant and Leicester wedding group against the magnificent sweep of the Holkham stairs. She was immediately struck by his impish smile and his size: he was just a few inches taller than she, whereas all her old beaux, Sunny, Johnny, Colin, Dominic, and Billy were well over six feet tall. She saw that he was not dressed in the formal three-piece dark suit and stiff-collared shirt that was the uniform for dinner parties when a dinner jacket was considered too formal. Armstrong-Jones preferred chukka boots and a casual jacket. He drank wine while she sipped a whisky, and they were placed next to each other at the dinner table. It soon became apparent to the solicitous Lady Elizabeth that her imaginative pairing was working. Tony, who called Margaret "Ma'am" throughout the evening and observed the protocol of bowing on being introduced and saying goodnight, was intrigued by the Princess, who quickly dispelled any preconceived notions of her he may have harbored. She was witty, informed, attractive and, he sensed, available. It was a challenge he did not intend to resist.

Before the dinner, Margaret knew little about Armstrong-Jones's background; her hostess had given her only a thumbnail précis: while he was on the fringes of being famous, he was not well known. The success of the Kent photographs had led to his taking the official portraits of Prince Charles, with his sister, for his eighth birthday in November 1956; the following year there had been a much-praised photographic exhibition of his work, featuring Marlene Dietrich, Sir Alec Guiness, Edith Evans, Claire Bloom, and other celebrities, and his work appeared regularly in the *Daily Express*, the newspaper which claimed to have "discovered" him. But of the man she knew nothing.

Margaret soon discovered that she was five months younger than Tony, who had an older sister, Susan, and that his father, Ronald Armstrong-Jones, was a successful barrister whose family home, Plas Dinas, was in Caernarvonshire. Ronald had married Anne Messel, the pretty heiress daughter of a millionaire stockbroker, and been divorced from her when Tony was five. Almost immediately, Anne had married the Earl of Rosse, a descendant of the Irish aristocracy with estates of 26,000 acres in County Offaly and near Doncaster in Yorkshire, where the family had made a fortune from coal mining. Ronald, who was to become a Q.C. [Queen's Counsel], had then married a blonde actress, Carol Coombe, daughter of an Australian, Sir Thomas Coombe, but they had separated and a divorce was being contemplated. Tony had been sent to Eton, where he contracted polio, and he had spent six months in the Liverpool Royal Infirmary, which was within driving distance of Plas Dinas. The illness left him with a withered left leg, one inch shorter than the other, and put an end to his boxing ambitions. When he went up to Jesus College, Cambridge, to study architecture, he took up the one sport in which success was still possible for him, coxing the college rowing eight in an effort to impress his father, who had rowed for Magdalen College, Oxford. Tony was awarded his blue in 1950, when, weighing 120 pounds and just touching five foot, three inches in height, he steered the Light Blues to a three-and-a-half length victory. It was in this race that he first displayed a streak of toughness: the boats had come perilously close on several occasions, and when they touched near Chiswick Steps, Tony had bawled at the Oxford cox, J.E.C. Hinchcliffe: "Why don't you fucking move over!" A dazed Hinchcliffe obliged, thereby giving the lead to Cambridge.

At Cambridge Tony had renewed friendship with an Eton friend, Jocelyn Stevens, millionaire nephew of Sir Edward Hulton, taking photographs and enjoying himself, to the detriment of his architectural studies. Eventually he left the university without a degree to concentrate full-time on his hobby. Margaret was told how he had gone to work in the Mayfair studio of Baron, the most fashionable portrait photographer of the day, after Ronald had paid a £550 "entrance fee" for the course, and had then started a free-lance career, setting up his studio in the basement of 59 Shaftesbury Avenue with a fellow photographer called David Sim, and hiring the Earl of Kinnoull's sister, Lady June Hay (now the wife of Tory M.P. Cranley Onslow) as a secretary and dogsbody. Commissions from the *Tatler* had followed, and when Jocelyn bought *Queen* magazine in 1957 as a twenty-fifth birthday present to himself, Tony was put on the payroll to help the new proprietor change the publication's staid image.

Soon Margaret was shown round Tony's studio home at No. 20 Pimlico Road, which he had transformed from an ironmonger's shop after his father had paid £1,000 for the lease. Between the Sunlight Laundry and an antique shop, and below a row of government-subsidized dwellings, No. 20 was on the ground floor with a spiral staircase descending into a basement patio area. As the Princess entered from the street, she was shown a rickety-looking ladder which led to a small bed perched in the recess above the front door. Tony told the Princess that he had slept there when he first moved in, clambering up a bookcase, but he had since converted another area into a bedroom, which allowed guests to use the nook—and take the risk of toppling down nine feet if they moved in the wrong direction during the night! Margaret saw Tony's darkroom and his secretary's office on the ground floor, and descending into the basement found it brightly decorated with Aubusson carpets, Regency gilt and lapis, with a parachute draped for effect, and an antique bicycle. What interested her most, however, was a large mirror on which Tony's honored guests had scratched their signatures with a diamond. But Margaret was not invited to add her name—Tony often entertained journalists, and he knew what inquisitive souls they could be.

Among Tony's more prosaic contemporaries, the reports of his parties and activities at No. 20 caused eyebrows to be raised—but he was a trend setter and Pimlico Road was a foretaste of the Permissive Society at a time when debutantes were expected to remain virgins and weekend house-parties were still strictly chaperoned to prevent "bed-hopping." A regular visitor to the studio, which she regarded as a second home, was Jacqui Chan, an exquisite model who had been born in Trinidad, where her father, of Chinese origin, was a photographer.

She sometimes stayed overnight and had enjoyed an un-committed friendship with Tony for more than a year at the time of his meeting with Margaret. Jacqui added exotic, feminine glamour to the mainly male gatherings at No. 20, and occasionally introduced black friends to Tony's circle. She had been a leading dancer in two musicals, *Kismet* and *The Teahouse of the August Moon*, in which Tony had photographed her. She had soon become his favorite subject, and a spread of his photographs was published by a Fleet Street newspaper in September 1957. When he went with her to London Airport, in June of the following year, to see her off to New York to audition for *The World of Suzy Wong*, there was speculation about a marriage. Tony told one reporter: "We are very, very good friends and she is a beautiful girl. We go about together and I have photographed Jacqui many times. But marriage—no."

Before Jacqui, Tony had been involved with an Eurasian beauty, introduced to him by his friend Patrick Pollen, a nephew of Lord Revelstoke. She caused his secretary, Heather Crawford, to resign. "Heather was also Tony's dark-room assistant," a close friend from the days at No. 20 recalls, "and one day she found a roll of negatives which she assumed Tony wanted developed. So she printed it and to her horror found that it contained pornographic pictures of the Eurasian with a lighted candle in a strategic position. Heather was very chaste and left immediately. The Eurasian stayed with Tony for a while, and eventually ended up with Eddie Maguire, an artist, and another friend of his."

During the early part of her romance with Tony the Princess had to share him with Jacqui—a novel experience for her. While she prepared for a family Christmas at Windsor, Tony was in New York with Jacqui. But he was a point of discussion in the Royal Family during the holidays. Margaret had told her sister and mother about her feelings for him, and he had recently taken official portraits of Prince Philip which would be released in January, at the start of a three-month tour of the Far East and Pacific. When Tony returned to London in the New Year it was to "do up" a hideaway he had found in Rotherhithe, where he could conduct his courtship of the Princess away from prying eyes and the gossip of his bitchier friends. No. 20 was out, not least because Jacqui felt able to drop in at any time of day or night. The place, anyway, had a risqué reputation out of keeping with his plans for the Princess.

Margaret, savoring Tony's noncomformist moods, told her closest friends that she felt "daring" being in his company and she was delighted that he persuaded an American journalist friend, William Glenton, to rent him the disused ground-floor portion of Glenton's riverfront house in London's dockland. There was only one drawback: Tony and his guests would have to share a first-floor landing lavatory with the landlord. Glenton was sworn to secrecy, however, and came to savor being a party to the clandestine arrangement. In March, Tony felt confident enough to end his relationship with Jacqui and took her on a final holiday to ski in Davos in

Switzerland, telling her that he had fallen in love. They parted good friends.

As the affair progressed, the circle of intimates who were invited to Rotherhithe expanded slowly, and those who were asked to join in cosy evenings—dinner was something simple like shepherd's pie with cheap wine to drink—found the couple calling each other "Tone" and "Pet," an intimacy which Margaret had allowed only one man before (others just being accorded the privilege of addressing her in private as "M"). Armstrong-Jones, it was noticed, had become the first man to peel from Margaret the carefully applied veneer of her royal upbringing.

Not all Tony's friends were pleased by the introduction to his new love, and some, like Jocelyn Stevens, who had married baronet's grand-daughter Jane Sheffield, a girl friend of the Duke of Kent, were horrified because they felt she was heading for a fresh and more wounding disaster. "Tony and I were friends at Eton but I went straight into the army for National Service and he went up to Cambridge because of his leg," says Jocelyn. "When I arrived at Cambridge two years later, we were out of step so to speak. I started a magazine there called *Cameo* with friends like Mark Boxer, and Tony used to take photographs for it. And when I took over *Queen*, Mark joined, and Tony became a regular contributor. I thought in 1959 that his work for me was beginning to go off and said to him one day, 'you must have some bloody bird!' Then he asked me down to Rotherhithe one evening, opened the door, and there she was, grinning. The next day Tony and I had an awful row. I told him the romance was madness but he wouldn't listen to me. He knew I was terribly against the relationship and acted, I thought, in an unreasonable way."

On May 26, 1959, Tony was spotted with the Princess for the first time in public but there were four other guests and no one made much of it because of his known involvement with Jacqui. It was assumed that the occasion was an extension of his position as a favored royal photographer. By the summer Tony's thoughts had begun to turn to marriage. When he spent a few days at Royal Lodge, taking the portraits which would be released in August for Margaret's twenty-ninth birthday, he felt confident that she would soon be ready to accept his proposal. Yet even the publication of the Armstrong-Jones photographs failed to alert Fleet Street to the situation, and their canoodling continued, unobserved, and without the intrusion of the telephoto lenses of cameramen which would haunt their movements later.

They were together at Balmoral in October, when Margaret's reverie was jolted. She received word from Townsend that he planned to marry on December 21, and wanted her to be among the first to know. He wrote that his fiancée's name was Marie-Luce Jamagne, that she was twenty, and her family came from Antwerp where her father, Franz, was a director of a firm which manufactured tobacco. They had first met in Brussels soon after he arrived in exile. She was a pubescent teenager who while competing in a horse show, took a fall at Townsend's feet. "I received a letter from Peter in the morning and that evening I decided to marry Tony. It was not a coincidence," Margaret, some years later, told Jonathan Aitken (now the Tory M.P. for Thanet East) on a holiday in Barbados. "I didn't really want to marry at all. Why did I? Because he asked me! Really, though, he was such a nice person in those days. He understood my job and pushed me to do things. In a way he introduced me to a new world."

Despite any reservations about Tony's total suitability, the Queen and the Queen Mother gave their immediate approval and blessing, but it was decided that no announcement would be made until the following February, after the birth of the Queen's third child. Nonetheless, just before Christmas, Tony gave Margaret an engagement ring, a ruby set in gold and surrounded by diamonds in the shape of a flower, which she showed off to her family at Windsor. Sister and mother continued to keep any nervousness about the proposed union to themselves. They were keenly aware that her one previous chance of marital happiness had been snatched from her, and now they were determined not to stand in the way of what might be her last opportunity.

The breathing space gave Tony and his family time to clear the decks and prepare for the inevitable spotlight. In April 1959, Ronald Armstrong-Jones had petitioned for a divorce from Carol after twenty-three years of marriage, citing a man named Lopez. He himself had become involved with a B.O.A.C. air hostess, Jennifer Unite, one year older than his son, and their marriage took place just before the announcement, which found them honeymooning in Bermuda. Prince Andrew arrived on February 19, and a week later, much to the amazed incredulity of all but a couple of dozen people, the Princess and Tony made their news public with a statement which read: "It is with the greatest pleasure that Queen Elizabeth, the Queen Mother announces the betrothal of her beloved daughter, The Princess Margaret, to Mr. Antony Charles Robert Armstrong-Jones, son of Mr. R.O.C. Armstrong-Jones, Q.C., and the Countess of Rosse to which union the Queen has gladly given her consent."

Jocelyn Stevens was at his home in Lyford Cay when Tony, to whom he had not spoken since the row, cabled the news to him the day before the announcement. "I sent a telegram back saying, 'Never has there been a more ill-fated assignment,'" says Stevens, who was full of premonitions and openly forecast disaster, as did Tony's father who, from the first moment he had been told, implored his son to change his mind. Indeed, he warned him of the folly of his intentions almost up to the wedding day, which was set for May 6, 1960. Peter Townsend, when contacted by the press for his comment, replied: "My wife and I are very happy. We wish Princess Margaret great happiness. In fact we have known about this event for some time. We rejoice with all of Britain. We immediately sent off a cable with our good wishes." And contacted in Paris, the Duke of Windsor said: "I do not know the gentleman but I wish my niece and her betrothed every happiness."

Asked how Fleet Street had been bamboozled into believing that there was nothing between her and Armstrong-Jones, although their names had cropped up together on several occasions—Tony had even spent part of January at Sandringham—Margaret explained some years later: "Because no one believed he was interested in women. We met at Lady Elizabeth's in the autumn, then we were together the next year at Royal Lodge for the photographs and Balmoral, and no reporter gave it a second thought."

The gossip about Pimlico Road blighted the weeks before the Westminster Abbey ceremony, in preparation for which, Tony had been moved into Buckingham Palace, taking a suite of rooms normally occupied by the Countess of Leicester during her spells as a lady-in-waiting to the Queen. Tony wanted Jeremy Fry, whose father, Cecil, was the head of the family chocolate firm, to be best man, but there was, naturally, opposition from official quarters when it was discovered that he had a homosexual conviction dating back to 1952. A regular at No. 20, Fry stood down a month before the wedding, pleading a diplomatic attack of jaundice although he was fit and tanned after returning from a skiing holiday. Another Jeremy—politician Thorpe, who was to become Leader of the Liberal Party—was then considered, but the Special Branch turned up evidence of his homosexual tendencies and he, too, was discarded. From a short list of five finally submitted by Tony, a less intimate friend, neurologist Dr. Roger Gilliatt, son of the surgeon-gynecologist to the Queen, was chosen. He was married to writer Penelope Gilliatt, who contributed to *Queen* and *Vogue*, and seemed refreshingly heterosexual.

"Whatever the stories, there were always girls around Tony," says one old male friend. "And what he had foremost in common with Princess Margaret could be put in three words, sex, sex, sex. Theirs was a terribly physical relationship, they couldn't keep their hands off each other even with other people present. Girls loved Tony. He was very well made and obviously that had a lot to do with it."

Friday, May 6, was a perfect late spring day, clear and sunny, and the good weather was a comfort to the thousands who had slept out overnight to reserve the best positions along the ceremonial route. By breakfast time, the Mall, with its distinctive red tarmac, over which fluttered flags with the intertwined monograms "M" and "A" on white poles topped with the royal crown, was suffocatingly packed. With Prince Philip beside her, Margaret rode to the Abbey in a glass coach, her every move being covered by television cameras from around the world, recording the first royal ceremonial occasion since the Coronation seven years before. Bride and groom were cheered every inch of the journey back to the reception at Buckingham Palace, and the crowds seemed to have thickened by the time she reappeared in her going-away outfit to drive through the City to the Tower of London, where the Royal Yacht *Britannia* was waiting to take them on a six-week honeymoon.

On that day Princess Margaret's allowance from the Civil List was automatically raised to £15,000 a year. The wedding cost £26,000, and questions were raised in Parliament over the use of *Britannia* with its crew of twenty officers and 237 other ranks, for which the taxpayer was contributing more than £10,000 a week. The Royal Yacht, with its gleaming blue hull, steamed to the Caribbean to take in Tobago, Antigua, Barbados and St. Vincent, retracing familiar steps for an excited Margaret, who had made a tour of the islands five years earlier at the instigation of Churchill, who was seeking to assuage the pain of her parting from Townsend. It also anchored for three days off the Grenadine island of Mustique, where Colin and Lady Anne Tennant were waiting for them.

Since Tennant had moved to the country after his marriage, contact with the Princess had become intermittent, although they remained great friends. He was a director of the family company in London, but had a taste for the West Indies, where his father owned a tea plantation in Trinidad. In 1959, Tennant sold the plantation for £44,500 and while sailing through the Caribbean heard of Mustique, a wild, undeveloped island near St. Vincent. It had been put up for sale by two Irish spinsters, the Misses Hazell, had a small resident black population, and consisted of 1,400 acres, three miles long and one and a half miles wide. He landed on the white beach of Endeavour Bay, discovered that there were no roads or fresh water, and only one house, but felt that the island had potential and bought it for £45,000.

"When I learned of Princess Margaret's engagement, I asked her if she would like something wrapped in a box from Asprey's or a plot of land on Mustique. She was obviously submerged by little wrapped boxes from Asprey's so she chose the land," says Tennant, who was involved at the time with business in Canada. "We arranged for her to see the wedding present on her honeymoon and Anne and I flew down from Toronto to welcome them. It was very primitive on Mustique then, and the only house was burned down the following year. The Royal Barge took us on picnics to otherwise inaccessible bays, and Anne and I went on board *Britannia* for a bath and dined once on the boat. Princess Margaret liked Mustique enormously, but we didn't decide exactly where her plot of land would be."

Margaret and Tony returned bronzed, with a suitcase full of film which recorded their idyll. They had to camp temporarily in her quarters at Clarence House while a ten-room grace-and-favor apartment in Kensington Palace was being renovated for them at a cost to the Treasury of £6,000. It had fallen vacant on the death of the Marquess of Carisbrooke, the last surviving grandson of Queen Victoria, and they moved in during the second week in July with a staff of seven whose annual wage bill was £6,000. Her financial affairs were looked after by Major The Hon. Francis Legh, the younger son of Lord Newton, who had been the Queen Mother's Equerry and became Margaret's Private Secretary in 1959, and her Treasurer later. All press inquiries concerning the couple's official life were directed to Clarence House where the Queen Mother had recently engaged Major John Griffin as her Press Secretary and extra Equerry.

They had decided not to start a family immediately, although both were looking forward to children, and there was an inevitable anticlimax for Tony after the heady excitements of the first half of the year, as he groped to find a role to which his talents were suited within the framework of a royal marriage ("I'm not royal," he used to say, "I'm just married to one") and his wife's official duties. Margaret was on parade two, three, or four times a week, pressing flesh, making polite conversation, opening or dedicating various places, or attracting charitable donations by lending her presence to an occasion like a premiere. He did not find the transition from top photographer to royal escort easy, and sometimes mourned the passing of No. 20, now in new hands.

"Tony went through a terrible time during the transference period immediately after the marriage," says a friend. "They were living in that small Kensington Palace apartment, which Prince Michael of Kent has now, and if you went over to dinner, Princess Margaret would make a terrible fuss over you and wouldn't go to bed while Tony, quite reasonably, liked everyone out by around midnight. But she insisted on staying up until 2 or 3 A.M. and there was nothing he could do about it. She very much had the upper hand and in the beginning he had no answer."

From the outset, Tony insisted on accompanying his wife on all her official engagements, so that the couple soon became an ersatz version of the Queen and Prince Philip, performing the second-league royal chores. Such was their energy that the satirical magazine *Private Eye* dubbed them "The two highest paid performing dwarves in Europe!" Philip, who would have preferred a more sportsmanlike brother-in-law, taught Tony to shoot, which he did off a stick because of his leg, and after Christmas with the Royal Family, Margaret and Tony flew on New Year's Eve to stay at Birr Castle, the Irish home of Lord and Lady Rosse. With them they took Billy Wallace—finally forgiven, Rupert and Micky Nevill, and Jeremy Fry with his wife Camilla. It was the first of only three visits Margaret made to Birr, and her antipathy to Anne Rosse (locally nicknamed Lady Rossecommon) was apparent from the start. "Princess Margaret used to joke rather cruelly that she had to pack her crinoline for Birr so as to compete with Anne dressing up for dinner every night. She was really wicked because she never told Tony's mother to call her anything familiar, although Anne was allowed to kiss her on both cheeks after curtseying. In the end she got over the hurdle by just calling Princess Margaret 'darling,' " says an Irish friend, "and that was found acceptable."

In March, it was confirmed that Margaret was pregnant, which caused the Cabinet of Tory Prime Minister Harold Macmillan, who had succeeded Eden in 1957, to discuss the subject of a hereditary title for Tony. The child, who would be fifth in line of succession, could not suffer the indignity of being the first to be born into the Royal Family as a commoner—plain Master or Miss Jones. Fleet Street had reports of another "rift," venturing that the Princess was insisting that her husband be made a Duke, level pegging with Prince Philip, while the Queen would have none of it. In fact Margaret made no demands at all. Margaret was only keen for Tony to take a title so that her children (they envisaged more than one) would have some future reflection of their birthright. Tony had rejected the offer of ennoblement on his marriage. He preferred to be known and respected in his own right, rather than lay himself open to the accusation of social climbing through the union, and Margaret had been proud of his decision. But now a baby altered matters.

Agreement was reached on an earldom, the lowest hereditary title by which daughters were able to prefix their name with the courtesy style of "Lady," and which always carried a courtesy title of a viscountcy or barony for the eldest son. Mindful of his Welsh heritage and prompted in part by his godfather, Sir Michael Duff, whose family had owned much of Snowdonia for many generations, Tony finally—after much riffling through works of reference like *Burke's Peerage* with Margaret—chose to become the 1st Earl of Snowdon. One wit was prompted to remark: "They have made a mountain out of a molehill!" For his secondary title he chose Viscount Linley, after his maternal grandfather, Linley Sambourne, who had been a noted cartoonist for, among other publications, *Punch*.

"Royal Rifts" are a favorite theme of the press, whose

members are never privy to firsthand, personal glimpses of Royal Family life, but the Princess is adamant that relations with her sister have never deteriorated to that extent. "In our family," she says, "we do not have rifts. We have a jolly good row and then it's all over. And I've only twice ever had a row with my sister." It is probable that both "rows" concerned Margaret's choice of men—certainly the final act of the Townsend affair caused concern which gave rise to anger, and, much later, the Queen tried to counsel a furious sister against her liaison with Llewellyn, which she was determined to continue. Both involvements led to gossip and controversy at times when the image of the Royal Family could least afford such criticism. The rows would have followed the pattern of their childhood days, with the elder sister reasoning against dark defiance from the younger, who would fall into a sulk which would end as suddenly as it had begun. A spoiled child takes badly to being thwarted, after all.

The birth was expected in the first week of November. Margaret broached the subject with her sister of a new, larger home: Tony was talking of finding more regular occupation outside royal duties and would need an office area. The Queen granted them No. 1A Kensington Palace which consisted of twenty rooms and had been unoccupied for many years. It had always been understood that Tony would make his home in his wife's house, so he felt no shame at improving his lifestyle. Margaret needed to be in one of the royal palaces with enough room for a staff to assist her in her role, and it was a provision of the Civil List that most of the cost would be borne by the Treasury. Tony, who had published a very successful book of his photographs, had been used to a handsome income, but had not amassed a capital sum anywhere near sufficient to support Margaret. He was prepared to pay his way, contributing to the housekeeping and rates, but could not complain when his wife referred to "my home."

The cost of renovation and redecoration of No. 1A was estimated at £65,000, to be paid by the Treasury, but the Queen, with a keen eye for public relations, disclosed that she would personally be meeting £20,000 of the bill. Even when the final account rose to £85,000, there was no censure or accusations of extravagance by the press, with whom the Princess was still enjoying a honeymoon. During building, Tony took to supervising the workmen, the architect in him coming to the fore, and occasionally took over the welding chores himself, as an office, darkroom and work area were constructed for his use in the basement. For privacy there were separate bedrooms and bathrooms, and the main reception room, which would hold more than one hundred guests at parties, was decorated with kingfisher-blue walls, gold and powder-blue settees, and chairs in gold and burnt orange to match the patterned carpet, which was designed by Tony's friend Carl Toms, made in Spain, and presented to the couple as a wedding present by the City of London. Two blackamoors stood guard by the richly polished wooden doors into the drawing room, which Margaret always kept shut—since childhood, perhaps to protect her privacy, she has always had an aversion to sitting in a room with open doors. A conservatory led onto a large, private garden and beyond were Kensington Gardens and the Royal Albert Hall. The new home filled all the couple's needs.

As well as accompanying Margaret on her forays, Tony had been working on a commission for an aviary, from the London Zoo in Regent's Park, and had taken on an unpaid consultancy at the Design Centre in the Haymarket. But there was no escaping it, he was underemployed, and Margaret encouraged him to seek some position involving his old love, photography, which would achieve the twin aims of giving him an income (there was the cost of a nanny and, eventually, school fees to consider), and curing his restlessness. Aid came from Mark Boxer. Married to Lady Arabella Stuart, daughter of the Earl of Moray, Boxer had moved from *Queen* to prepare the launch of a color magazine for the *Sunday Times*, a great journalistic innovation for Britain. He brought Tony together with Roy Thomson, the forthright owner of the newspaper, and seeing mutual advantages, Thomson suggested the job of Artistic Adviser, with a salary of £5,000 a year, plus liberal expenses and international travel. Thomson did not know much about journalism—he regarded it as what went between the lucrative adverts—but he was angling for a hereditary peerage to add to the millions he had made in his later life (he had been virtually bankrupt at fifty), and he was not slow to appreciate the advantages of having the Queen's brother-in-law in his camp.

Tony's earldom was gazetted in October, in time for the birth at Clarence House on November 3, of a son weighing six pounds, four ounces. The infant Lord Linley was christened David Albert Charles Armstrong-Jones in the Music Room of Buckingham Palace on December 19, with the Queen, Lady Elizabeth Cavendish, Lord Plunket—Master of the Queen's Household—Lord Rupert Nevill and the Rev. Simon Phipps (now the Bishop of Lincoln) for godparents.

The New Year found Margaret and Tony taking a three-week break in Antigua, to the clucking of the press which labelled the Princess callous for leaving her baby with a nanny and a nurse. And while the parents were in the Caribbean, the exultant *Sunday Times* revealed that the new Lord Snowdon was joining their payroll, extracting apoplectic noises from the rival *Observer*, whose Editor, the Hon. David Astor, regarded the upstart Thomson with a mixture of horror and envy and wrote: "It will inevitably seem unfair to rival newspapers and magazines that the Queen's close relative is used for the enlargement and enrichment of the Thomson empire." The Queen had been consulted and she approved: it did not do the image of the family any good for any member, even by marriage, to appear to be idle, supported by the State via the Civil List.

Servant problems apart—their third butler in two years departed, muttering that the couple was hard to please (the first, Thomas Cronin, had quit to sell his story to a Sunday newspaper), and a maid, Ruby, left after five months. Margaret and Tony were establishing a pattern of life, moving between town and country, attending first nights of plays, ballets and operas, and giving dinner parties or going to those of similarly well-heeled friends who had inherited fortunes and an urge to enjoy themselves. Weekends were spent with couples like Jocelyn and Janie at their Hampshire home near Longparish, or the Frys (who separated and divorced after thirteen years of marriage and five children), or at Royal Lodge with the Queen Mother, who was proving a doting granny and had become immensely attached to Tony. Confounding the Cassandras, the marriage seemed to be working well, although with two similarly strong-willed partners, there were bound to be rages and following Cronin's betrayal, the staff was required to sign assurances that nothing seen or heard would either be communicated to the press or used later as part of a book of memoirs. To "do a Crawfie" was the ultimate sin, although Elizabeth and Margaret had come to realize that their governess had spilled the beans solely to ease the hardships of her retirement and had forgiven her.

On May 1 their second child, a daughter, was born and christened Sarah Frances Elizabeth Armstrong-Jones, in the Private Chapel at Buckingham Palace by the Dean of Westminster, Dr. Eric Abbott. Her godparents were Mrs.

Eric Penn (Jocelyn's sister Prue), Janie Stevens, who had become a lady-in-waiting, Marigold Bridgeman—the elder sister of artist Gerald—the Earl of Westmorland and wine shipper Anthony Barton, a friend of Tony's from Cambridge days. Like her brother, David, she was small, but with a mother who was barely five feet and a father only inches taller, medical opinion was that their offspring would be fortunate to achieve medium height. Margaret, everyone who saw her agreed, was a marvellous mother, breast-feeding her children at the beginning and, despite the presence of a nanny, getting up in the middle of the night to answer cries and involving herself in diapers and bottles when time permitted. If she had felt that she could have wheeled them around Kensington Gardens without drawing attention to herself, she would have done so. Being a mature mother, and having the advantage of staff, Margaret was able to enjoy her children and their love for her reflected this.

As part of her exercises to regain her figure, after adding almost three stone with each pregnancy, Margaret was exhorted by Tony to take up his passion for water-skiing. She herself had learned the sport in the brilliant waters of the Caribbean and then continued, wearing a wetsuit to ward off cold, on Sunninghill Lake in Berkshire, close to Royal Lodge, where Tony kept a speedboat and their equipment. "I really don't like sports at all," says the Princess, who used to refuse to accompany Townsend stalking at Balmoral, his favorite pastime. "But water-skiing was such fun and I became rather good at it. Then Tony sold the boat and I didn't do it again."

Introduced to Tony's artistic friends before marriage—like Cranko, Toms (who helped with Prince Charles's Investiture in 1969) and photographer Bob Belton, whose task it had been to escort Jacqui Chan to the wedding—as the new liberated mood of the sixties grew, Margaret found herself and Tony being feted by more conventional acquaintances. Greek shipowner Stavros Niarchos played host to them on his private island of Spetsapoula in the Aegean, where the couple was delighted to find Sunny Blandford and his new wife as fellow guests. Sunny's marriage to Sue had ended in divorce after nine years and in 1961, he married Tina Livanos, the ex-wife of Aristotle Onassis, whose sister Eugenie was Mme. Niarchos. The island was stocked with game birds specially imported for shooting, and the Niarchos yacht took the party on sight-seeing forays to Delphi and Corinth.

In the August following Sarah's birth, the British-born Aga Khan, who was struggling to get his Costa Smeralda (Emerald Coast) development off the ground in bandit-ridden Sardinia, invited Margaret and Tony to stay. Their acceptance was a considerable publicity coup. Tony, who was to accuse Tennant later of "exploiting" the Princess's connection with Mustique, appeared not to object to the royal couple's presence being subtly utilized to boost the prestige of the £80 million resort. "K," as friends call the Aga, whose first name is Karim, was a generous host, even to the extent of despatching his personal Falcon Fanjet plane to fetch his guests, who were put up at the Hotel Pitrizza in Porto Cervo, as the Aga's villa nearby was deemed too small. In Sardinia, with its unpolluted waters, they swam before breakfast, water-skied after, and, lest boredom set in, the Aga laid on his sleek yacht, *Amaloun*, so that they might explore the coast and go snorkelling. When the yacht was grounded, after confusion among the Italian crew, Tony donned a rubber suit to dive down and investigate the damage, returning to report that the white and brown hull had been holed. For the attendant British press, of which he was now a card-carrying member, he had a short statement:

"This is the most beautiful place for a holiday. We are enjoying ourselves tremendously."

On August 27, the day after the yacht mishap, Margaret and Tony were flown in the Aga's plane to Treviso, in northeast Italy, en route to stay with Jocelyn and Janie who had rented a Palladian villa, La Malcontenta, at Maltenza near Venice. "We were very heavily into culture in those days and we used to go off extremely early every morning on expeditions to places like Vicenza," says Jocelyn. "And when we got back in the evenings we would be debriefed by Princess Margaret who keeps these beautiful diaries. She would ask things like: 'Now what did we see in the Giotti chapel?' knowing full well herself, but making sure the rest of us had taken everything in as well." In the evenings the foursome would venture into Venice, dining with friends like Countess Marina Cicogna, granddaughter of Count Volpi, who had been Mussolini's Finance Minister, at her palazzo just off the Grand Canal, or in Harry's Bar, a cramped but fashionable restaurant close to St. Mark's Square. Margaret and Tony attended the Anglican church in Venice on the first Sunday of their visit but were less welcome a few days later in Padua, when the Princess tried to enter a Roman Catholic basilica in a sleeveless dress and was stopped at the door by the keeper.

The year ended, literally, with a bang. Visiting Abbey Leix, the home of Tony's sister Susan and her husband, John, the 6th Viscount de Vesci, and their three young children, Margaret and Tony found the route from the airport to County Leix strewn with leaflets by I.R.A. sympathizers, and one small country road was completely blocked by tree trunks. At the house itself there was a minor explosion but no one was harmed. In due course the Security Services warned the Princess against trips to Ireland, official or otherwise, and they ceased altogether, without much regret. The Irish, she said, were too boisterous for her, and relied too much on an outdoor life.

Many of Tony's old friendships faded, to be replaced with new pals, like Peter Sellers, whom he had met on an assignment to photograph the Goons, Derek Hart, a B.B.C. television reporter, with whom he eventually teamed up to make three documentaries, and journalists like Francis Wyndham of the *Sunday Times* (Colin's cousin), and Quentin Crewe, an Old Etonian writer who was confined to a wheelchair, with a crippling disease. From the arts there were performers like Rudolf Nureyev, who would stun guests at Kensington Palace (colloquially called K.P.) parties by turning up in head-to-toe leather or in full-length fur coats. After a party for Marlene Dietrich, Margaret was furious to discover that four bottles of a type of vodka then a rarity in Britain, which had been brought as a present for her, had disappeared. She spent the whole of the next morning telephoning guests to ask if they had seen anything. "She soon uncovered the culprit," says a guest who was interrogated.

As the so-called "Swinging Sixties" gained momentum and shape, Margaret and Tony became the totem for the new achievers, mixing easily with "trendies" like designer Mary Quant or hairdresser Vidal Sassoon, and giving royal recognition to the pop world led by the Beatles. Tony enjoyed the change of direction more than Margaret, who said: "When we married, I pressed him to keep up with his old chums, but the funny thing about Tony is that he is a friend dropper. After the marriage nearly all his old friends vanished and I never saw them again. I'm not like that, I don't discard people. My friends are old friends."

Tony's official role as consort to the Princess on her public engagements, began to become secondary to his business commitments. These were organized by his secretary Mrs.

Dorothy Everard, who had arrived at No. 20 in 1959 some time after Heather Crawford's outraged departure. Tony's early struggle was to prove to the world and to himself that he was his own man and not just an appendage of his wife. His father Ronald used to say: "Perhaps, with my three marriages, I didn't give him the stability he needed. But I gave him freedom and without freedom and the ability to do what he wants, he won't survive."

Splendidly rehearsed by Prince Philip, Tony had adopted the hands-clasped-behind-the-back posture as he limped an obligatory pace or two behind the Princess on her rounds but, away from protocol, he would don leather to ride his powerful motorbike out of the Kensington Palace gates into the High Street traffic, occasionally—to the alarm of her Scotland Yard detective—with Margaret on the pillion in dark glasses and a scarf tightly binding her hair.

Sellers, with whom the Princess was to become very involved emotionally, and his second wife, Swedish starlet Britt Ekland, soon counted themselves the couple's best friends. They were invited to Royal Lodge and were taken over to the Castle for tea with the Queen and Prince Philip, much to the delight of Prince Charles, who was a great fan of the Goons and would practise his impersonations with Sellers. Like Tony, Sellers became a keen shot, taking part in the pheasant shoots from Royal Lodge, and in turn, Sellers and Britt would entertain Margaret and Tony at their spacious house in Elstead, near Farnham, in Surrey, which had paddocks and a rural setting. When Britt became pregnant (her daughter Victoria was born in January, 1965), Margaret was full of advice and, says Britt: "When our daughter was born they sent flowers and gave her a fluffy Teddy Bear which she adored, but Sellers read too much into the gestures. If Tony just happened to say he liked a new camera or lens which Sellers had bought, then he would make him a present of them. Sellers sold Tony our silver blue Aston Martin at a fraction of the price it cost. After our divorce in 1969, Ringo Starr bought our house and Sellers was there to arrange to pack our things. He saw Victoria's Palomino pony, Buttercup, grazing in the field and telephoned for a horsebox and had the pony delivered to Kensington Palace as a present for Princess Margaret's children. Buttercup was special, four feet high with a silky coat the color of champagne and Victoria was devastated."

Peter and Britt were guests when Margaret gave a thirty-ninth birthday party for the Queen, in April 1965. First there was a visit to the theater to see Spike Milligan in *Son of Oblomov* with repartee during the performance between Sellers in the middle of the royal party and Milligan in bed on stage ("Why does Prince Philip wear red, white and blue braces?" "I don't know," replied Sellers. "Why does Prince Philip wear red, white and blue braces?" "To keep his trousers up!"). Then there was dinner at K.P., followed by more Goonish behavior, aided and abetted by Harry Secombe and Michael Bentine, to the especial delight of Prince Charles and Princess Anne.

The high point of the evening was the "Royal Premiere" of a home movie directed by Jocelyn, photographed by Sellers and Tony, and starring Margaret, Tony, Sellers and an eight-months-pregnant Britt. "Princess Margaret impersonated Queen Victoria, Tony hopped along as the One Legged Golfer, Sellers did his Indian doctor "Goodness Gracious Me" moments from the film *The Millionairess* and I was an old movie screen vamp," says Britt. "For the final curtain, we all linked arms and sang, "We're riding along on the crest of a wave" in the best Gang Show tradition." Sellers, generous as ever to royalty, had paid £6,000 to have the film edited and to add on a soundtrack. He presented a copy to the Queen, which is still brought out at family gatherings.

Sellers and Britt went to Rome during the summer, extending an invitation to Margaret and Tony to look in on the set of *After The Fox*, the film they would be making following their Sardinian holiday in August. At the end of another cosseted stay with the Aga, Margaret and Tony flew to Southern Italy to meet up with Jocelyn and Janie, and stay with the Count Martini Carissimo at his thirteenth century castle situated atop a hill in the middle of Oria, a town near Brindisi. Tony's Aston Martin had been delivered there, and followed by Jocelyn and Janie, who hired a car, he drove Margaret through the changing countryside to Rome, where there was the added pleasure of seeing Judy Montagu, who had moved there permanently in 1959, and, three years later, married American art critic Milton Gendel. When a daughter, Anna, had been born the following year, Margaret was delighted to become a godmother. The highlight for Margaret and Tony was a private audience with Pope Paul at Castel Gandolfo, his summer residence outside Rome. They then went with Jocelyn and Janie to stay at Villa di Maser, a beautiful Palladian house with Veronese frescoes, in the foothills of the Dolomites near Treviso. Their hostess at the villa was Countess Marina Luling Buschetti, the elder daughter of Count Volpi. It was all a great success and Margaret was to remark a few years later: "That was the last really happy holiday Tony and I spent together."

There was work, too, that year, official visits to Uganda, in March, where Margaret and Tony were received by King Freddie, the Kabaka of Buganda, an honorary colonel in the Grenadier Guards, and his Prime Minister Dr. Milton Obote; and late in the year, to the United States where they were welcomed to the White House by President Lyndon B. Johnson, and opened British Week in San Francisco. Along the way Tony was able to promote his new photographic book *Private View*, and in Hollywood they met superstars like Paul Newman, Steve McQueen and Gregory Peck. It was Margaret's first trip to America, and had its origin in a private invitation extended by Sharman Douglas, who had met the Princess when her father, wealthy Lewis Douglas, a copper heir, became Ambassador to the Court of St. James's in 1947. Sharman was a founding member of The Margaret Set, accompanied the Princess to the Derby and Royal Ascot, and had kept closely in touch through occasional visits to London after her father returned to America in 1950. Her suggestion that Margaret might like to visit Pontano Farm, the Douglas spread near Tucson, Arizona, led to an official flag-waving tour being arranged, but the jaunt unfortunately ended in adverse publicity in Britain.

Willie Hamilton, the Labour M.P. for West Fife (now Fife Central), and a man noted for his fierce republican leanings, criticized the cost (£31,000) in Parliament, and the tour ended on a sour note when there were angry scenes over the return flight on a scheduled B.O.A.C. aircraft. Apparently there had been a mix-up over seats, and ordinary passengers were forced to make space for the twenty-six strong royal party, who were charged an extra £5,000 for excess baggage. The theme of unnecessary royal extravagance was one to which Hamilton, who came from a mining background and represented a mining constituency threatened with many layoffs, was just beginning to warm.

On a personal front, too, there were problems for Tony, whose father had become seriously ill during the summer of 1965. Ronald, whose health had started to decline two years earlier, when he was taken off the *Empress of Britain* during a Mediterranean cruise was suffering from cancer. He had been forced to resign his post as the Lord Chancellor's Legal Visitor and spent five months in the hospital at St. Mary's, Paddington, before being released in October to rest at Plas Dinas, a beautiful sixteenth century house, where he was able to join the fifth birthday celebrations of his son Peregrine. By New Year's Day it was obvious that the end was near: it came on January 27. Tony organized the funeral, still deeply distressed at his father's courageous but painful fight to live. "Tony worshipped his father and whenever Ronald was in evidence, he acted straight as a die," says a close friend. "He was always doing things to please his father, like the rowing. Tony wanted his father to be proud of him and was devastated by his death even though Ronald never really came round to the marriage."

In his grief Tony sought to get away, and the *Sunday Times* arranged an assignment for him in India with writer David Holden, who was later murdered in Cairo in circumstances which are still unexplained.

6

THE EARLY WEEKS OF THE YEAR, BEING THE least busy in terms of official work for members of the Royal Family, present an ideal opportunity to go winter sporting—a favorite relaxation for keen bobsledder Prince Michael and skier the Duke of Kent—or to the sun to escape the dreary British weather. (Only the Queen, at Sandringham in 1966, mixed business with pleasure, sharing her holiday between her family (a third son, Prince Edward, had been born in March 1964) and the onerous task of "doing the boxes" (in reality, scuffed old leather dispatch cases) which are delivered to her every day, wherever she may be, for key Government documents to be read, initialled, signed, and returned.) With Tony away, only the odd engagement to fulfil, and the children in the capable hands of Nanny Sumner when their mother tired of playing with them, Margaret was looking for diversions and was glad when Anthony Barton, Sarah's godfather, called to inquire if all was well and to ask for news of the grieving Tony.

An archetypal tall, dark and handsome Briton, Barton had met Tony at Cambridge through his elder brother, Christopher, who was at Jesus College. Christopher had become a rowing hero for Armstrong-Jones when he stroked the 1948 Cambridge Eight to victory in the Varsity Race, and went on to captain the British boat that year in the Olympics. The Barton family had lived in Ireland, but their business was wine production and shipping in Bordeaux, where the firm of Barton et Guestier had been established since the beginning of the nineteenth century. Christopher was expected to inherit the company from his uncle, Ronald Barton, who ran the business from Château Langoa, a typical eighteenth century house of the region, but after a difference of opinion he went to New Zealand where he became a farmer. His brother, who was slightly younger than Tony, became the heir. With his wife Eva, who was Danish, and their two children, Anthony went to live in Bordeaux. The Bartons and the Snowdons became firm friends, sharing holidays and meeting regularly.

"They were a great foursome and their children were of similar age, but when Tony came back from India he discovered that Princess Margaret had become emotionally involved with Barton. Perhaps she had been lonely or feeling insecure, but he was a very attractive man," says a Barton family friend. "The first Eva knew about anything was when Princess Margaret rang to confess her feelings for Anthony and to say how sorry she was and how guilty she felt. But for that call, no one might ever have known, but Princess Margaret obviously enjoyed the role of *femme fatale*. She is a typical Leo —devious, destructive and jealous. I don't think Eva has ever forgiven her, but they did get back on speaking terms eventually. Ironically Princess Margaret and Tony soon made it up. They were very tactile and I can remember seeing them soon after the Barton business and they could not keep their hands off each other. Then they went to some West Indies Independence celebrations, looking happy." If the Barton episode came as a surprise to her friends, it was also a shock to Princess Margaret who had never believed herself capable of such an emotional attachment. So far she had regarded herself as a model wife and mother, and it had never occurred to her that she would not continue to be so. Having married relatively late, she felt that both she and Tony had the experience to make it work, yet here she was shaking the foundations of their relationship. Because of his personal problems. Tony had been understandably difficult to live with and, while every woman needs occasional reassurance as to her attractiveness, she had taken matters too far and was contrite, resolving never to let it happen again. She knew, however, that Tony could regard her lapse as providing him with a license to misbehave himself, but his ardor for her did not seem to have dimmed and she dismissed those thoughts.

Those who had been apprised of the sensitive situation were soon surprised to find that Tony and Barton had apparently returned to bosom friendship. On July 25, following a hospital checkup for Tony, Anthony and Eva Barton gave a dinner party for ten, including Margaret and Snowdon, in the revolving restaurant, run by Butlin's, at the top of the Post Office Tower in Marylebone. Among the guests were wine expert Alexis Lichine and his wife, Hollywood star Arlene Dahl, who read Tony's fortune from tea leaves as the party drew to a close at 1:30 A.M. As a godfather, Anthony continued to be welcome at Kensington Palace to see Sarah, who, like her brother, had her father's looks, but the situation did put an end to the shared holidays the two families had so enjoyed.

"I've no doubt that Barton was originally encouraged by Tony," says Jocelyn Stevens. "If you yourself are playing around, then your conscience is eased if your partner does the same. Tony has a very complicated character."

If, after six years and a brief hiccup, the couple appeared to be enjoying an idyll, it was not to last, and the household soon divided again, this time over Tony's choice of a country retreat. Living as he had been, in his wife's domain, he wanted somewhere of his own, which owed not a penny to the Civil List or handouts from the Royal Family, a place where he could spend the children's holidays without servants and continuous social traffic, and invite his friends to relax, as in the old days of Pimlico Road. Financially he was in good shape, having made an estimated £30,000 from his book and now earning around £10,000 a year from the *Sunday Times*. He chose Old House, little more than a cottage, at Nyman's, a Sussex estate with thirty acres of gardens featuring rare conifers, shrubs, and plants, which had been handed over to the National Trust by the Messel family, for whom the burden of its upkeep was proving too much. Originally woodsmen's dwellings, Old House dated back three centuries and was virtually uninhabitable, although friends like Cranko and Bob Belton occasionally camped out there during warm summer spells, drawing water from an outside pump. Tony obtained permission from the Trust to modernize the building and make a lake down the hill in front of the house, in the middle of which he planned an island with a pagoda, to be reached by a replica of a gondola.

Tony invested his income from *Private View* (which not surprisingly had sold well in America) in Old House, cannily employing enthusiastic but cheap student labor during the holidays. When it was at last ready for occupation, Tony asked the Queen Mother down to cut a ribbon for a mock-ceremonial opening, while the Queen looked on applauding, and he snapped the occasion with all the enthusiasm of a Fleet Street cameraman. But Margaret soon found faults with the house, and voiced them. It was, she told the designer, too functional, without the sort of comforts she would expect, and clearly built to his wishes without catering to her needs. It was obviously not the sort of place she was going to enjoy staying in and, perhaps, that had been Tony's Machiavellian scheme all along? In return, he disapproved of the long-term retention of a nanny for the two children (they had decided not to have any more), who he felt should be allowed to stand on their own feet more.

"Tony has a theory about bringing up children," says a friend. "For instance he insisted that toys had to be constructive. When he was at Eton, boys were banned from having wirelesses or gramophones in their rooms unless they made one themselves, which Tony did—from the beginning he was a genius at designing and knocking up things. He did not think children would evolve to their limits with a nanny always on hand and in the row over how long Nanny Sumner should stay, he had a lot of support from friends."

While British tourists were restricted by the Labour Government in 1966 to taking just £50 a head abroad with them in an effort to preserve the balance of payments and prop up Sterling, Margaret and Tony, fortunately, were able to avail themselves of a free holiday—courtesy, again, of the Aga Khan, who ferried them on August 10, to Sardinia in his jet. They arrived at the height of the island's worst wave of banditry—two people had been shot, five policemen held up and tourists had been robbed in three ambushes—and "K" laid on armed guards for the royal couple. While David and Sarah were at Balmoral, with their aunt and grandmother, Margaret celebrated her thirty-sixth birthday at sea—the Aga provided a cake with thirty-six candles in the shape of the Hotel Pitrizza, where they were again staying—before rejoining the children in Scotland at the end of the month.

But in contrast to the surface image, it was not a happy time. The Barton affair had taken its toll, and friends, like Jocelyn, had noticed a certain edginess in Margaret and Tony. In the months to come, Stevens was to think back on the accuracy of the prescient telegram he had sent on learning of the engagement. "The row over Old House was not so much the cause of the eventual break-up as a sign," he says. "It wasn't so much a stupid squabble over who lived where, but the seeds had been planted a long time before and now they were being reaped." But Margaret sees it differently and says: "Tony broke up the whole marriage by going there. We were going to build a house at Sunninghill by the lake where we waterskied and then, without telling me, he went off and started Old House."

Against a background of bickering, Margaret sought the company of people to amuse her, and, unlike Tony, to share her interests and appreciation of music—her connection with the ballet had reawakened her love of the classical music and composers like Tchaikovsky and Prokofiev. A chance meeting reestablished her friendship with Robin Douglas-Home, a gifted piano player who, in the fifties, had performed nightly in the cocktail lounge of the old Berkeley Hotel in Piccadilly. His name had then been linked with Princess Margaretha of Sweden. Despite Robin's being the nephew and heir-in-line to the Earl of Home, a mooted marriage had been banned by Margaretha's autocratic grandfather, King Gustav, and in 1958 Robin had married top model Sandra Paul, an acknowledged beauty of her generation. They had separated, however, after the birth of their only child, a son named Sholto, largely because Robin—despite his charm—was inconsistent and unreliable.

Robin, whose uncle Alec had renounced his titles to become Prime Minister in 1963, gave up the piano to follow his writing ambitions, took up photography, and started a weekly column in the *Daily Express*, writing sophisticated notes about international society. He had published a biography of Frank Sinatra, who had become a close friend, and during that autumn and winter, Margaret either saw him or spoke to him most days of the week. Occasionally, too, he contrived to be included in her country weekends, while Tony involved himself elsewhere, unconcerned it would seem by the infatuation that others saw in Robin for the Princess. Robin told friends he was very much in love with Margaret and felt she reciprocated his passions. He hinted that she was delighted when Tony left for Japan after Christmas, for a month with journalist Brian Moynahan, to shoot a lengthy profile of the country for the *Sunday Times* color magazine.

In the Orient, Tony grew a beard and behaved more like a carefree bachelor than a married man, but Moynahan did not detect any signs that his cameraman might be concerned with events at home: "We were both staying at the Tokyo Hilton and working together every day, but he never once mentioned Princess Margaret," he says. "He was in contact with London but if there was anything going on, he didn't seem at all concerned. The first I knew about a rift in their marriage was when I read about it on my return. It surprised me."

The British newspapers had scented the whiff of scandal (Robin had been a Fleet Street colleague, after all) and piecing together the clues, seized on Snowdon's absence abroad to back up the claims that a separation of a more permanent nature was imminent. Their suspicions were seemingly confirmed when Margaret was announced to be unwell and, on the advice of her physician, Sir Ronald Bodley Scott, was admitted to the King Edward VII for a complete checkup. The Fleet Street grapevine had it that the Princess had taken an overdose of pills. While she was in the hospital, Tony flew from Tokyo to New York and, under pressure to make a statement concerning the growing press speculation, held a conference on February 27 at the Manhattan offices of *Vogue*, another of his regular employers: "Talk of a rift is totally unfounded," he declared in his most innocent manner, drawing heavily on a cigarette. "It's news to me—and I would be the first to know. I am amazed."

It was a typical example of dousing the media's curiosity by outright denial, sure in the knowledge that nothing could be proved. Both Margaret and Tony had known from the outset that much of their life together would be conducted as if in a goldfish bowl, but that did not mean they had to perform all the time. Tony was versed enough in the wiles of journalism to know that in the face of silence, a story soon dies, and he was not about to provide Fleet Street or anyone else with tomorrow's headlines. Besides, it was the proper form to present a united front to the world, and as far as he was concerned, his disapproval of Margaret's behavior with Robin was only going to be voiced in private. The incident had its advantages for him—it served to allow him greater freedom in the future in his own actions.

Margaret remained in contact with Robin, who was given to write her poetic letters, couched in intimate terms which left no doubt as to the intensity of his feelings and hopes for the future. On February 14—St. Valentine's Day—the Princess wrote to him. It was affectionate, loving even, but seemed to draw back from the commitment Robin demanded. When shortly afterwards, Sir Ronald recommended a sunshine recuperation for his patient, Margaret contacted Tony in New York and suggested a meeting in the Bahamas. Jocelyn had offered his Lyford Cay house, and it was arranged that the Princess would fly out, collecting Tony en route at Kennedy Airport in New York on March 10, to join him and Janie. For Margaret the days and evenings with Robin had been a joy, as well as a welcome fillip for her morale when it was low and still sinking. She had encouraged his protestations of love and, it had to be admitted, reciprocated them in some measure. "Tony couldn't understand about Robin Douglas-Home because he couldn't understand about music," says the Princess. "I had the devil of a job convincing Tony, who was convinced that it was all about you-know-what, that the basis was music. One of the letters to Robin was a very long musical joke, done in code."

Nassau was a reunion, but not a rapprochement. It solved

little in the long term, but the tensions were eased considerably by the presence of the photographer Earl of Lichfield, Margaret's first cousin once removed. "Patrick is frightfully keen to make money on any basis and knew that a photograph of Princess Margaret would sell round the world and kept badgering for Tony and me to set one up," says Jocelyn. "So we decided to play a trick on him and said we would arrange a fantastic picture of PM waterskiing if he split the proceeds three ways with me and Tony. My house was on a crescent bay with points on either side like the horns of a bull and we told Patrick to situate himself in some bushes on one of the points and we would bring the speedboat in very close with PM skiing behind so he could get great shots without her knowing."

As soon as Patrick placed himself and assorted cameras in the bushes, Jocelyn telephoned the police who had been doing their utmost to ensure the Princess's privacy and informed them that he and Lord Snowdon had just seen a French photographer skulking in the bushes, and asked for him to be arrested. No doubt, added Jocelyn, the man would pretend to be the Earl of Lichfield, but the Police were to take no notice of this subterfuge. From the window of the house, Jocelyn and Tony then watched in great glee as Lichfield was dragged off struggling.

"That evening Patrick had not reappeared, and at dinner Princess Margaret asked, 'Where's my cousin?' We told her we had no idea and that he was probably off chasing women. Then she said we ought to find him but we replied that we wouldn't know where to start and left it at that," says Jocelyn. "But we relented that night and called the police and told them that there had been a frightful mistake and the man was, after all, Lord Lichfield. Patrick loves telling the story against himself to this day!"

On another occasion the Bahamas' Minister of Tourism

arranged a visit to see how his illustrious visitors were getting on, and just as he was due to arrive at Jocelyn's house, Carina, the heavens opened and a tropical rainstorm started. "We decided that we would pretend that it was a wonderfully sunny day, and when the Minister came he found us all wearing bathing suits, the Princess and Tony lying on deckchairs reading, despite the terrific downpour, and looking as if we were soaking up the sun although water was dribbling off our noses. The poor man couldn't work out what was going on and just stood there getting frightfully wet. When he left we couldn't stop laughing—it was always like that when Princess Margaret and Tony were getting on well. We used to have such fun and never stopped laughing, that was what was so sensational about the marriage when it worked."

Before she left the Bahamas, Margaret telephoned Colin Tennant and asked him if his offer of the wedding present had been serious because, if so, she wanted to avail herself of his generosity. He confirmed that it was, and arranged to bring a map of the island to Kensington Palace for her to choose a ten-acre plot. It was the first intimation that Margaret was preparing for a life without Tony, who loathed islands, swimming, and sunbathing, but, as far as the public was concerned, the reconciliation had been effected.

When Margaret returned, she found Robin more persistent than ever. He refused to believe that anything had changed between them, but Margaret had made up her mind to persevere with her marriage. David was five and Sarah about to be three and "Mummy" and "Daddy" as they called their parents (unlike the more usual royal "Mama" and "Papa") had to stay together whether they liked it or not. Divorce, even a separation, was unthinkable as well as against the edicts of the religion, which Margaret still held dear, and which comforted her. What such an action would have done to the image of the Royal Family did not bear contemplating. So the Princess sat at her cluttered desk in the drawing room of Kensington Palace (she calls it her "system of mess") to compose a final letter to Douglas-Home which, without being harsh, would spell out to him that the affair could not, must not, continue. She had thought deeply about it, she wrote, and thanked him for the times they had shared, but she felt her responsibility lay with her husband and children and, in that realization, she had to sacrifice their friendship to make a go of the marriage. They must not meet again.

Robin was shattered. Later he took a job, at £50 a week, playing the piano in the early evening at the Clermont, the Berkeley Square gaming club founded by wildlife expert John Aspinall, but he began to talk, even to casual acquaintances, of suicide. He started writing a new novel (the first had achieved a minor success), but his world began to disintegrate when he lost his job, a year after Margaret dismissed him from her life. He had taken photographs of Aspinall with his animals, mainly gorillas and Siberian tigers, at the private zoo at his estate near Canterbury and, foolishly, had been persuaded by the gossip column of the *Daily Express* to sell, for £50, one of Aspinall in his swimming pool with a tiger. When it was published, Aspinall sacked him, calling his action a "betrayal." Robin, whose depressive personality had alienated him from many of his old friends, committed suicide in his country cottage when he was accused of another act of betrayal—some of Princess Margaret's letters to him turned up for auction in New York.

Meanwhile, Sellers, whose own marriage had been through a separation and stormy reconciliation, had observed the turmoils of his great friends with foreboding, and suggested they might all have some fun that summer on his new toy: he had paid £150,000 for a fifty-foot yacht, naming her *The Bobo* after the film he had been making (Britt had a supporting part), and wanted to sail her to Sardinian waters in August, for Margaret and Tony's annual visit to K. While the party was billeted in the new Cala di Volpe hotel, on the opposite side of Porto Cervo to the Pitrizza, with Margaret and Tony occupying the Presidential Suite, *The Bobo* was moored in a favored place in the harbor and, temporarily at least, "Captain" Sellers was the panacea they needed. He worked overtime at his antics and Goonery to diffuse sudden tensions and moods, and long, lazy days were spent on the yacht, with friends like Kirk Douglas and his wife Anne, whom Sellers had invited along after meeting them en route in Monte Carlo. Angus Ogilvy and Princess Alexandra were also visiting the Costa Smeralda—another coup for the Aga —and Margaret stayed on to celebrate her thirty-seventh birthday at a party given by her host. Competing as photographers, Tony and Sellers snapped away, throughout the holiday, often using their new Polaroids. When the royal suitcases were unpacked, the Kensington Palace staff were taken aback to discover several rather indiscreet snaps which had been taken, obviously, on the boat out at sea. . . .

Margaret's mind was on Mustique during these months and she had formed an ambition to build a house there to use as an escape hatch. Early in 1968, she flew with Tony to Barbados to stay with his uncle Oliver Messel, Lady Rosse's bachelor brother and the noted theatrical designer, who, for reasons of declining health, had made the Caribbean his permanent home, in a beautiful colonial residence called Maddox. In the belief that he retained some enthusiasm for architecture after three years at Cambridge, Margaret asked her husband to design a house for her. Tony said it did not interest him, so Oliver, gallantly, took over the project without fee. "One might have thought that Tony, as a failed architect, would have enjoyed doing it," says the Princess, "but he was being difficult."

Mustique was then in its infancy of metamorphosis from jungle to jet-set retreat, and Tennant had even put the island up for sale for "much more than £1 million," but there were no takers at that price. He had lost his job with the family firm when it had been sold in 1963, for £2 million to Consolidated Gold Fields, and had been involved in various leisure enterprises, including the promotion of the multi-million-dollar development of Grand Bahama, which had been transformed with hotels, condominiums, villas, a Jack Nicklaus designed golf course, and a marina. Mustique was a much smaller proposition, but without water, roads, or an airstrip, it still needed considerable capital investment to make it a commercial entity. Margaret's presence was to be a key factor in the transformation, and Colin was waiting for her at the jetty when she arrived by boat from St. Vincent to inspect her present, having flown the first stage of the journey in a light aircraft.

"I had duly gone to Kensington Palace with the map and together we chose a site above Gelliceaux Bay. Then I formally gave her the land by deed of consideration in marriage which meant that there would be no tax," says Tennant, who was on the island with his partner, the Hon. Hugo Money-Coutts, son of Lord Latymer. "She arrived without any trousers to protect her legs so we kitted Princess Margaret out in a pair of my pyjamas and Hugo and I cut a path, rather like grouse beaters, up to her land. It overlooked one of the bays where we had picknicked on her honeymoon and it had a marvellous view. She said she was very pleased with her present. At that time I still had no idea what I was going to do with Mustique and when I suggested the wedding present, I had no plans to develop it."

Accused, and not only by Tony, of using the Princess, Tennant does admit that her association was "obviously helpful" in promoting the venture, but it had sprung up from innocent beginnings and, in a way, her determination to put down roots in Mustique gave him the impetus to develop the island. "Tourism after the war was the setting up of large hotels—white reserves, imposed from the outside. They thought people wanted cocktails and cha-cha-cha beside the pool, waited on hand and foot by grinning negro servants. In Mustique I tried building from the inside outwards and events proved I was ahead of my time. In Antigua, where the villagers were ignored by the tourists, the people turned against the whites. I made sure the villagers in Mustique enjoyed the same confidence they would have enjoyed at Glen. I was able to employ most of them, when before there was no work at all, and those too old to employ were given pensions which helped them to retain their status in the village. Almost more important, they are protected by my standards of behaviour."

To match Margaret's mood of independence, Tony was to be seen out in London lunching with attractive, flattered women, mostly associated with his work for glossy magazines. Among his companions were American writer Pamela Colin, who was approved of by the Princess and, in 1969, after a short romance, married widower Lord Harlech, the former British Ambassador to Washington; author Angela Huth (an ex-wife of Quentin Crewe), who contributed to both *Vogue* and *Queen*; and several comely ex-debutantes who worked as assistants at *Vogue* offices in Hanover Square, and regarded an invitation from Tony as a feather in their cap. Lunch invitations for the fortunate would progress to evening meetings, and one buxom conquest even spent part of her honeymoon at Old House with her unwitting Old Etonian banker bridegroom. She still carries a duplicate of the front door key as a memento of the liaison.

After a dozen or so visits to Old House, Margaret pronounced it "too clinical" and stayed away altogether. Tony, as if in retaliation, gave up the shooting in which Prince Philip had so conscientiously instructed him, explaining that he had lost the appetite for killing. He was thus absent from the Royal Lodge shooting parties, at which Margaret became host to guns like Sunny Blandford, Patrick Lichfield and, occasionally on his own, Peter Sellers. While the Princess weekended with her mother during school termtime, Tony would retreat into Old House, conveniently situated for David Linley's new boarding preparatory school in the Ashdown Forest. From an early age, David took after his father in character, as well as looks, while Sarah was more her mother's child. Brother and sister were loved equally but there were some occasional hints of favoritism displayed by Tony towards his first-born. The children were openly affectionate, well-mannered but, perhaps on account of their size, and distance from the real world, they were both shy when presented to it, and Margaret was relieved that they would never be required to jump through the public hoop as she was: "My children are not royal," she explains. "They just happen to have the Queen for an aunt."

Like many of their married contemporaries, Margaret and Tony had come to an arrangement which would need all their sophistication and verve if it were to work harmoniously. As long as the children, on whom both doted, were not affected, and the public did not discover the arrangement through the gossip columns, they would go their own ways in the private hours, keeping up a united appearance at public functions—around three a week—during school holidays, and on family occasions at Windsor and Sandringham (Balmoral, with its heavy emphasis on shooting, stalking and fishing held no appeal for Tony). Some marital arrangements work for a lifetime, but others are soon destroyed by jealousy, and Margaret and Tony were heading for trouble. Even at Sarah's christening, Ronald Armstrong-

Jones had looked at the infant's parents and said sighing: "They are too alike. It won't work."

In August 1969, they were back in Sardinia enjoying K's largesse. The Aga was more animated than on their previous holidays, principally because he was entertaining an English beauty, Lady James Crichton-Stuart, whom he planned to marry, but since the royal couple seemed at odds from the beginning, sniping at each other, it was difficult to cater to their moods. When Lady James (who had been born Sally Croker Poole and was the ex-wife of the Marquess of Bute's younger brother) married the Aga in October, she was not surprised, therefore, to see Margaret arrive at the reception in Paris without her husband, escorted instead by Patrick Lichfield and Jocelyn. Stevens had caused consternation at the British Embassy, where the party was staying, by bringing along—on the plane which the Aga had sent—an Australian whom he had met only the night before at Annabel's. The British Ambassador, Sir Christopher Soames, quickly had her shipped back to London.

Spending an increasing amount of time on his own at Old House, Tony was taken up by his neighbors, the most sociable of whom were also the nearest: the Marquess of Reading, a stockbroker in London who occasionally commuted to the City from nearby Haywards Heath station, and his wife Margot, a statuesque woman with a truly schoolgirlish sense of fun which coincided with Tony's. They had two grown-up sons, Viscount Erleigh, known as Sy, and Lord Antony Rufus-Isaacs; a daughter, Lady Jacqueline, who was twenty-two, and their youngest son, Lord Alexander, who was twelve and called Xan. Tony had introduced himself to Michael Reading before work commenced on Old House, asking a favor. His new home was in the woods and in a fairly inaccessible part of the Nyman's estate, and could only be reached, without a lengthy detour, by a private path which went past the Reading establishment, Staplefield Grange. In winter the path was impassable except by four-wheel drive vehicles, and Tony asked if he might lay two parallel concrete tracks, at his own expense, along to his home. Michael, a benign, pipe-smoking lover of classical music and the piano, readily agreed and soon Tony was dropping in, without needing to be invited, for tea or drinks, amusing Margot when her children were away during the week. On weekends the boys would help with the rebuilding, and Tony had become so friendly with the Reading children by November 1969, that when Jackie celebrated her twenty-third birthday, he sent her a card and a small present.

Princess Margaret had met the Readings and their children during her cursory stays at Old House and came to like Antony and Jackie enough to add them, no doubt at Tony's suggestion, to the Kensington Palace party list. She had learned that Jackie worked at Piero de Monzi, a fashionable clothes shop at the South Kensington end of the Fulham Road, and thought her pretty, although, as she remarked to Tony, she had neither a model's figure nor face and was inclined to spots. And when Margaret agreed to grace the charity premiere, on December 11, of the new Peter Sellers film *The Magic Christian* at her "local," the Kensington Odeon, she did not object that Antony and Jackie were included in the list of those invited afterwards to a party at her fifties haunt, Les Ambassadeurs.

When Margaret arrived at the cinema she found Sellers waiting to welcome her with his son Michael, who was fifteen, daughter Sarah, twelve, both from his first marriage, and Britt, from whom he had been divorced for a year. He explained that he had rowed with his new love, Miranda Quarry, a daughter of Lady Mancroft, and Britt was a last-minute replacement. After the film Sellers led the party, which included his costar Ringo Starr and his wife Maureen, Jocelyn, Lichfield and Tommy Sopwith, to Park Lane.

There were fifty guests placed at five tables, and Princess Margaret sat between Lichfield, on her right, and Jocelyn, while Tony contrived to be next to Jackie at another table where he went on to monopolize her attention. Sometime after 1 A.M., it was suggested that the nucleus of the party go on to Annabel's, five minutes away, for some dancing and a nightcap and Tony, in a velvet jacket with a scarf tied loosely around his neck, made sure that Jackie was not left behind. Sellers did not stay long, declaring his intention to go off and find Miranda and smoke some marijuana (a habit he had picked up the previous year in Hollywood making the flower-power film *I Love You Alice B. Toklas*), but Britt hardly noticed. She had been on Lichfield's other side at dinner and had been agreeably surprised when he devoted most of the evening to her, to the exclusion of the guest-of-honor. They had met only two days before when Sellers had brought her to Royal Lodge, where Patrick was staying for the pheasant shooting. He was amusing, handsome, rich, titled and unattached—just, in short, the kind of man Britt had been searching for. Whether he was sexy as well, she intended to find out quickly. She was delighted then, when Lichfield, instead of taking her up the road to her Mayfair flat, drove her in his Rolls directly to his Kensington studio house on top of Campden Hill in Aubrey Walk.

Although Margaret observed that Tony was making an effort, too much of an effort, she thought, with Jackie, she was not unduly concerned. She had seen too many sexy women flutter their eyelashes at her husband, and bask in his company, to worry enough for it to spoil her evening. As the official car took Tony and her back to Kensington Palace, Jackie made her way, Cinderella-like, to her Pimlico flat, situated, as Tony was to point out later, just fifty yards from the back of his old studio. Among the close-knit group who comprise London Society, the night of the premiere provided two items of hot gossip to be relayed around the drawing rooms of Belgravia and Chelsea. Lichfield had started an affair with Britt, and Lady Jackie, it was said, was very much in love with Snowdon. If the Princess suspected anything at this stage, she played a remarkably cool hand and invited Jackie and her brother Antony to Kensington Palace for a New Year's Eve party. As the new decade was rung in, Tony made his way to Jackie's side and, conspiratorially, squeezed her hand as he pecked her cheek.

7

LORD SNOWDON'S EX-LOVERS, INCLUDING
Princess Margaret, have only good words for him. They say he
is tender, unselfish, versatile and has great stamina. His affair
with Jackie lasted a little longer than a year, and was conducted with such discretion that few of their friends or family
knew about it until it was all over. It took place in Sussex
during weekends, when Jackie would slip up the lane from
the Grange, and in her second-floor flat in Cundy Street, just
off Ebury Street. Jackie's previous experiences had been
with contemporaries of her two elder brothers; she was entranced by Tony's consideration and gentleness but entertained no long-term hopes. In time, as the relationship
remained undetected, Snowdon became bolder, parking his
Aston Martin or his motorbike outside her block—one of
four in a private circle—and even turning up at Piero de
Monzi, where he would be taken into the back garden for
coffee or a glass of wine. Occasionally they would contrive
to meet at San Lorenzo, a fashionable Knightsbridge restaurant in a basement in Beauchamp Place. It was owned by
mutual Italian friends, Mara and Lorenzo, who would ensure that the coast was clear, since journalists sometimes
looked in, hoping to find big names for the gossip columns.

Tony continued to pop into the Grange—it would have
been suspicious if he had curtailed his visits—and made an
elaborate pretense of being distantly friendly with Jackie in
front of her parents. He became close to Antony, who had
changed his job from working for a gems firm, in Hatton

Garden, associated with Hambros Bank to being an assistant with an advertising company, Garrett's, in Farm Street, Mayfair, specializing in making television commercials. Antony was the first to share the secret, and if Snowdon wanted to meet Jackie nearer to Kensington Palace, he would arrange a rendezvous in Antony's dark basement flat in Ennismore Gardens near Knightsbridge Barracks.

While Margot Reading was aware that Tony's marriage was less than satisfactory—he made no bones about it—she had no inkling that her daughter, whose happiness was of great concern to her, was in the throes of an illicit affair. And no alarm bells sounded when Tony boasted one afternoon at the Grange that he would have no difficulty gaining a divorce. "He was always saying he could get rid of Princess Margaret, but it was difficult to believe," says Lady Reading. But Jackie did believe him, maybe only for appearance's sake, and told her brother more than once that Tony wanted to marry her. How and when were not discussed, but by the winter the affair had reached an impasse. The novelty of fleeting and secretive meetings away from public places was wearing off for Jackie, and she resolved to take a long holiday abroad, starting in the New Year.

On December 15, Tony entered the London Clinic for a second operation on his hemorrhoids, timing it, so friends said, to avoid the family Christmas at Windsor. The nurses noticed that Jackie was a more frequent visitor than the Princess, the two fortunately contriving to miss each other, once by a matter of seconds. "Tony tried to ban me from visiting him," says Margaret. He was discharged on December 30, in time to join Margaret for the New Year's Eve festivities. Jackie, her thoughts on Snowdon, spent New Year's Eve at a fancy dress party in Cadogan Square, to which she was escorted by Sy and Antony. Over Christmas at Staplefield, she had finalized plans to stay in Gsteig in

Switzerland at the chalet of a Sussex neighbor, Mrs. Hylma Payn, who would be there for the first two weeks with her daughter, and then leave Jackie to remain as long as she wanted. She arranged to drive out with her eldest brother, who had at the last moment invited another Sussex neighbor, Anita Fugelsang, to accompany them. Sy had met her at a party at the Grange on Boxing Day, had been instantly smitten by her blonde, blue-eyed Nordic looks and had high hopes that a romance would develop in the mountains.

They set off in the first week of January. The car broke down during the icy night on a mountain pass, and they arrived late to join Mrs. Payn and her red-haired daughter, just as 3,500 miles away the *New York Daily News*, America's largest selling newspaper, broke the story of Snowdon's affair with Lady Jacqueline. Lord Reading, alerted by a Fleet Street friend of the impending bombshell, telephoned his daughter and received, comfortingly, her denials and, thus armed, prepared himself for the inevitable press onslaught. He counselled Jackie not to give any interviews or make even a short statement. Contacted early by the two London evening newspapers at Staplefield, and asked for his comment on the *Daily News* disclosure, Reading dismissed it out of hand. He was quoted as being "outraged" and added that Snowdon and Princess Margaret were neighbors and, like other neighbors, dropped in from time to time; Jackie was a friend of both the Princess and Lord Snowdon, he said, and talk of a romance was preposterous.

As midday placards in Fleet Street proclaimed the rumor, Jackie was taking to the nursery ski slopes in Gstaad, the fashionable skiing resort five miles from the much smaller village of Gsteig. An early bird photographer from the *Daily Express* snapped her in a relaxed and unconcerned mood, which was to alter that evening when her parents telephoned her to say that the story was front-page international news, and was being broadcast on all the TV and radio station news bulletins.

At lunch that day in a party of twelve, on the terrace of the restaurant at the foot of the Eggli ski run, Jackie took aside a male friend, who had just arrived to stay at the Palace Hotel and had Fleet Street connections, to ask him what she should do, and if there was any point returning to London. He matched her father's advice and told her to deny everything if she should find herself confronted, as was likely, by journalists. "But it's all true," she blurted: "I love Tony and he wants to marry me. I don't care who knows—I must call him." Instead of telephoning from the Payn chalet, which was full of people she did not know terribly well, Jackie went to the Palace and rang Tony from the friend's room on the seventh floor. The conversation lasted about twenty minutes and began with Tony inquiring if all was well with her and telling her that he missed her. He said that his office would not be making any statement to dignify the story and agreed with her that the best policy was to say nothing. For convenience, he added, he was going to Barbados where Princess Margaret would be joining him. She rang off, reaffirming her love, and promising she would telephone again before his departure.

"It's all a bit of a giggle," Jackie said as the chalet was besieged for three days by the press and *paparazzi* photographers from the Continent, but she held her counsel until the story became old news, calling Tony twice more. They left it that they would meet when they both returned from their respective holidays, but the realization was there between them that the affair was over, killed stone-dead by the headlines.

If Jackie was sad, she did not show it. The romance had to end sometime, somehow, and this, she felt, was as good a way as any. In Gsteig life was enlivened by Erleigh's eccentric courting of Anita, a budding show jumper who had given it up to train as a photographer, and who would not reciprocate his advances. Anita's bedroom had twin beds, pushed together: one night as she was getting into one of them they parted like the Red Sea, and Erleigh, totally naked, appeared from the chasm: Anita's shrieks were heard by Jackie in the next room. The situation was smoothed over, but Anita, who later married the Earl of Suffolk and Berkshire, decided to cut short her stay.

Life was more sober at Staplefield, where Lord and Lady Reading were facing up to facts, having extracted a confession from their daughter. They turned on Snowdon, accusing him of seducing an innocent and impressionable young girl. He was, Lord Reading told him in a rage, banned henceforth from their house; forbidden ever to contact any member of their family again. The stormy scene stopped just short of the threat of horsewhips.

Margaret, who had been white with rage when she had first found out about Jackie, secretly enjoyed Tony's discomfiture. She had warned him that it would all end in tears and now it had, and, worse, had been dragged in front of the public whose affection for the Princess, she knew, diminished every time she was tainted by scandal. In an effort to redeem her image she had agreed to go to the Caribbean and act as if nothing had happened, but privately her mood was, "I'll show him." Tony flew from London with his sister on January 21 to stay at Maddox. On the evening of his departure, Princess Margaret went ostentatiously with Lichfield to the Mayfair Theatre to see Alec McCowen in *The Philanthropist*, with Lord and Lady Harlech making up the party. A week later she followed her errant husband to Barbados, and on arrival at Grantley Adams Airport was happy, for once, to pose for pictures with Tony, embracing him for the cameras as if to demonstrate to the world that the marriage was fine, the rumors rubbish. A few days later Margaret and Tony agreed to another photographic session on the beach, with Tony in a skimpy pair of trunks while the Princess wore her usual one-piece costume with its decorous skirt hiding any possible trace of the upper thigh.

Tony took up parachute water-skiing and crashed from a dangerous height on his debut flight, shaking himself, but causing no injuries. Still presenting a united front while the vapors of the Jackie business finally dispersed, Margaret showed concern. "She begged him not to go up again but he insisted on doing so immediately," says Johnny Kidd, who was driving the boat. "He was quite mad and kept on screaming at me, 'faster, faster'."

Kidd, a grandson of Lord Beaverbrook and a 6 foot 5 inches tall show jumper, was staying with his mother Janet at Holders, their home above Sandy Lane on the St. James coast, which is considered one of the finest residences on the island. Janet, elder sister of Sir Max Aitken, who had inherited Beaverbrook Newspapers on his father's death in 1964, had agreed to lend Holders for a ball in aid of the local Red Cross, and Margaret offered to attend as a spur for people to buy tickets, knowing that charity functions attract greater crowds when graced by a royal presence. On that night she was suffering from one of her migraines, an affliction she had borne since teenage days, but stoically insisted on turning up so as to not let the guests, both white and black, down. She smiled bravely through the evening, dancing a couple of times, but at midnight decided it was time to go to bed. When she looked around for Tony to take her home, he was nowhere to be seen, and Margaret, who was sitting with Jonathan Aitken, a cousin of the Kidds, asked him to seek out Tony.

Aitken enlisted the aid of Margaret's Scotland Yard detective, Inspector Falconer, but he returned from a search saying that Lord Snowdon was nowhere to be found. "It was obvious to me that Falconer knew where Tony was and had been told to go away. Princess Margaret drummed her fingers for a few minutes more, hoping he would turn up—it was past twelve and apart from anything else, none of the guests could leave before her," says Aitken, who did his best to keep her amused. "Then she asked me to look and I got Falconer to show me where he was. I found Tony, literally, under a table giggling with a pretty girl who worked in the boutique in the arcade of the Sandy Lane Hotel. I told him Princess Margaret was desperate to go and he replied, 'Fuck off, arselicker.' So Falconer and I reached under the table, grabbed him under the armpits and propelled him towards Princess Margaret. He wasn't best pleased."

When they returned to England, Tony did make one comment, which was included in a newspaper series on the Snowdon marriage, when reference was made to Jackie: "Yes, there were some difficult years at the beginning but now, do we look as if we're breaking up?"

Jackie resolved to stay on in Gsteig, where her mother had arrived for a brief visit—Lady Reading did not ski—and when the Payns and the other guests had left she was delighted to receive a call from Dai Llewellyn, who was at a loose end in London and asked if he might invite himself out for a couple of weeks. "Jackie was an old chum and when I saw her at that New Year's Eve party, she told me she was off to ski and that there were plenty of beds if I wanted to come," says Dai. "So a week or ten days after that kerfuffle, I rang and booked myself in and just as I was setting off in my new white Mini 1275 GT, my brother Roddy said he wanted to come along too. When we arrived there was just Jackie and Margot, who went after a couple of days leaving us with the place to ourselves."

Dai, born in 1946, is the elder son of Lt. Col. Sir Harry Llewellyn, who achieved fame with his show jumper Foxhunter, winning a gold medal for Great Britain in the 1952 Olympic Games in Helsinki. At that time he was working for Horizon Holidays, after a two-and-a-half year jaunt around the world. His brother Roddy, eighteen months younger, having given up an apprenticeship in a brewing company of which his father was a director, was running a mobile discotheque which had been financed from the proceeds of a legacy. Dai had a formidable reputation, of which Jackie was well aware, as a ladies' man, while—according to his brother—Roddy had yet to lose his virginity and seemed to show scant sexual interest in women, although there had been a teenage romance with a girl who lived near the Llewellyn estate in Wales.

"I thought I would pair off with Jackie, now that she was free, but I broke my right leg the very first day I went skiing, showing off as usual. I didn't let it cramp my style, however," says Dai. "Then I had this marvellous idea of pairing Rods with Jackie and it was a great success. Every morning I used to make a pitcher of Martinis for breakfast, mixing it with snow—it's my skiing holiday ritual. The morning after I had got them together, I had just made the Martinis when Rods came down the stairs, grinning sheepishly. I cheered! All Jackie would tell me was they had formed an "understanding," but there was no doubt in my mind that something had happened. She knew the Snowdon thing was over because of the publicity. We left after a couple of weeks and I remember we all had lunch with David and Hjördis Niven on the last day. Despite my leg, I drove, with the front seat full back. I didn't want to let Rods near my precious car."

Jackie went home in March, back to work at Piero de Monzi. She did still see Tony from time to time, but only for casual meetings at the shop, where he would drop in after lunch for a chat, or at San Lorenzo, joining up for a drink after lunching with other people, as Mara hovered to ensure privacy. She saw more of Dai though, and she was with him in the Royal Enclosure, in June, at Royal Ascot races, as members of the royal party passed by. "She suddenly saw Tony and sent me to fetch him over for a drink," says Dai. "They chatted and I remember it cost me a couple of bottles of champagne! At the time I was having a bit of a walk-out with Jackie and the Snowdon thing really was over." On the occasions Tony reappeared to stay at Old House, Margot Reading took great delight in persecuting him by promenading her weekend guests along the public footpath which passed within a few yards of his front door, wended down around the lake and completed a circle past one side of his back garden. If anything, Margot now evinced sympathy for the Princess, whom she used to label a "monster" after swallowing Tony's propaganda.

The real casualty of the Jackie Affair was, inevitably, Margaret's standing and popularity: any scrutiny of her private life, she was aware, provided ammunition for her persecutors among the leftwing in Parliament who, unable to attack the Queen for fear of drawing howls of outrage, pounced on the Princess's every indiscretion as a means of cavilling at the Civil List and the growing cost of the Monarchy. The realization that Tony had been bragging openly that he would be able to end the marriage also disquieted her, since in discussing the matter with her sister she had been told that divorce so close to the throne was impossible

(105)

in the prevailing climate. Educating the public to accept change took time; while the divorce and remarriage in 1967 of their cousin George, the Earl of Harewood, had partly paved the way, Margaret had to appreciate that her situation was different.

During the summer a tense Tony was in a difficult mood, often going his own way, but when H. J. "Jack" Heinz II, whose family owned the "57-Varieties" business, gave his annual fancy-dress dance on July 7, at his Mayfair mews house behind Berkeley Square, Tony escorted Margaret. That night he appeared to be drinking more than usual; clearly his social judgment was awry when he clumsily tried to cut in on the dance floor on urbane Old Etonian Peter Cazelet, who was dancing with the beautiful Jane Westmorland, wife of the Earl of Westmorland, a Lord-in-Waiting to the Queen since 1955. One of the old guard who did not approve of Tony, Cazelet, who was in his sixties and trained the Queen Mother's National Hunt racehorses at Fairlawne, his stately home in Kent, rebuffed Snowdon sharply as he attempted to take over: "This is not America. Fuck off."

Tony retaliated by tipping a glass of red wine over Cazelet's white silk dress shirt and when the startled couple circled the floor and came past again, Tony followed up by throwing a glass of white wine. The undignified incident was witnessed by several dozen of the four hundred guests who were horrified by Snowdon's behavior. The Heinzes tried to smooth over the incident, but it was noted that Margaret and Tony were missing from their party the following year.

As if to dispel any lingering doubts harbored by the public over the stability of their marriage, Margaret and Tony took their children to Sardinia for the first time. David and Sarah were treated to a ride in the Aga's new Grumman Gulfstream II, the world's most advanced executive jet and a major improvement on the chugging, propeller-driven Andovers of the Queen's Flight they were used to. With the children to consider, the couple appeared outwardly to have settled their differences, but in reality they had travelled too far down their diverging paths to turn back. Tony's career had expanded in another, lucrative direction, and he had just completed his third television documentary with Derek Hart, *Born to Be Small*, which was due to be shown by ATV in December. It followed the success of *Don't Count the Candles* which had been made in 1968 for CBS, and *Love of a Kind*, commissioned by the BBC the following year. The themes, about midgets, the aged, and pets, sprang from Tony's genuine concern for the disadvantaged and the handicapped, and the series won numerous prestige awards for him and Hart.

Whether by design or luck, an old flame from the fifties, Dominic Elliot, now came back into Margaret's life. A year younger than the Princess, "Dommie" had married Countess Marianne Esterhazy (nicknamed Bunny), in 1962, but she had left him after the birth of two sons, Alexander and Esmond. Elliot, who had given up the insurance business for property, had been awarded an uncontested divorce in 1970, and was keen to renew ties with Margaret. She had always retained a great affection for him—he had stepped in when Tennant had bolted, been at her side at Balmoral as she made plans to marry Townsend, and, in early 1959, as she became secretly involved with Tony, had acted as her public escort, accompanying her to the theatre twelve times in one month alone. By Christmas his relationship with the Princess had been reestablished to the extent that she seemed to be more with him than Snowdon, and after Margaret made an official four-day visit to the British Virgin Islands at the beginning of March 1972, Dommie flew out to join her in Mustique, as a guest of Colin and Anne Tennant. "We are, of course, old friends," he told reporters at Heathrow. "I am going out for two weeks, but I don't know how long the Princess will be staying."

Margaret had good cause to distance herself from London —in London there had been an attempt in Parliament to axe her allowance from the Civil List completely, but it had been defeated by 148 votes to 34 (a majority of 114) with, ironically, its perpetrator, Willie Hamilton, absent because of illness. The furor had arisen from proposals to make massive increases in the Civil List allowances for the first time in years, because of inflation. Margaret, who had been receiving £15,000 a year since her marriage, was to have a raise to £35,000, while the Queen's allowance was to go up from £475,000 to £980,000, with proportionate rises for other members of the Royal Family. In the House of Commons, a motion to stop the increases was defeated by 300 to 27 (a majority of 273) after Hamilton ranted: "This is the most insensitive and brazen pay claim made in the last 200 years." Even the Queen Mother did not escape his ire, and he alienated the Commons when he added: "It is obscene that this House should be spending its time giving an old lady like that £95,000."

Hamilton's failure to find many allies is explicable in view of the fact that the Civil List system, originating with King George III, involves the Sovereign's surrender of all the Crown Estate revenues in return for a regular income from the treasury for members of the Royal Family; it is an undeniable fact that the Estate administration produces a good deal more income for the taxpayer than the taxpayer provides under the Civil List—a matter of several million pounds surplus annually. But that does not prevent some Members of Parliament, invariably with fragile majorities and in need of garnering publicity, attacking Princess Margaret as the weakest link in the royal chain. As she points out, they consistently blur the facts about the Civil List to make it sound as if the money goes straight into the royal pockets to spend on high living, joyrides and personal extravagances. It is provided, rather, to reimburse members of the Royal Family for the cost of fulfilling official duties, for the salaries of their staff, such as secretaries and chauffeurs, and for the upkeep of royal households (although the Queen personally pays for Sandringham and Balmoral).

Margaret felt at that time that her record should speak for itself: in 1970 she had undertaken 177 official engagements, including eleven to the Armed Forces. She was adamant that it was her inalienable right to have an allowance from the Civil List as long as she continued with her public duties. That was what she had been brought up to do and she felt that the great majority of her sister's subjects wanted her to keep on. In 1955, she had been given the choice of giving up her position and the allowance, and at considerable heartbreak to herself had opted to continue. It was not, she argued, as if the money went to her to pay for her cigarettes or liquor, which along with her personal entertaining came out of her personal account. The annual sum, in fact, nowhere near met her overhead and the difference was consistently made up out of her private fortune.

On Mustique Margaret felt safe from her detractors and was busy planning a house on her land. Oliver Messel had flown over—a rather bumpy earth airstrip had been prepared to allow light planes to land and take off in daylight hours—with his designs. Tennant soon discovered that his wedding gift was going to be decidedly more costly than something wrapped in a box from Asprey's: "Because I had the labour force and all the materials in Mustique, I didn't think Princess Margaret's house would cost me anything," says Tennant. "But then Oliver did the design and there were other little refinements and in the end it worked out at

£25,000. When I gave her the land I hadn't really thought about building anything on it. Then one day Princess Margaret said: 'What about the house . . . ?' "

On the island were Patrick Lichfield, alone although his affair with Britt was still going strong, and his best friend, the Hon. Brian Alexander, who worked there several months a year as Colin's assistant in the Mustique Company, formed to develop the most accessible parts of the 1,400 acres, which had been zoned into nearly 100 lots for sale at prices up to £40,000. Alexander, younger son of the wartime Field Marshal who was ennobled as Earl Alexander of Tunis, was in charge of the sales force and on hand to be pleasant to potential purchasers, as well as help promote the concept of Mustique overseas, in places where there might be prospective customers. The men acted as sounding boards as Margaret discussed decor, furniture and the possible addition of two small gatehouses at the start of her drive, and the choice of servants. The Princess chose a name for her house, Les Jolies Eaux, which reflected the sparkling waters below, and went into the feasibility of letting her property during her absences to defray the cost of upkeep and give employment all the year round. She was not, she told anyone who asked, a rich woman.

Elliot had been a perfect holiday companion, swimming with her by day, sharing evening pastimes before they dined (either at the Tennants or with some of the other British people who owned houses, like Guinness heiress Lady Honor Svejdar) and, more often than not, ending the evening with her at the Beach Bar, where there was a phonograph and a bit of life. Even the second time around, being with Elliot was fun for the Princess, and it was with some trepidation that she went back to Kensington Palace and her crumbling relationship with Tony. Divorce she knew was still not feasible, nor was a separation. She felt trapped living under the same roof as a husband who had strained to be rid of her. There seemed to be no escape from the strait jacket of a marriage which had seemed so promising at the outset. For solace she had been able to turn to Dommie, and before him, Sellers and Derek Hart (much to Tony's obvious chagrin) but she wanted some comfort, some sense of permanence, and her future promised neither.

Matters were exacerbated by Tony's burgeoning success outside their life together. He made his fourth documentary, *Happy Being Happy*, for ATV in 1973, and his photography for the *Sunday Times* and the various international editions of *Vogue*, the world's top fashion magazine, demonstrated that he was still in the forefront of his art, hailed as a photographer in the mold of Cartier-Bresson and Beaton. By contrast, Margaret was being dressed down more and more for the way she performed her job. At a time when she needed understanding and bolstering, she was receiving none.

Almost like somnambulists they returned to Sardinia in August, again with David and Sarah, who had, alas, become old enough to be aware of the tensions between their parents, but too young to do anything about it. This time the holiday was a disaster. Princess Margaret recalls: "Tony was bolshie from the start, late for meals or not turning up at all, that sort of behaviour. And worse than anything, he was rude to me in front of the children. It was the last straw." There was also an unpleasant incident when Tony insisted on taking Margaret aboard the yacht of Krupp steel heir Arndt von Bohlen: the Princess was horrified to find their host wearing a wig and made up with mascara, eye shadow and face powder, with a touch of lipstick. On another occasion, a fellow guest of the Aga's observed, K's yacht put into Porto Cervo harbor, and when Margaret stepped ashore and made for her car, which was surrounded by jostling, camera-toting tourists, Tony moved as if to follow, but then stayed on the yacht from where he watched Margaret's discomfiture with a smile, as, hot and sticky after a day at sea, she was ogled and all but pawed. Only after two or three minutes did he rescue her.

Relations continued to deteriorate for the rest of the year, and it was with relief that Margaret heard that work on Les Jolies Eaux was almost finished. She arranged to spend three weeks there in February and March, to coincide with an invitation to open British Week in Barbados on March 11. Sensing her low morale, Tennant, whose self-appointed task it was to see to Margaret's entertainment on the island and provide her with a variety of interesting companions to help while away the tropic days, determined to make her stay memorable. He invited Lichfield and a friend of his, American writer Jon Bradshaw who worked for *Queen* magazine, commissioning them to produce a history of Mustique. Along with them he also invited his young cousin Lizzie Paget and her Old Etonian boyfriend, Richard McGillycuddy, who held the quaint Irish title of The McGillycuddy of the Reeks. A former Mustique Company partner, Gerald Ward, whose father had commanded the Household Cavalry, booked in for a week with his wife Rosalind, and among the island regulars were lawyer Sir Harold Cassel, who lived in a native-style hut, and another Irishman, Rory Annesley, who had taken over the Beach Bar with his mistress Meg Stenham, daughter of the former Conservative Party chairman Lord Poole.

As Tennant intended, the pace was relentless and he himself was an early casualty, wilting visibly by the start of the third week, and greeting one new arrival with the words: "Thank God you've come. I've had thirty-four consecutive lunches and dinners with Princess Margaret and I need a rest. She stays up most of the night because she has no reason to go to bed and it's simply exhausting for the rest of us."

Margaret was filling every day, determined to make the most of the lull in her domestic woes. Every morning she would sunbathe in the privacy of Les Jolies Eaux with Lichfield and the Tennants, who were staying with her, and then either have a picnic lunch on one of the beaches (mostly deserted as there were less than sixty visitors to the island) in a group or join a lunch party in one of the villas. An hour's swimming would follow, with Margaret leading a small flotilla in a gentle breaststroke, then there would be a late-afternoon siesta to prepare her for what little there was of Mustique night life. Such as it was, it was enlivened once a week on Wednesdays with a "Jump Up" at Rory's Beach Bar, which now boasted a more sophisticated stereo system. Wherever the Princess went, she was shadowed by her Scotland Yard man, attired in holiday mufti, or a black police officer seconded from St. Vincent, who was in uniform and armed. Neither seemed concerned by the blatant lawlessness of Colin's eldest son, Charlie, who was in his sixteenth year, and was living on the island after being taken away from a British boarding school for experimenting with drugs. He was to be seen openly smoking marijuana, sometimes in front of the Princess, and when drugs were discussed one day—she had learned that a male relation had the cocaine habit—she expressed concern at bringing up children in a drug-oriented society: "My vices are cigarettes and drink," she said. "And I don't see myself giving those up."

For her last evening, Tennant arranged a dinner party for forty at The Cotton House, the island's only hotel, which curiously enough did not have any bedrooms: guests were placed instead in villas whose owners were away (one such was the modest two-bedroom bungalow owned by ballerina Nadia Nerina). They took their meals on the veranda of The

Cotton House, which had one large reception room with a bar at the far end, manned by Basil Charles, who owed his life to Colin and Hugo Money-Coutts: they had found Basil, almost dead, by a roadside in St. Vincent after a hit-and-run incident, and had taken him to the hospital where he had lost a kidney. When he recovered, he was offered a job in Mustique and had quickly learned the barman's art.

Colin had imported a band from St. Vincent to play for dancing after dinner. Margaret was an eager partner to friend and stranger, black and white, capping the evening by performing a cabaret with Basil, in which she sang "Walk On By," which they had been rehearsing in secret all afternoon. As the audience, swelled by other guests who had not been at the dinner, burst into applause without any trace of sycophancy, Basil rewarded the Princess with an affectionate hug, and she thanked him with a mock curtsey.

The party broke up a bit after 2 A.M., as the Princess was flying in the morning to perform a ceremony in Barbados. Tennant had ordered two eight-seater aircraft as several other guests, including the Wards and Bradshaw, were also departing. They were told to meet back at The Cotton House at 9:30 A.M. for take-off half an hour later. After an early breakfast, Basil was back behind the bar mixing rum punches for some jaded revellers, when Tennant arrived with the news that one plane had reached St. Vincent, where it had run out of fuel, and the other's start had been delayed so there would be a forty-five-minute wait. A group formed at the bar, passing the time, and Basil was in the middle of refilling glasses when Princess Margaret came in. Bidding everyone a good morning, she stood expectantly waiting for someone to light the cigarette she inserted into her holder. After an awkward moment or two, she turned to Bradshaw, motioned to his glass, and asked him what he was drinking. "Rum punch, Ma'am," he replied. "May I get you one?" The

Princess declined: "I'll have a gin and tonic, please. A large one."

There were two refills before the planes—a mauve one for the Princess—buzzed low over the hotel to land on the airstrip a quarter of a mile away, where everyone on the island assembled, workers excepted, to wish her farewell. As if she was making an army inspection, Margaret went down the line, while the women curtseyed and the men bowed, saying goodbye, and as the planes took off in convoy, those left behind jumped up and down like animated puppets until the craft disappeared over the hill. Tennant, who accompanied the Princess to Barbados, with Anne acting as her lady-in-waiting, pronounced himself well-pleased with events, but there was one vital ingredient missing. "Princess Margaret," he said, "needs a man."

8

WHILE THERE HAD BEEN A DALLIANCE, NOW
over, with Patrick Lichfield ("It's all right," Margaret reas-
sured a quizzical friend, "He's a kissing cousin!"), and she
had enjoyed the platonic company of other young bucks like
brewing heir the Hon. Timothy Tollemache, the eldest son of
Suffolk landowner Lord Tollemache, the Princess was really
on the lookout for a loyal companion as much as a lover to
share her nights. There were long periods in her calendar
when there was little to do. Royal duties tend to be com-
pressed into spurts and she needed a man whose employment would be on a similarly *ad hoc* basis, allowing him
time to fit in with her free moments, to share her pursuits
and interests. It followed that the man would need to have
independent wealth, and if such a paragon existed, Margaret
was more and more despairing of meeting him. Sympathizers like Colin and Jocelyn had attempted to produce
suitable partners, but to no lasting effect, and when Tennant
invited the Princess to Glen for a few days early in September
—he had inherited the estate in 1967 when his father
had gone into tax exile in Corfu—she refused.

At the beginning of September, Colin Tennant was
thrown into a panic. Margaret, who had been in Rome the
previous month with Tony and the children, before taking
them to Balmoral, had called to ask if she might change her
mind and accept his kind offer after all. Although Colin pre-
tended to be delighted, and arranged to meet her with the
children for lunch at the Café Royal in Edinburgh on Tues-

day, September 5, before driving them on the fifty minute journey south to Glen, Margaret's call had presented him with a terrifying problem—he had no man for her and, worse, was not able to think of one. He turned in desperation to Mrs. Violet Wyndham, his great-aunt by marriage and a London hostess of advancing years, knowing that many young men passed through her house in Notting Hill. Colin outlined his needs and asked if she knew anyone who fitted the bill. Violet suggested Roddy Llewellyn, explaining that she had not seen him for a while and would have to ring around to locate him. Tennant urged haste.

Violet had met Roddy, then working as a researcher tracing people's genealogy at the College of Arms, the year before, when he had been brought to tea by an old friend of hers, Nicky Haslam, an interior designer. A cousin of the Earl of Bessborough, Haslam had been educated at Eton where he had been a precocious teenager, forming friendships with social figures many years older (including Tony), and had moved, in the sixties, to New York. He had lived on a ranch in the West before returning to London, where he was prominent among the city's effete crowd. A self-confessed homosexual, he made no bones about his proclivities.

Haslam was at his South Kensington studio flat, where Roddy had been living, when Violet rang to explain her quest: "Princess Margaret is going to stay with Colin after all, and he hasn't got a spare man. I thought of you first, but how about darling Roddy? Do you know where I can find him?" In fact Roddy had moved out three months earlier after a fight. Haslam gave her the Abergavenny number of his parents, Harry and Teeny Llewellyn, which she called, only to be referred on to a number in Looe, a picturesque fishing village in Cornwall, where Roddy was spending a few days with a friend and her children. Violet's ring was answered by Belinda Jenks, a hefty divorcée whom Roddy had met through Jackie Rufus-Isaacs in Gsteig. Belinda passed the telephone to her houseguest, and Violet explained her predicament, asking if he was free to spend five days with the Tennants and others at Glen, Princess Margaret being the principal guest. After some hesitation, Roddy agreed, and Violet told him that Colin would be calling him with instructions.

By the time Tennant telephoned, Roddy was giving the matter second thoughts. He felt ill-equipped for such a sudden confrontation and did not think he would be able to cope. A smooth-talking Colin managed to dispel his doubts. He told Roddy to fly from Heathrow Terminal One on the morning of September 5, so as to arrive in good time for lunch at the Café Royal, just off Princes Street opposite the station, where a table had been booked for 1 P.M. in Tennant's name. Colin advised him to pack a dinner jacket as well as informal clothes, as there would be walks and picnics by day, dinner parties and visits to the Edinburgh Festival by night. He told him not to worry about the fare, adding reassuringly that both he and Anne were looking forward to meeting him.

As Princess Margaret was travelling south from Balmoral to Edinburgh with her children and Nanny Sumner, Roddy arrived in the city with more than an hour to spare. He thought it looked grimy, probably the fault of having sited the railway station in the center, and wandered around the castle to kill time, constantly checking his watch. Precisely at 1 P.M., he walked into the Café Royal to find everybody already seated, which gave him the appearance of being late. Princess Margaret, sipping a gin and tonic, was facing the door and saw him before the others. She immediately thought that he reminded her of a younger Tony.

A few inches taller than Tony and slightly heavier, Roddy was still on the small side. He wore a tweed jacket and gray trousers, and as he bowed on their introduction, Margaret noticed his longish fair hair which was shaggily cut. His handshake was gentle but masculine, and she liked the softness of his voice as he answered introductions around the table—the group was completed by Colin's younger son, Harry, and his first cousin Matthew Yorke—before taking the empty chair beside the Princess. As he relaxed with a vodka, making small talk with Margaret about his journey and his father, whom she had known for nearly twenty years, he was handed the à la carte menu and quickly ordered his favorite lunch of lamb cutlets. Such was their ease with each other that by the time they started eating they sounded like old friends. The angst with which Tennant had been living for days evaporated in minutes, and he says: "It was obvious that something happened as soon as Princess Margaret saw Roddy. She was taken with him immediately and devoured him through luncheon. It was a great relief."

Roddy had been brought up with some experience of how to conduct himself with royalty—his father had been involved for many years in the equestrian world with Prince Philip—and found he was unable to eat more than a few mouthfuls as Margaret, after fiddling with her food, preferred to make conversation. "It's a frightfully outmoded convention that when you are with royals, you must stop eating when they do," he says. "Princess Margaret just nibbled away and then put down her knife and fork. I had only just started and was starving but had to leave all those lovely cutlets."

During lunch Colin mentioned to Roddy for the first time, the outdoor swimming pool at Glen, which was always heated above eighty degrees, and he said he had not packed any bathing things. Margaret told him that she would take him shopping that afternoon in Edinburgh. Together they chose a pair of swimming trunks emblazoned, fittingly, with a Union Jack, before driving on to Innerleithen. More baronial than Balmoral, Glen House is set in rolling country which Roddy describes as "magnificent." Turreted, and with large reception rooms furnished with typical Scottish touches and ancestral portraits, the house has more than twenty main bedrooms. For one month a year, from mid-August to mid-September, Colin and Anne entertained constantly changing house parties to make up for their lengthy absences in the West Indies.

The family has been part of the landed gentry for no more than a century. The first titled Tennant was Charles, born in 1823, who became Liberal M.P. for Glasgow and then, in 1880, for Peebles and Selkirkshire, and was rewarded with a baronetcy. His fourth son became Lord High Commissioner to the General Assembly of the Church of Scotland and was created Baron Glenconner in 1911. "My grandfather was an amateur scientist who wanted to stamp out speech. At meals we never spoke. He encouraged us to sing madrigals instead and it's where I got my passion for songs, particularly music hall numbers of the 1880s, which I'll perform at the drop of any hat. What a splendid man my grandfather was—he would whistle and hum at the same time," says Colin, whose father, Christopher, inherited the titles and estate sixty years ago at the age of twenty-one, on his father's death.

Margaret's visit provided the finale to the Tennants' "At Home." Fellow guests included Drue Heinz, the wife of H. J. Heinz II; Lucia Santa Cruz, the daughter of the former Chilean Ambassador to London and Prince Charles's first love, and Lizzie Paget with Richard McGillycuddy. Charles Balfour, twenty-two and a descendant of the Victorian statesman, came later in the week. Tennant had originally invited him as a precaution, in case Roddy did not hit it off with Princess Margaret, but Balfour arrived to find them holding hands at table and displaying open, and rather embarrassing, affection, with eyes only for each other. David and Sarah, who did not stay up for dinner, seemed to take the development in their stride. Their mother explained that she had met someone whom she liked very much and she hoped they would like him too. She was open with them and they appreciated it. It made them feel grown-up.

The Princess was two weeks past her forty-third birthday, while Roddy was a month shy of his twenty-sixth, and the budding romance hit exactly the right note the first evening after dinner when Margaret was joined by Roddy at the piano. They swapped favorite songs and tunes, eventually singing more to each other than their audience. When Margaret took out a cigarette to place in her holder, Roddy, who smoked almost as many, would light it. Towards the end of the evening they sat on the sofa almost touching, with a late-night glass of whisky. A man with limited sexual experience, Roddy was totally captivated by Margaret, following every move she made, almost as if to convince himself that she was real and he was there, feeling vibrations that had not existed before. What had seemed beyond the bounds of imagination twenty-four hours before, was now happening to him. Destiny appeared to guide his footsteps as Margaret bade everyone good night and Roddy followed her from the room.

As if to bless the birth of their love for each other, the weather was marvellous, so that their days were spent walking through the estate taking in the wonderful early autumn hues, picnicking beside the lake, and swimming in the steaming pool, the heating of which Tennant refused to turn down. Margaret's children reacted as favorably as she had hoped to the situation, displaying all the sophistication of their upbringing. They had observed their mother being affectionate with other men before and had been taught by both parents, in the wake of blazing rows, that marriage was a series of readjustments to fit in with circumstances. David and Sarah trusted their mother, and because their standards were a reflection of her actions, they did not find it odd or humiliating that the man occupying all her attentions was not their father. There was comfort, as well, to be derived from the fact that their parents were still married to each other, unlike the families of many of their contemporaries at school.

Before the house party broke up, there was a visit to Edinburgh for the Festival, with dinner in a restaurant on the journey back, and on the last night there was a party at Glen, with guests invited from neighboring estates. This was climaxed with a singsong in which Margaret and Roddy showed off their new repertoire, including their favorite, "The Bells Are Ringing For Me And My Gal." After lunch the next day, Sunday, Margaret and Roddy made their separate ways back to London, having exchanged telephone numbers and made plans to meet again as soon as practicable.

Roddy returned to the flat in Onslow Gardens, South Kensington, where he had been staying with Dai since his parting from Haslam (according to his brother, he had arrived on the doorstep "Looking a mess and with tufts of his hair pulled out"). Hotfoot from Glen, and glowing with the satisfaction of his unexpected conquest, Roddy burst into the second floor flat to find Dai engrossed in an old film which was being shown on television, *The Spy Who Came In From The Cold*, starring Richard Burton. "I've just had the most wonderful week of my life. I can't wait to tell you what has happened," he blurted out to his brother, who, not really listening, told him to shut up as he was concentrating on the movie. Crestfallen and deflated, Roddy went to his bedroom and unpacked, carefully placing a memento of the Princess on the table beside his bed. "Damn Dai!" he thought. "Here am I in love with the Queen's sister, and she with me, and he does not want to hear about it."

"When the film ended, I went to Roddy's room and asked what it was all about. I couldn't understand why he was making all this commotion, and then he told me about Princess Margaret," says Dai. "I was amazed for obvious reasons. But it was clearly true, because she started telephoning him at the flat. How it happened, God knows, but it did and I was very pleased for him. He'd been through a very depressing time, had twice tried to commit suicide, and then had got caught up with Haslam. Now he had a chance to build a new life with, of all people, Princess Margaret."

To follow up the initial euphoria, the Princess sought every opportunity to see Roddy. This required the assistance of friends like the Tennants, who had London homes and would invite them to dinner parties and, should the couple wish, provide them with a room afterwards where they would be left alone. Margaret had first hit on this system at the beginning of her romance with Townsend, when Billy Wallace played discreet host at his Mayfair house. Kensington Palace was unsatisfactory, unless Tony was away, but Roddy did have two encounters there with a surly Snowdon after calling on Margaret. Of course, there was no possibility of infiltrating him into the Royal Lodge weekends until the relationship achieved a degree of permanence and acceptance. But, with a husband on whose company she could no longer rely, Margaret had at last found the person she had been searching for: whether others would consider him suitable did not worry her. As far as she was concerned, Roddy was "my darling angel."

Obviously Margaret's friends, particularly the old guard like Blandford, Elliot, and Wills, and the Penns, would find him totally unsuitable, and not just because of his age. They agreed with Snowdon that he was a "lightweight": the little they knew about him was enough to create an adverse opinion, and as more facts emerged about Roddy to confirm first impressions, it became difficult to listen to Margaret's enthusiasm without contradicting her with hurtful truths. Perversely, the more the Princess learned about Roddy, the more attached she became to him. He was one of society's victims and so, in a way, was she, and to her role of lover she added, in course, that of protectress. When friends like Jocelyn sought to criticize Roddy, she cut them short. It was not their place to try to poison her against him and she made it plain that she would hear none of it in the future. If they did not like it, they could lump it.

Apart from the chores at the College of Arms—a job paying £15 a week which he had got after meeting socially with John Brooke-Little, who held the resplendent position of Richmond Herald—Roddy had been working part-time at the DM Gallery in the Fulham Road as a sales assistant. The DM was an addition to the spreading Piero de Monzi empire, of which Jackie Rufus-Isaacs was now a director, and he had got the job after bumping into her a year after the skiing holiday, and complaining that he needed work and money. It was Jackie, also, who had introduced him to Nicky Haslam in that summer of 1972, during one of the *al fresco* lunches Piero de Monzi used to host in the adjoining gardens at the rear of his row of shops, serving cold foods and white Italian wine under the baleful stares of two liver-colored Wiemaraner hounds, Bugatti and Mozart.

"When we met, Roddy was trying to buy a flat in Fulham," says Haslam. "It was a real hole which was reached by going down a dingy passageway and he took me to see it after that lunch. I told him it was too awful for words and suggested he move into my studio in Roland Gardens with me."

At the time, Roddy was living in a three-bedroom flat in

Ashley Gardens, near the Houses of Parliament, with his first cousin Colin Prichard, his copartner in the mobile discotheque, "Elevation Entertainment." Roddy had inherited £3,000 in the will of his maternal grandfather, Lord de Saumarez, who had died in 1969 in South Africa, where he lived; Colin, the younger son of Harry Llewellyn's middle sister Elizabeth, had been given around £20,000 by his parents when he was nineteen, and they had both invested a small part of their windfalls in equipment. They had travelled abroad with it, played at functions in London and the country, and had a lot of fun, but it was never a money spinner. When it was finally disbanded, Roddy had looked for other work, remaining in his cousin's flat, where he had decorated his room with black paint and turquoise lampshades. It was in this room that he had tried, on two occasions, to take his own life during an emotionally muddling time, when he was having doubts about his sexuality. In an effort to alter his environment, his parents had offered to buy him a flat of his own with a price ceiling of £20,000.

Roddy's search for a place was interrupted by a nine-month interlude with Haslam who, in contrast to the expensive and spacious homes he decorated for wealthy clients, lived in one large, high-ceilinged studio room in a rather seedy building, which had once been fashionable among artists because of the north light. There were a small kitchen and bathroom leading off the room, which was overlooked by a loft area containing a double bed.

They had lived in varying degrees of harmony, bought a Honda motorbike and helmets, and during his stay with Haslam, Roddy gave up the DM to concentrate full-time on the College of Arms. Used to a mundane life, divided between working in London and weekending in Wales, Roddy found Haslam's camp world a revelation and was excited when, in February 1973, Nicky took him for his first visit to

America, to stay in a house he had rented in the Bel Air district of Los Angeles. He had his ear pierced and wore an earring, like Nicky, and turned up at parties in punk leather gear and chains, a trend which Haslam helped to pioneer. But confined in such stifling proximity, the friendship was bound to suffer and when it did, he sought refuge with Dai. "They had terrible fights and we all totally disapproved of Haslam and what he did to Rods. There were certain things for which I will never be able to forgive him. Rods had left Colin's to live with Haslam and seemed to depend on him. The only woman he ever saw was a huge fat lady called Ju-Ju and Rods used to bring her down to the country," says Dai.

Although he had moved out, Roddy soon resumed his friendship with Nicky, and by the time Violet called to seek Roddy's whereabouts, they were back on amicable terms. "I'd known Violet forever but never realised until then that she was any relation of Colin's. She was only being polite when she began by saying that she had thought of me to fill the vacancy. Can you imagine me being considered for Princess Margaret?" Haslam says. "Long afterwards when we discussed events, Violet said to me: 'In our tiny way, darling, I do believe we might have changed the course of history!' "

With the affair with Margaret taking on more permanent implications, Roddy decided to move from Dai's and renewed his efforts to find a flat, choosing almost at once a basement with its own small garden in Walham Grove, a leafy avenue wider than its neighbors, leading into the heart of Fulham, where the Broadway meets the North End Road, with its cluster of street-market traders. The price of the two-room property was £19,000 for a 99-year lease. Harry and Teeny arranged to meet the cost out of their Marriage Settlement Trust, and contracts were exchanged in late October 1973.

The new home was a short distance from the "dingy" flat he had been shamed out of purchasing by Haslam and, as fate would have it, in the house next door to where Tony's old friend Bob Belton lived. Margaret was shown the place —she had known royal servants with more spacious accommodation, she thought—and offered advice and assistance, even recommending builders who had carried out work on Kensington Palace. "Women are far more practical than men and Annabel Whitehead, my lady-in-waiting, and I used to go off to places like Peter Jones to order things for Roddy," says the Princess. Roddy bought a Bechstein upright for £250, and spent a further £400 on its renovation. A Welsh dragon was painted on the mahogany lavatory seat in the tiny bathroom, and he furnished the L-shaped sitting room with a desk, loose carpets, an orange sofa and comfortable chairs. It looked out on to an unkept garden at the bottom of which was the back of a row of new government-subsidized houses, and to block out any view of his activities, he erected a high wattle fence on three sides.

For Margaret, the first months of her new affair wrought several changes in her. She slimmed down, found a new zest for other areas of her life, and immersed herself in Roddy, who was totally unlike anyone she had ever met before. On weekends, he told her, he would sometimes to to a "commune" in Warwickshire on the estate of the Hon. David Verney, heir to Lord Willoughby de Broke. Roddy explained that it was run by an artist, Sarah Ponsonby, who was closely related to the Earl of Bessborough, and among the group living there were her stepbrother, Prince George Galitzine, who painted and was often visited by his girl friend, Helen Mirren, a Royal Shakespeare Company actress based at Stratford-Upon-Avon; an Australian writer, James Darling, with his wife Angela; Bob Whittaker, a photographer who had worked with Brian Epstein and The Beatles, and Isaac Guillory, a musician. Roddy had been introduced to the group, who lived in a cottage called Parsenn Sally, after a breed of Swiss Dairy Cow, by John Rendall, an Australian whom Dai had first met in Sydney on his travels, and who had become Sarah's lover.

Roddy, during the hours, evenings, and the occasional weekend he was able to share with the Princess, told her about his life, his illnesses (one of which had kept him bed-ridden for six months), and his family, painting a rather lurid picture of Dai as a detrimental influence, almost a bully, and the person who stood between him and the family fortune, estates and title. Margaret, the younger sister, was able to empathize with Roddy, the younger brother, and sympathized with the vicissitudes of his life.

If any friend of Harry and Tenny Llewellyn had been asked to forecast which of their two sons would one day capture the heart of a princess, they would have pointed unhesitatingly to the elder. Dai was named David St. Vincent after his grandfathers, Sir David Llewellyn, who had made a fortune in coal, and Lord de Saumarez, owner of a great estate in Suffolk and a landlord in the City of London. He developed into a father's son, while the younger, chris-tened Roderic Victor, took after his mother in looks and temperament. Both were short for their ages (at Eton, Dai remained the smallest boy in the school for two humiliating years) and were brought up in a household which revolved around horses, the star being Foxhunter. Dai took to riding at once, but Roddy showed minimal enthusiasm: "My rela-tionship with horses was always less than a love affair, trea-sonable words in our home, I fear," he says.

Harry was the younger son of the baronet, Sir David, who was given his title in the New Year's Honours List of 1922 for helping avert a coal strike the previous year, and was reputed to be the owner of the largest coal mines in Wales.

He had seen action in Iraq, North Africa, Sicily, Italy and Northwest-Europe during the war, was twice mentioned in dispatches, became a Lieutenant Colonel, and in 1944, on leave from the Italian campaign, married The Hon. Christine Saumarez, the younger daughter of the 5th Baron. When Sir David died in 1940, the title passed to Harry's bachelor brother, Rhys, but as a result of the war and the subsequent nationalization of the mines, the beneficiaries of his seven-figure estate were unable to collect their inheritance until 1952, by which time it had diminished considerably.

Another multimillion-pound sum disappeared in 1946, when Lord de Saumarez, who was 57, and feared that the Labour Government would nationalize land as well, sold all his estates and houses, except one, for a twentieth of what they are worth today, and emigrated to Rhodesia before moving on to South Africa. It was remembered by the family that when the 4th Lord de Saumarez died in 1937, the bells rang in seventeen parishes, all of which were on his land. "If my Llewellyn grandfather had died either before or after the war, we would have been worth millions," says Dai. "But his death could not have come at a worse time for realising his assets and after the war there was a long wait for compensation for nationalisation."

The Llewellyn family mansion, St. Fagan's Court, Bwllfa, was sold and turned into a home for old people, and Harry based his family at Gobion Manor, a fifteenth-century house near Abergavenny, before he bought Llanvair Grange, a few miles away, in 1954. Llanvair had 1,000 acres, 380 of which were agricultural with the rest a hill sheep farm. Both boys were put down for Eton and were sent first to Hawtrey's, a preparatory school in a stately home in the Savernake Forest, boasting a deer park and formal gardens. But when they were eight and six, they were injured in a car accident which nearly killed their mother: a Land Rover Teeny was driving, taking her family to Bognor Regis for a summer holiday, crashed head on with a truck at a bend in the road. "The impact rammed our mother against the reinforced steering wheel and she broke all her ribs, dislocated a hip, wrenched her jaw apart and had her face pitted with glass. Her teeth were smashed in and it was a miracle she lived," says Roddy whose face went through the windshield and needed thirty-nine stitches. "But she was tough, physically strong and with fantastic determination. When she was showjumping she broke eighty bones in her body and her back twice. She spent six months in plaster after the accident."

In his childhood Roddy found an interest in gardening and was given his own small greenhouse at Llanvair, where he cultivated only cacti—much to the horror of Mervyn the gardener—eventually winning first prize in the class at the Abergavenny Show. At school he learned to play the piano, sang in the choir, and won a poetry prize, while Dai was more of a games player. The brothers were separated when the elder went to Eton a few days after his thirteenth birthday. The following year Roddy sat his entrance exams, but his grades were not quite up to standard, and with many more applicants than vacancies, he was asked to take common entrance again during the Christmas term of 1960.

"It was terribly unsettling for him because he had said goodbye to all his chums at Hawtrey's thinking he was leaving, then had to go back the next term and go through it all over again," says Dai. "The fact that he couldn't get into Eton wasn't really to do with grades, which weren't super good in his case, but with The Bulge which everybody was talking about in those days. A lot of people decided to start families after the war or only marry when it was over so there was this gap and then a huge baby boom and Roddy was born plum in the middle of The Bulge. There never had been so many boys, as in 1960, looking for public school places. I can remember David Macindoe, my housemaster who was terribly sweet, coming into my room and saying, 'The awful thing is your brother is in the middle of The Bulge and we're just not going to be able to fit him in.' "

The bad news was broken gently to Roddy who was devastated, as only adolescents who have set their heart on something can be, at being robbed of his chance of going to the world's most exclusive school. After scouring the country, Harry eventually placed him at Shrewsbury, having by chance met the headmaster of the Shropshire private school at a cocktail party. "Not going to Eton was the greatest disappointment of my life," says Roddy. "It was a shame because at Eton you make a network of friends to last the rest of your life, whereas I have only a couple from Shrewsbury. That place was so priggish, humourless and uncivilised. In winter the water beside your bed froze."

While Dai cut a swath at Eton, Roddy's five years at Shrewsbury, by all accounts, were of unremitting gloom. It was a hearty school, where prowess at cricket or other games was a passport to popularity, and it failed to bring out any particular talent in Roddy, who was regarded as a snob—his favorite bedtime reading was *Burke's Peerage*, a fat red tome which details the genealogy and history of all Britain's titled families. "I was always crying down the telephone to Mummy, asking to be taken away, but no doubt I would have encountered similar problems and conditions elsewhere. We fagged for the senior boys for the first two years and I can remember being beaten by a prefect after he hid a teaspoon behind a radiator which I had cleaned and then asked me why I hadn't done it properly—I was framed. I survived Shrewsbury absolutely numb."

To the joint relief of the Llewellyns and the school, Roddy left in 1966 with "A" levels in French and German, and in October that year followed in Dai's footsteps and enrolled at

University at Aix-en-Provence to study French philosophy for a one-year course. In May 1967, just before the academic year ended, Dai appeared at Aix driving his new Austin Healey 3000 convertible sports car, with a blonde debutante, Caroline Blunt, a baronet's daughter, in tow. He took Roddy to Monaco for the Grand Prix, in which Italian driver Lorenzo Bandini was killed, burned alive in his car in front of their vantage point. The weekend was typical, a vignette of the years to come, producing in Roddy a sense of inferiority and insecurity—Dai, with money to burn, a fast car and a pretty, sexy woman, while he traipsed along unable to make an impression. He was even too small, at 5 feet, 9 inches tall, to join a Guards regiment as Harry had wanted. For a holiday job, he worked in one of his father's companies, Davenco (Engineers) Ltd. at Newport, dipping push buttons for telephones into electroplating vats.

Then, while Dai swanned off to South Africa to stay with their de Saumarez grandparents, Roddy was discovered to have Jeep's Disease, a pilonidal cyst caused by an ingrowing hair in the anus, which affects the lower spine and can lead to paralysis. He went to St. Joseph's Nursing Home at Malpas, a suburb of Newport, and underwent an operation which is now no longer practiced. "They cut a three inch hole just above the cyst, and there were three women at St. Joseph's having the same operation and they told me it was more painful than childbirth," says Roddy. "The hair in the cyst grows and forms a ball, which forms a ball and so on and nowadays they just inject. But when I went to the loo after the operation, blood just poured out for days."

For convalescence he joined up with Dai in the Cape, and they toured southern Africa before Roddy returned to England to become an apprentice brewer at Tennants, in Sheffield, a subsidiary of Whitbread's, of which Harry was a director. Meanwhile, his elder brother sailed for Australia to seek his fortune. In Africa Roddy had worked at an asbestos mine near Bulawayo, earning £60 a month, which seemed a fortune compared to the pittance he was being paid at Tennants, but he stuck it out, not being able to think of an alternative occupation, and lived in a third-rate hotel opposite the main gates. "I was literally on the shop floor, humping, cleaning out the mash tubs, throwing in the yeast," he says. "At the end of my training, I used to walk round in a Dr. Kildare white coat, carrying a clipboard and pen. Once I dropped them into a huge fermenting vessel and kept very quiet about it until the vessel was due to be cleaned, and then I mentioned it to the chap who was cleaning it. All that was left was the bulldog clip and the ballpoint part of the pen. Strong stuff, beer. Actually they test it for colour and I was terrified it was going to turn out with a pinkish hue, but they didn't notice. I suppose millions of people drank it."

In the autumn of 1969, Roddy moved south to "head office," the Whitbread Brewery in Chiswell Street in the heart of the City of London. He found a dark, noisy basement flat at 114 Old Brompton Road which was convenient for South Kensington tube station, and Dai, after two and a half years away, returned to London, moving in with his brother temporarily. "I've still got the letters he sent me from Sheffield and he hated, loathed, and detested the place. There was not one person with whom he had anything in common and all he could think about was the big move to London. At first Rods was terribly keen about Chiswell Street, but then it got him down. He had been having bouts of depression which returned and he threw the job up. I don't think he lasted three months."

While Dai was amusing, able, according to his father, to charm the birds out of their trees, and an extrovert (he once considered standing against Michael Foot at Ebbw Vale in a

General Election) who enjoyed a stunning success with girls, Roddy was tongue-tied in their company and would listen at night to the sound of his brother's conquests with envy. There had been a teenage "love" for Sheila Cameron Rose, who lived near Llanvair, but Roddy was still a virgin at twenty-two. When he took out girls, he discovered, their feelings for him were distressingly platonic, as were his for them. He put this down to a dormant libido, finding his male friends better company, and after Dai brought John Rendall down to the country for a weekend, having met him again at a cocktail party in the Boltons, Roddy was to be seen more and more in his company.

"John had a very broad accent when I first knew him and said his parents were graziers and had estates down in New-castle," says Dai. "But he was really from a small town called Bathurst where they had a dry cleaning business. He used to drive an old silver Porsche, which was considered chic, and his exclusive reading matter before he left for Australia was old copies of Queen magazine. He used to leaf through the social diary with the pictures at the back and say, 'Dai, see this lady over here, is she worth getting to know?' He always wanted the English social scene. In those days he acted very camp—he was the first person I knew who used to get a laugh out of queening it around. When he came to Llanvair, he got on well with Rods and they've been best chums ever since."

This, then, was what Princess Margaret learned from Roddy in those early days, about his life, his experiences, and who he saw. The blame for his lack of success, he laid firmly at the door of a domineering father and an insensitive, selfish brother. There were, he told Margaret, three women in his life, whom he worshipped: his mother, his sister Anna, who was nine years younger and who used to refer to herself jokingly as "a mistake," and his Nanny Rebecca Jenkins, who still lived in Llanvair.

By Christmas, less than four months after the miracle meeting at Glen, Margaret had decided to take Roddy with her to Mustique where they would be able to be together, without constraints and subterfuge, for three weeks. They arranged to travel separately, and Margaret told Roddy, who was earning less than £70 a month from the College, even after a small raise, that it would be her treat: all he would need was money for tipping the staff at Les Jolies Eaux.

Before she left for the Caribbean, Margaret saw David into a new school, Millbrook House near Abingdon, which specialized in tutoring boys to pass the common entrance. Put down at birth for his father's old school (the only way of being guaranteed a place at Eton), David had been a boarder for four years at Ashdown House, after attending prepreparatory school at Gibbs in Kensington. At Ashdown it had become increasingly apparent that his grades would never be up to the stiff Eton entrance exam, and Margaret and Tony were invited down to the school to discuss the matter and find out what options were open to them. David was more artistic than academic and seemed a natural for Bedale's, a freewheeling coeducational establishment at Petersfield in Hampshire, which allows greater freedom than Eton, and, with his approval, it was decided to send him there with the thought that Sarah might join him later. But first he had to pass its common entrance, so he went to Millbrook to bone up. In any case, he told his parents, he had never really wanted to go to Eton.

As the small plane, to which Roddy had transferred in Barbados, came in to land on Mustique, with him craning to catch his first glimpse of the paradise Margaret had described, it was exactly six months to the day since the fateful lunch at the Café Royal, and he chuckled at how his fortunes had improved. His thoughts went back five years to the consultation he had had with a clairvoyant and psychometrist called Madame Carnel, when he had been at Whitbread's with ambitions no higher than a steady job at head office. Fingering Roddy's watch for divine inspiration, Madame Carnel had told him that one day he would meet someone whose name began with "M" and spend a lot of time with her in the West Indies. He had laughed in disbelief, but now it was all coming true.

He was collected after landing by the Princess and Tennant who, with Anne, was also staying at Les Jolies Eaux, and driven the two miles to her house in the Land Rover she kept on the island. At the entrance to her land, she pointed out the two lodges, explaining that one had been bought by Patrick Lichfield and the other was for her Scotland Yard detective.

The frenetic pace of the previous year's visit was not repeated. The Princess had good reason to stay at home at night and mostly entertained at Les Jolies Eaux, venturing out from the sanctuary for picnics and afternoon swims with a small group of island regulars whose intimacy with her allowed Margaret to display tender touches to Roddy, such as coating his back with suntan lotion. Over an evening glass of whisky, the lovers would play games like Scrabble and tune in to the BBC World Service or local stations for the news, so as to keep abreast of events—Mustique did have a telephone system but it was not reliable, and occasionally lines were down for a day or two. Later, as at Glen, they would sing, expanding their repertoire, and once a week they would celebrate at the Beach Bar Wednesday Jump Up. To live up to his boasts of having green fingers, Roddy experimented with half an acre of Margaret's estate, planting shrubs and vegetables and aided by her gardener. He was resigned to temporary success at best, as Mustique, without its own water, relied on rainfall which was nothing like as plentiful as on neighboring St. Vincent with its volcano, and the gardener tended to disappear when his mistress was not in residence.

The holiday was almost a honeymoon and did not have one jarring moment. It ended on March 26, and Margaret flew with Roddy to Barbados, where she caught a connecting flight to Heathrow alone, leaving Roddy to follow a day later. He knew the island well—his father had a house above Sandy Lane near Holders—and its variety made a change from the claustrophobia of Mustique.

During his wife's absence, Tony, who had never been back to Mustique since the brief honeymoon visit, had celebrated his forty-fourth birthday with a lunch party at Scott's, a Mayfair restaurant noted for its fish. Among the all-male group were Derek Hart, Quentin Crewe, and Billy Hamilton, an Anglo-Irish friend from the Pimlico Road days. As if to draw attention to the fact that he was slogging away in frosty Britain while Margaret lazed in the sun, Tony had an item fed to a gossip column so that readers would sympathize. And when the Princess arrived at Heathrow, she was informed that Lord Snowdon had come to meet her and was waiting in the Alcock and Brown VIP suite. She had travelled in summery clothes in the economy section of the British Airways jet and, displaying a touch of consideration, Tony had brought Margaret's mink with him. When they emerged to be driven back to Kensington Palace, the Princess looked less than cheerful for someone reunited with her husband after three weeks, even allowing for jet lag and the early hour. Tony, it appeared, knew all about Roddy's stay in Mustique and had been preparing for Margaret's return with mixed emotions.

9

ALWAYS OPEN WITH HER MOTHER AND SISTER,
Princess Margaret had told them at an early juncture about
Roddy and her feelings for him. They had watched the slow-
motion collapse of her marriage without interfering or taking sides and knew that no one could put the pieces back
together again. The Queen Mother had been particularly
sad, for she had grown as close to her son-in-law as she was
to Townsend, and viewed the present course of events with
alarm. Family conferences always came back to the same
point: Margaret and Tony would have to stay ostensibly
together and make the best of a not very enviable situation.
In the meantime their concern was for David and Sarah, who
were brought even closer into the family circle, being taken
by their grandmother to Ascot races, sharing holiday moments with their cousins Andrew and Edward, and wanting
for nothing in emotional comfort.

For Margaret's romance to prosper, Roddy needed constant organizing and cosseting by those in whose interest the
Princess's emotional stability and well-being lay, in particular, Colin Tennant, who was soon able to declare of his inspired matchmaking: "I have done Princess Margaret a very
great favor." It was to Tennant, with twenty-five years of
royal experience, that Roddy was able to look for guidance
about his courtship and advice over problems which arose
from his new status; from Colin he was able to assemble an
aide-mémoire about Margaret's likes and dislikes, whom she

regarded as her allies or foes, and what her reactions would be to certain situations. Roddy, who had told Haslam on several occasions that it was his greatest ambition to meet Princess Margaret, applied himself diligently to securing his position, and making friends with David and Sarah, more as a big brother than as usurper of their father's role in the home. But inevitably he made a fast enemy in Lord Snowdon who, on learning of a visit by Roddy to Kensington Palace while he was abroad, telephoned Haslam and hissed: "Tell your friend to keep out of my house."

It was important for posterity's sake to play down the circumstances surrounding Margaret and Roddy's initial introduction, and when asked by a reporter, Lady Anne Tennant vouchsafed: "Roddy was meant for another girl, much younger. He wasn't invited as Princess Margaret's partner, or date, or anything. One doesn't actually try to pair young people off at Glen, but obviously it is much better to have an even number—that is why he was asked. I suppose no one knows what qualities people see in each other, but something seemed to happen between them and they do seem to make each other happy. I remember thinking what a quiet, shy young man Roddy was when I met him."

In an early interview, Llewllyn said: "We were not paired off as if we were all trooping abroad The Ark for a stormy voyage. I was invited because the Tennants were a man short of the right balance and the story goes that Mrs. Wyndham suggested me because of my looks, wit and generally amusing character—some of which I would like to believe! My parents had met the Princess in the past, but this was my first encounter. I discovered a warm and witty woman, possessing a strong sense of duty and dedication to her country's interests, who has honoured me with her friendship since that first house party that was so filled with fun and laughter. We found that we were fond of charades and singsongs and I sang to Princess Margaret's accompaniment on the piano."

Financially, Roddy was in no shape to be a Princess's paramour. He lived frugally, by necessity, although the general expenses of Walham Grove were met out of his parents' trust and he still had part of the inheritance from his grandfather, he relied solely on the college for an income. When he asked for a raise, he was offered £2 a week, pronounced himself insulted, and complained to Tennant, who came to his aid by arranging an interview with J. "Algy" Cluff, the son of a self-made Northerner, who was in the process of making several million pounds through risky speculation in North Sea Oil. Cluff, seven years older than Roddy, had joined the Grenadier Guards after being educated at Stowe, the Buckinghamshire private school, and made friends with brother officers like Patrick Lichfield. He went into banking after completing his short-service commission (during which he was chosen to carry the standard during the Trooping the Color ceremony), formed a company, with blue-blood backers including Lichfield and Sunny Blandford, to bid for blocks when the North Sea oilfields were opened up, and was rewarded with success. Colin told Cluff, a bachelor with a penchant for escorting black ladies, that it would be a service not only to him, but to Margaret, if Roddy were to be given a job, and he was taken on as Algy's personal assistant.

Margaret and Roddy returned to Glen for their "first anniversary," and then, on September 13, the Princess was welcomed to Llanvair, for the first time, to spend a weekend, bringing Sarah with her. She was given a twin-bedded room, with its own bathroom, at the top of the front stairs, with a view down the drive, away from Harry and Teeny's suite of rooms, which were at the rear of the house. Dai, who had been to a wedding in Kent on the Saturday afternoon, drove down for dinner to help welcome the royal guest. While everything went off well, and Margaret and Roddy gave the impression of being more in love than ever, Dai was soon to notice that his brother was experiencing pressure on two fronts. The physical side of the relationship was proving difficult to sustain, and Roddy was becoming depressed about his involvement in a business world which was totally alien to his easygoing nature. He complained about "commuting," although his daily journey was only from Fulham to St. James's, and told Dai he was feeling "very odd, very fidgety."

"It was obvious to everyone at Cluff's that I didn't have a clue what was happening," says Roddy. "I was hopeless from the beginning and didn't know what anybody was talking about. Not having any business acumen, I wasn't of much use. I was whisked around the City all day by Rolls, and occasionally asked to produce pieces of paper. Perhaps I could have made something more of it, and enjoyed it more, if I had been helped along.

"One day I was having lunch at Morton's in Berkeley Square and tried to analyse why I felt so peculiar. I wasn't interested the slightest bit in my job and I was finding other things quite difficult as well. So I leapt up, went back home to pack a suitcase and headed for the airport, planning to catch the first plane, wherever it was going."

He telephoned Princess Margaret and then his mother and told them he was going away, did not know where and had no idea when he would be back and went to Heathrow carrying, Dai remembers, a pair of riding boots. "They were the rubber kind, not the expensive leather boots and Rods gave them away without a word of explanation to a puzzled Pakistani lavatory attendant!"

As it happened, the "first plane" went to Guernsey, but Roddy may have selected it subconsciously as the Channel

Island was the home of his de Saumarez ancestors, and their house there was open to the public. Within two days he was back at Heathrow, this time in transit for the more exotic Istanbul. He entertained the notion of travelling at length and leisure through the Far East and had withdrawn a few hundred pounds from his nest egg at the bank. Wearing jeans and a flying jacket, an unshaven Roddy joined a Turkish Airlines 707, seating himself near the back of an almost empty aircraft. Soon after takeoff he moved a few rows up the plane to where a tall, middle-aged man, obviously British, was seated alone.

"I was in the row behind the wing and had noticed this solitary figure further back, but I was surprised when he suddenly appeared next to me and asked if I was English. I said no, I was Scottish, and he replied, well, that's all right because he was Welsh. He asked my name and when I told him it was Rory McLeod, he guessed the Rory had been shortened from Roderick and told me, 'I'm a Roderic too. My name is Roddy Llewellyn.'"

Roddy explained that he had been having an affair with a married woman, and that it had all got too much for him and the sex had become a problem. He said he was growing a beard as a disguise, and was fleeing abroad to escape the situation. He said he had been to Guernsey, which was a futile gesture, and was now planning to reach India, after exploring Turkey. "Why India?" asked Rory. Roddy replied that he did not know. A homosexual of taste and refinement, Rory had moved in aristocratic circles for many years—at least one Duchess was a close friend—and Roddy soon discovered as they talked over several drinks, which Rory bought, that they had many mutual friends and acquaintances. "It seems you know the people I'm trying to get away from," said Roddy. "I've put the keys of my flat through a friend's letter box and told everyone I don't know when I'll be back."

As the flight neared its destination, Roddy gave in to a brief moment of panic and demanded a razor from a stewardess to shave off his stubble: he had recalled that the Immigration authorities had been conducting a crackdown on unkempt foreigners after hordes of hippies had been apprehended attempting to bring drugs back to Europe from Afghanistan via Turkey. No razor could be found. Instead Rory, who was in hotel management and was travelling to Istanbul as a delegate to a conference of the Universal Federation of Travel Agency Associations, suggested that Roddy borrow one of his badges and pose as a fellow delegate. "I had been issued with several and told Roddy to mix in the general melee at the airport as lots of delegates were arriving from different places at about the same time and just follow the crowd. He had a cover, just in case, that he was a freelance journalist but all went according to plan and we congregated in a VIP reception area set aside for delegates and were then herded on to official buses and driven to Istanbul. As Roddy didn't have a clue where to stay, I invited him to share the double room I had been allocated at the Hilton. He hadn't a lot of money so he was grateful for the offer."

At the Hilton, Rory met up with a friend, a travel writer called Jemima, who had been living in Turkey, and explained Roddy's difficulty. She agreed to back up his story in case any problems arose, and they all dined that evening at the Facyo, a well-known fish restaurant in the Tarabya area of the city. "We had a lovely time and the next day, Roddy said he was off in the general direction of India," says Rory. "We had discovered that we were both invited the following month to a dance in a castle in Wales and Roddy's last words to me were: 'I doubt very much if I'll be back for the party, but tell my brother you've seen me.' I haven't met him since."

In fact, Roddy never reached India. For nearly three weeks, without contacting anyone, he travelled around Turkey by bus, visiting Izmir and Ephesus, and stayed for a few days on the coast. Eventually he felt he had things "straight" in his mind and could bear to return. When he got back, he found, to his relief, that his job had not been kept open for him. "But it was horrible having to go back to my office at Cluff's to pick up my bits, with everyone giving me funny looks. I lasted just two months and it's a miracle it wasn't two days. I can't really explain why I went off, but I just had to get the hell out. I thought if I'd stayed in London just one minute longer, I'd shake so violently that I'd fall into a million pieces."

Princess Margaret, understandably, was the most affected by Roddy's precipitate action, and she took a handful of fairly innocuous sleeping pills, the aftereffect of which caused her to cancel a couple of engagements, in Wolverhampton and London. On November 15, her office disclosed that she was suffering from a "severe cold," and no one sought to remark on it. "It was more a *cri de coeur* than a serious attempt to harm herself. She swallowed no more than half a dozen and felt woozy for a while, looking rather sheepish when she was visited," says a close friend. "Perhaps she had expected too much of Roddy, and he had been unable to cope."

Whatever Roddy, who was still in a tremulous state, had decided about his immediate future, Princess Margaret was not to be a part of it. She explained that her sister was making a Caribbean tour in the New Year: it would be wholly inappropriate for Roddy to be nestling in Mustique while the Queen passed by, and while she did not believe that the affair was finished, she knew that a breathing space was called for. She spent Christmas with Tony and the children, presenting the appearance of a united family to her relatives at the Windsor Castle festivities, while Roddy went home to Llanvair to make elaborate plans to tour South America for five months with a Junoesque Welsh friend, Louise Macgregor. He had Walham Grove repainted, made plans to let the flat, and in early February, set off with Louise for Barbados, where Harry's house was up for sale for $165,000. Roddy told his father he would repaint it and the swimming pool and try to find a purchaser. In the event of success, he would get a commission. He arrived to find that the house was denuded of furniture, the electricity had been cut off, and the pool was empty.

He rented an orange Jeep and started calling on neighbors and friends to "borrow" furniture, beds, and lamps to make his father's house, which had had the electricity reconnected, habitable. Roddy found a bed for himself and left Louise to sleep on an air mattress. He started wearing an earring in his left lobe again, and after a while, would buy only dark rum on the daily forays he and Louise made to the supermarket. When the Queen arrived in Barbados on February 18 (among other engagements, to knight cricketer Gary Sobers), Roddy was part of the colorful crowds lining her route, excitedly waving a Union Jack at the royal cavalcade.

"He was on a permanent high, behaving very irrationally, drinking rum and hardly eating anything," says a girl who knew Louise and stayed in Harry's house for a few days. "One night we went to Alexander's, the discotheque, and Roddy fell in with two local boys, one of whom was an artist. They invited us back to their place which was in the middle of the island and the Jeep ran out of petrol about a mile from the house. And although they said there was some petrol at the house, Roddy insisted that we push the car all the way there. We stopped from time to time, and the boys would rush into the canefields and cut off some cane to eat."

Louise, who had been terrified by Roddy's maniacal driving, realized he was heading for a breakdown and discussed it with Janet Kidd, an old friend of Harry's, who recommended a psychiatrist, Dr. Patrick Smith, whom Roddy started to visit. Any chance of recovery was lost as a Sunday newspaper came out with a revealing series about himself and Margaret, and Tony and Jackie, copies of which were distributed on the island.

According to Roddy, a "friend" had given him an air ticket to Mustique, telling him that she had spoken to Princess Margaret and she wanted to see him. Tony was away in Australia for eight weeks, making a television film in the "Explorer" series for the BBC, but his stepfather and mother, Lord and Lady Rosse, were visiting Margaret. They were all surprised at the sudden, unheralded arrival of a crazed-looking Llewellyn in white jeans and a T-shirt. Margaret was returning to London via Barbados that day and took him back from Mustique on her plane, saying goodbye at the airport. Still confused, Roddy arrived in the middle of a party at the house of Geoffrey Edwards, who lived next door to Harry and had made a £5 million fortune as an arms dealer.

"He came dashing in wearing sneakers and leapt on to the table as we were eating a barbecue dinner and shouted: 'Here I am!' Then he said: 'I'm feeling marvellous, I've had a wonderful day. I went to Mustique and had a blissful time. We walked along the beach and talked and we laughed and laughed.' He didn't mention Princess Margaret's name but we all knew who he was talking about. Geoffrey told him to get off the table and he was effusive for a while, then he went next door with Louise," says a guest.

Princess Margaret with Group Captain Peter Townsend during the
South African tour of 1947. (*Popperfoto*)

Princess Margaret with the Marquess of Blandford at a charity Hallowe'en Ball at the Dorchester, 1949. (*Popperfoto*)

Princess Margaret with Lord Ogilvy (wearing kilt) and the Earl of Dalkeith at the Perth Hunt Races, September 1950. (*Popperfoto*)

Princess Margaret, Princess Elizabeth, and the King and Queen at a Royal Command Variety Performance at the London Palladium, November 1950. (*Popperfoto*)

Princess Margaret with Billy Wallace in 1952. They became unofficially engaged four years later. (*Popperfoto*)

The Royal Box at Royal Ascot, 1952. The Queen is looking through field glasses, with Princess Margaret on her left. Group Captain Peter Townsend, hatless, stands to her right. (*Popperfoto*)

Princess Margaret with Colin Tennant at a charity dinner at the Dorchester, as engagement rumors gained momentum during her "dizzy summer" of 1954. (*Popperfoto*)

The official twenty-ninth birthday portrait, taken at Royal Lodge, Windsor, by Antony Armstrong-Jones. Two months after its release they became secretly engaged at Balmoral. (*Camera Press*)

Camera slung around her neck, Princess Margaret in an informal pose shortly before her engagement was announced in February 1960. (*Jack Esten, Camera Press*)

The Marchioness of Blandford (formerly Mrs. Aristotle Onassis), Lord Snowdon, and Princess Margaret, after disembarking from the yacht *Creole* during their summer holiday in 1963 as the guests of Stravros Niarchos on his private island of Spetsapoula. (*Camera Press*)

Princess Margaret with Peter Sellers in 1965. They became close friends after Lord Snowdon photographed the Goons. (*Solo*)

Britt Ekland and Lord Snowdon aboard the yacht *The Bobo* in Sardinian waters, August 1967. (*Solo*)

Lady Jacqueline Rufus-Isaacs and Lord Snowdon at the Les Ambassadeurs dinner party following the premiere of *The Magic Christian*, December 1969. (*Camera Press*)

The first photograph taken of Princess Margaret and Roddy Llewellyn in a group with their hosts Colin and Lady Anne Tennant in September 1973. (*Syndication International*)

Princess Margaret with Lady Lichfield at the Gold Night Ball held in Mustique for Colin Tennant's fiftieth birthday, December 1, 1976. (*Camera Press*)

Lady Frances Armstrong-Jones's christening in October 1979 at Stapleford, Sussex. Viscount Linley stands beside the Countess of Snowdon. (*Camera Press*)

Norman Parkinson's photograph taken at Kensington Palace to mark Princess Margaret's fiftieth birthday, August 21, 1980. (*Camera Press*)

Princess Margaret with Lady Sarah Armstrong-Jones and Viscount Linley—a Norman Parkinson photograph published as she began her visit to Canada in July 1981. (*Camera Press*)

The next morning Roddy was acting like a zombie and told Louise, who alerted Patrick Smith, that he had taken "quite a few" Valium during the night. Janet Kidd was consulted. She telephoned Harry in Wales to inform him of the situation. Roddy was given an injection and taken to Holders, where a lunch party was about to start beside the swimming pool. "He was obviously in a pretty crazy state and after talking to Harry, it was arranged that Patrick would fly back to London with Roddy and see him into hospital—there was nothing else we could do," says Johnny Kidd, who was staying with his mother to compete in a polo tournament. "We put Roddy on a sofa and every now and again one of us would get up from lunch and see if he was O.K. We were very worried about him."

Roddy does not recollect much of what happened during his stay in Barbados but remembers the final day. "I certainly did not feel I was going mad or anything. I wasn't a screaming lunatic, but I was given this injection which I am sure white slave traders use. It makes you compliant and afterwards it was all 'Roddy get up,' 'Roddy get dressed,' 'Roddy come to the airport,' 'Roddy get on an airplane,' and I obeyed. While I was at Janet's, I was put on a chaise-longue on the terrace and there was some cocktail party going on. Everyone took it in turns to come and have a good stare at me."

The plane journey became livelier after a stopover at Antigua, where Roddy had disembarked and managed to buy a copy of the Sunday newspaper, which carried the second part of the Margaret story. On the next stage of the flight, he wandered up and down the aisles pointing to his photograph and telling total strangers: "Look, that's me, that's my picture!" Patrick Smith finally put his patient into the new Charing Cross Hospital in Fulham, after a mix-up at a clinic which had no beds. During Roddy's three weeks of treatment, Princess Margaret, feeling partly responsible for his condition, asked to be kept informed of his progress but did not venture a visit. Roddy tried to cheer up the ward, which contained some patients with serious mental disorders, by appearing for meals in his multicolored West Indian dressing gown and wearing a hat which he decorated with tulips sent by a friend. He told friends that no one had turned a hair, and he was shortly pronounced cured, and discharged before he drove any of the other patients madder.

Roddy returned home to Wales and the calming ministrations of his mother and Nanny Jenkins. He gave up all thoughts of international travel, and whenever he contemplated his future, he could see only bleak horizons. Margaret did telephone from time to time and sent him letters of encouragement, for his breakdown had served to reawaken all her motherly feelings for him. But her parting from Tony, which lasted eleven weeks, did nothing to improve the tense atmosphere of Kensington Palace, where the two of them were leading increasingly separate and hostile lives. Into this simmering situation, Tony brought the news that while he was filming in Australia, he had fallen for the willowy brunette, Lucy Lindsay-Hogg, who had been his assistant on the project, which involved retracing the disastrous expedition of Burke and Wills in June 1861, into the arid and furnacelike Australian hinterland.

Tony had met Lucy at the beginning of the winter in London, at the preplanning conferences, and love had blossomed in the dry heat of the outback as shooting, scheduled for six weeks, progressed. Born at the beginning of World War II, Lucy had been brought up in Ireland where her father, Donald Davies, had started a fabric and design business in the eighteenth century County Wicklow manor house which he had bought during the war for £400. He had made a success of humble beginnings, so that by the time Lucy left school and began working for him, he had laid the foundations for a clothing empire stretching from Tokyo to London, where his headquarters was a prestige address in Mayfair.

Lucy had other ambitions, however, and went to work for Radio Telefís Eirann, the Irish broadcasting network, before she graduated to independent television in London. There she had met Michael Lindsay-Hogg, a contemporary, who had achieved success in his early twenties directing the top pop show, *Ready! Steady! Go!* Michael's father was the younger brother of a baronet and an amateur sportsman who had married Geraldine Fitzgerald, the Irish actress, but Michael used to like to romance that his real father was Orson Welles, whom, as an overweight teenager, he did resemble. After a two-year romance, Lucy married Lindsay-Hogg in 1967, in Mayfair, but the marriage was a failure and they divorced, without recriminations, four years later. "We didn't have any children and it was very amicable," says Michael, now a noted stage and film director.

After breaking up with Michael, Lucy had a brief affair with the best man at her wedding, the Hon. Colin Clark, and worked for his independent film company as a production assistant, staying on when the romance ended. She was still engaged on projects with Colin, when the opportunity to work with Tony arose. Clark, the younger son of Lord Clark, who made the BBC TV *Civilisation* series, says: "I was very sorry to lose her. She was terribly good at her job and ideal for Lord Snowdon."

Lucy lived in a small flat in Kensington Square, a five minute walk from the Palace. Tony would meet her there, often staying out for most of the night, much to the impotent fury of his wife, whose own affair was at an impasse. "There he was, living in my house, thinking he could have a lovely affair. I asked him for a separation but he laughed in my face. I would only know he was back at night when I heard him banging about in the bathroom—it was all hours," says the Princess. "And he was drinking a lot of vodka in the morning, a bottle of wine at lunch and he even used to take a bottle up to his room afterwards. He was like an alcoholic. He was becoming a virtual stranger and we would meet on the stairs and growl at each other. And I had to go on behaving as if nothing was happening."

Able to count on Tony's company for official events only, and with Roddy continuing to languish in the country, Margaret began seeking out new friends. One of her new favorites was Ned Ryan, a tubby, balding son of a Tipperary farmer, whom she had first met a year or so previously at the Holland Park house of actress Anouska Hempel. They were spotted at 6 A.M., one Friday morning, the Princess in a plain overcoat and wearing a headscarf, at chilly Bermondsey Market, where dealers congregate to trade among themselves. Soon Neddy was invited more and more as a spare man to dinner parties she attended. With a thick Irish accent and unprivileged background, he was an unlikely escort, but he was courteous and amused the Princess no end. Also, they shared an interest in antiques, and Margaret liked to browse around the Portobello Road, where Ryan ran a stall on Saturdays, looking for bargains.

Margaret used to hoot at Ryan's stories about his life and the variety of jobs he had held, usually briefly. He had worked at Cleary's, a department store in Dublin, and had then taken the ferry and train to London to learn the ropes at the Harvey Nichols store in Knightsbridge, while working in a local pub at night to earn extra money. One summer, he had gone to Jersey to be a barman in a holiday camp and then returned to London for a spell as a bus conductor on the No. 19 route, ending up selling fabrics in Liberty's, which he left in 1964, after a year, to become a buyer at the Army and Navy Store in Victoria.

In those days Ryan was living in a £3-a-week room in an Earl's Court hotel, where he became friends with another resident, Constantine Hempel, whose father had been the German Ambassador to Ireland. Hempel had worked as a reporter on the *Sunday Dispatch* before he went into property and prospered. He married Anouska after picking her up one Sunday in Belgrave Square, the day after she had arrived from New Zealand with her sister. An introduction to Margaret, during a Barbados holiday with Verna Hull, had been followed up by meetings for dinner or the theater in London, at which Ryan was usually present; but in 1973 Constantine had been killed when the car he was driving, with Ryan as a passenger, plunged into a basement in Pimlico. Anouska took over the property business, which included Blake's, a chic hotel in South Kensington, with help from Ned, who had left the Army and Navy following a disagreement with his boss, a woman, who objected to his Portobello Road activities: he had often sold goods, like furs and silver, bought cheaply from the store.

While Ned, and friends like him, were a welcome diversion, Margaret's thoughts were with Roddy. She had seen him a couple of times when he had been up to London, and he had told her how he was bringing order to the Llanvair gardens and greenhouses, but was no nearer finding an occupation. Harry had given up making suggestions, and Roddy spent days with his mother, occasionally walking on the Brecon Beacons where Foxhunter, and the horse's scrapbooks, had been buried in 1959.

"Roddy was always at his best in the country," says Dai. "Ma and he both suffer from a sort of Swedish melancholia, which you get in that country from the long winters with no daylight. They wear it like a Mafia badge and I can never break it. When Ma is having one of her difficult times, I'm apt to say, 'Pull yourself together, darling.' But if Roddy is there when she is upset and goes and lies down in the middle of the garden and refuses to get up, he will go along and just lie down beside her. He's marvellous with her and is also much closer to Nanny because he was her child. She came when I was a year old and calls me, 'Old Dai,' but with him it's always, 'Darling Roddy.' When Rods was born the doctors pinched him and said he was dreadfully emaciated, but Nanny loved him from the start. She is one of eleven children and is the seventh child of a seventh child, and Roddy was her seventh charge. Because our parents were away jumping so much in our childhood, she was the most important person in our lives and when we go home now, it is as much to see Nanny as anything. She has been the only person we have been able to rely on, year in, year out, and whatever is good in us is due to her."

To Margaret's relief, Roddy's problems were resolved in June when he received a telephone call from John Rendall inviting him to join a commune he and Sarah Ponsonby were starting at Surrendell, a farm with forty-seven acres at Hullavington, near the Wiltshire town of Malmesbury. David Verney had asked Sarah and John to leave Parsenn Sally, following a reconciliation with his wife Petra who disapproved of the setup, and they began searching for a cheap property to restore, part of which they wanted to convert into a recording studio for pop groups, to provide themselves with an income. Among the places they inspected was Bayham Abbey, a Victorian house in Kent owned by Marquess Camden (now married to the former Mrs. Peter Townsend), who had refused an offer of £600,000 for it at the height of the property boom, but Surrendell matched their pocket and it was purchased for £47,500 with the help of a £10,000 loan from the Countess of Bessborough. The house itself was three-storeyed, with three gables, and a ninety-by-forty-foot tithe barn attached.

"At Ditchford we had a mobile studio parked in the grounds and musicians would come and stay with us at Parsenn Sally to use it and we would charge them," says Rendall. "It made money so we thought we could improve on the idea for the new house which was perfect because Surrendell had an enormous barn on the side of it. The place was derelict with lots of outbuildings but had great potential. The roof was sound, although the lead had been pinched, and the tenant farmer had moved out twenty-five years previously because there was a spirit in the house which haunted and upset his young daughter. When we bought it we thought of Roddy and asked him to come and help us put the place together."

Surrendell was formed into a trust, and all the people who were going to live there were required to put up an entrance fee of £1,000. As an extra source of income, they decided to open a restaurant in Bath, the nearest large town—to be called Parsenn Sally in memory of the happy days at Ditchford. Michael Tickner, a designer responsible for Parson's, a pretty restaurant in the Fulham Road, was placed in charge of the project, while a Portuguese called German, who had been the manager of another fashionable London restaurant, Nikita's, was deputed to run the venture. It would be served by fresh vegetables and produce from a kitchen garden Roddy was going to organize. He arrived with most of his possessions in his blue Ford transit van, and set to work with an enthusiasm that was fuelled by the best summer weather Britain had known in years, which made up for the primitive nature of Surrendell, which had no plumbing and only an outside water tap.

"When John rang me and said, 'Come and join us,' it was

the start of the best year of my life," says Roddy. "The place was perfectly lovely, in the middle of nowhere with acres of land and at the end of a two-mile drive. The trouble was that it had been deserted for years and you couldn't walk up to the front door except armed with a machete. It was an absolute jungle and the first thing to do was clear it. I started with a two-acre walled garden, with everyone pitching in at various stages. It was full of brambles and nettles and elders and logs and all the usual."

From time to time, Roddy would drive his transit up the M4 for an evening in London, where he saw the Princess, who was infected by his enthusiasm for the task and asked to be invited down one day to see for herself. Roddy told her he had been alloted one of the eight bedrooms in the main house, while Tickner had taken the largest and installed a bathroom and lavatory two doors away. Sarah and Rendall had ensconced themselves in the "grand room," which had been converted from a granary and had a platform supporting a double bed, over a bathroom. There was no telephone, but calls could be made from one which belonged to the neighboring farmer, John Rawlins. It was placed in a box in a field 100 yards away from the house, and to reach it you had to negotiate a barbed-wire fence, a gate and an electric fence—the joke at the commune was that by the time the bell had been heard and the assault course completed, the other end had usually rung off.

Margaret was invited to lunch. She arranged to drive down John Phillips, the American singer and composer who founded the Mamas and Papas singing group, and his second wife, South African actress Genevieve Waite. "Teeny and Anna Llewellyn came over from Llanvair, and we got Lady Edith Foxwell, who lived nearby, to pop over and be on hand. At that stage we had actually got into the house, but work was still going on all around us—we had a plumber there, an electrician, everyone, and it was a working lunch," says Rendall. "Princess Margaret just came down to have a look. It was a beautiful day—the whole summer was—and the place suddenly looked fantastic. She enjoyed herself tremendously and said she would like to come back and stay a night."

During the early part of the winter, Margaret returned for a weekend, taking over Tickner's room which, with its double bed and proximity to the only bathroom, was adjudged the most comfortable in the main house. "I went down to help with the garden and arrived bearing all the things they hadn't got, like secateurs [garden shears]," says Margaret. She found Surrendell slowly emerging from the process of transformation—the greatest change had been in the garden, around which she was conducted by a proud Roddy. Margaret went to Bath, where she had once browsed with Tony, during their stays with the Frys, to see the restaurant, which she found "very pretty." Around a dozen people sat down to lunch, and dinner, which always ended in a singsong led by the Princess and Roddy. It was all very jolly, but spartan and quite unlike anything Margaret had ever experienced. It was also very cold, despite the constant fires, and she did not repeat the experiment, although she sent a generous letter of thanks. "It was absolutely primitive but she mucked in, put her Wellies [boots] on and loved it," says Tickner. "When Roddy told us Princess Margaret was coming to stay, we weren't thrown into a panic. She had a nice clean bed at Surrendell, and there she was in the evening in her pearls, muddling along with a game of Mahjong which she said she hadn't played since she was a child. She endeared herself to all of us."

Margaret had particularly enjoyed the industry of Surrendell where, apart from the rebuilding, Sarah was painting and sculpting, as was Prince George Galitzine. His girlfriend, Helen Mirren, stayed for various lengths of time, governed by her acting commitments, and Rendall's sister Toni Furley, separated from her husband, moved in to work as a waitress in the restaurant. The recording studio enterprise was put in the hands of Simon Heyworth, who had produced a very successful record called "Tubular Bells," and neighbors like Lady Edith, and Diane Cilento, who lived in a nearby farmhouse with playwright Anthony Shaffer, were regular visitors, as was Richard Courtauld, a member of the fiber family, whose own manorial house forty-five minutes' drive away was run on similarly freewheeling lines.

Roddy's happiness among them was evident, and Margaret was thankful that her relationship with him benefited from his new-found composure. They decided on a visit to Mustique in February, as a welcome break for Roddy from the hard physical exertions of the winter months, but Margaret did not repeat the experiment of the previous November when, with Jean Wills, she had economized by flying the cheapest way to Barbados, via Luxembourg. The Princess and Mrs. Wills had had to endure a cramped flight and the curious stares of the hoi-polloi. The urge for economy had added a tedious four hours to the journey, and instead of relaxing on a British Airways plane with cabin staff dancing discreet attendance, she "roughed it." In a strange, but understandable way, the Princess had been proving to Roddy that she, too, could "slum it." He had declared himself delighted at her stoicism.

On Mustique, they were greeted by further signs that Colin's plans were prospering from the investment of nearly £1 million of his personal fortune. New villas were under construction, most of the plots had been sold. The Cotton House had gained a bedroom extension nearby, and its own swimming pool. In a seemly fashion, tourism was being encouraged. All-inclusive packages to include flights and American-plan board had been introduced, so that no one took any notice when Ross Waby, a New Zealander who described himself as a schoolteacher, booked into the hotel with his wife for a fortnight. In previous years Tennant himself had met flights and turned back journalists, who were easy enough to spot, to safeguard Margaret's privacy, but Waby managed to slip through the safety net. He worked for the New York bureau of News International, Rupert Murdoch's network of sensation-seeking newspapers, which includes the *Sun*, the *News of the World*, and the *New York Post*. Waby had organized the "holiday" for the sole purpose of taking a compromising photograph of the Princess together with Roddy.

Because Margaret and her guests, shadowed by her detective, usually kept themselves away from the other holiday-makers, there was only one place where she could be guaranteed to appear during her stay—the Beach Bar. Annesley had fallen out with Tennant and had taken over the neighboring island of Bequia's hotel, selling the bar back to him. Colin had offered it to Basil, who had become the Assistant General Manager of the Mustique Company, and his new girl friend, Viscountess Royston, had urged him to take it on. Widowed in 1973 when her husband "Pips," heir to the Earl of Hardwicke, had died of a heart disorder, aged thirty-five. Virginia Royston had fallen in love with Basil on a summer holiday in Mustique and had subsequently moved to the island from London. Her two children—a son, who became the Earl on the death of his grandfather in 1974, and a daughter, Lady Jemima Yorke, who was then six—came with her. The Beach Bar was an ideal opportunity, Virginia had realized, to involve themselves and make a steady income

(157)

besides. It was there that Waby stationed himself daily, his inconspicuous wife as cover, with a typical tourist's camera innocently at their side.

Basil and Virginia had become good friends of the Princess, dining at Les Jolies Eaux, and when she took a small group one day for a drink at the bar, Waby's patience paid off. He took a photograph, which although it was rather blurred, was printed on the front page of the *News of the World*. It showed Margaret and Roddy sitting at a table in beach clothes; the rest of their party, including Anne Tennant's cousin Viscount Coke and his wife Valeria, was chopped from the picture to imply that it was an intimate occasion. Publication of this doctored photograph was to lead to the official separation of Margaret and Tony, after nearly sixteen years of marriage, but in the meantime, Willie Hamilton, inevitably, took full advantage of it to attack the Princess in Parliament. He suggested to Denis Healey, the Chancellor of the Exchequer, that Margaret be "sacked" and added: "Even when she is here, a lot of her so-called engagements are audiences which last perhaps a couple of minutes. There are charity balls and premieres, which are really entertainment, yet which are called official engagements. The figures show that very few of these engagements are outside London."

Although they had been meeting for two-and-a-half years, this was the first time Margaret and Roddy had been photographed together. It gave Tony the lever he had been waiting for, and he greeted the publication with moral indignation, claiming that he had been "humiliated" and that his position had been made "quite intolerable"—which drew a wry smile from Princess Margaret, since for nearly fourteen months her husband had been involved with Lucy Lindsay-Hogg. But there had not been one word of publicity about Tony's own affair, and now she, Princess Margaret, was being branded the guilty party in the breakup of their marriage. "Lord Snowdon," says Margaret, "was devilish cunning."

When Snowdon had assured the Readings in 1970, that he was able to obtain a divorce, it had been a vain boast. In truth he had not been able to see a way out, so the intervention of Roddy was a godsend, in that it placed public opinion firmly behind him. The advisers to the Royal Family were at last in a position to inform the Queen that the climate was right for a separation, with the eventual possibility of a divorce. On March 19, Kensington Palace announced: "H.R.H. The Princess Margaret, the Countess of Snowdon, and the Earl of Snowdon have agreed mutually to live apart. The Princess will carry out her public duties and functions unaccompanied by Lord Snowdon. There are no plans for divorce proceedings."

Tony was en route to Australia for an exhibition of his photographs in Sydney when the statement was released, and on arrival he agreed to be interviewed on television. He was emotional, smoked heavily, and begged everyone's understanding for Princess Margaret and the children. He thanked the Queen for her sympathy and help. Sitting in the emptiness of Kensington Palace as Tony's clothes and effects were being moved to his mother's house close by in Kensington, Margaret was forced to marvel at the moist-eyed performance when it was shown on the British television news. "I had never seen such good acting," she says.

To the less sophisticated, it is difficult to comprehend how Margaret and Tony had blithely seemed to tolerate each other's liaisons for so long before mutual antipathy set in over Roddy and Lucy. Tony had been quick to forgive Barton; he displayed admirable sang-froid through Margaret's crushes on Sellers and Hart, who had been his friends; he had felt a genuine pity for Douglas-Home; neither had he resented Elliot; and Lichfield had sparked more of a professional than personal jealousy: "He should make up his mind whether he wants to be an earl or a photographer," Tony had said, perhaps unaware of the irony. According to Tony's friends, Roddy was the first of the Princess's lovers to get to him, and from that moment he was determined to get out of the marriage.

"The sex between them was always good and that is what confused Princess Margaret," says a close friend. "Because it was so marvellous for her, she couldn't understand why the marriage was going wrong. Maybe it was naive, but that is the way she thought. Even towards the end, when they weren't meant to be speaking to each other, people would telephone and the way they answered, it was obvious they were in bed together."

Yet to many friends, the miracle was that the marriage had lasted as long as it did. "They had a show-business quality and when it worked, it was sensational," says Jocelyn. "But when it didn't, there was an atmosphere you couldn't kick your way through." Lichfield remembers one dinner party which was particularly acrimonious, and at which: "They traded insults like machine-gun fire." And Haslam opines: "They were too alike, almost the same person. Sometimes it works in a relationship, but in their case it didn't."

10

AWARE OF THE IMPENDING FUROR, MARGARET had returned from Mustique before Roddy, to thrash the matter out with her sister and break the news to her children that their father would be setting up a home on his own. David was enjoying Bedale's, where Sarah had joined him the previous September, after four years at the Francis Holland (Church of England) School near Sloane Square, and had settled in without problems, even though their parents' visits incited great curiosity among their fellow pupils. Margaret explained that the separation meant that their holidays, in the future, would be divided equally between her and Tony, and although their parents were still fond of each other, because they did not love each other it was impossible for them to live under the same roof. She did not broach the subject of divorce, nor did she mention Lucy, to whom she referred privately as "that thing." The final parting of the ways brought one realization home to the Princess: her future lay with David and Sarah and, eventually, their children. About Roddy, she could not be too sure. There were too many imponderables.

He was lying low at Walham Grove when the harsh spotlight turned on him, and a small army of photographers and reporters, some carrying thousands of pounds in bribe money, converged on Surrendell seeking interviews, photographs, anything in fact to associate the farm, which the press dubbed an "upper class commune" with Margaret. Roddy was labelled a "hippie" and the *Daily Express* came up with an offer of £6,000 in cash for a simple group picture of all the Surrendell regulars. Rendall telephoned the news to Roddy and said that if he was interested, he should gather a few friends together and drive on down because there weren't too many "regulars" in evidence.

"I said why not? So we all piled into the van and went back to the farm where we agreed to this photograph. Like a fool I only kept £500 for myself and put the rest into the restaurant which was in trouble. It was a silly gesture, but the sort of thing one does in a commune. I suppose," says Roddy, who roped in chums like Ben Carruthers, a black American actor, Susie Allfrey, a half-sister of the Earl of Caithness, Richard Courtauld and Katie Windsor-Lewis, a niece of the Marchioness of Abergavenny, to pose with Sarah and John and a few others. As he counted the money, which came in a brown paper bag, Roddy said pompously to the *Express* reporter: "Now I hope to be left alone to continue my work at the farm. My family of friends would also like to be left alone in peace."

But it was not to be—the story was too good to be left at that, and around twenty journalists started a vigil, taking it in turns to drive up to the house to beg for interviews. When they were rebuffed, they retreated over the fields, only to set up telephoto-lensed cameras, hoping for a candid shot of the "hippie" whose bizarre association with the Princess had led to the end of her married life. While Roddy remained a silent prisoner at Surrendell, Harry told one newspaper: "It was a perfectly innocent association." Cousin Colin Prichard also made a contribution, proclaiming: "The relationship between Roddy and Princess Margaret started as a bit of fun. At first Roddy enjoyed the prestige—that was probably the main thing in his mind at the time. I know that as the relationship developed, Roddy took it seriously. He is a serious person and would not have maintained the relationship for too long just for prestige. If there was a divorce and he felt it would be expected of him to marry the Princess, then he would go ahead and do it."

Even President Idi Amin of Uganda contrived to get in on the act, announcing through Radio Uganda that the breakdown of Lord Snowdon's marriage "will be a lesson to all of us men not to marry ladies in a very high position."

Shortly after the group photograph appeared in the *Daily Express*, Jocelyn was lunching with Princess Margaret who referred to Roddy's plight. "Well at least he's making some money out of it," said Stevens. "We've just paid him £6,000 in cash." At first the Princess refused to believe it, but when Jocelyn convinced her by producing a receipt signed by Roddy, she changed her tack. "It's not enough!" said Margaret, laughing, and the subject was never brought up again.

Cut off from Margaret as the siege of Surrendell reached stress proportions, Roddy decided it was time to get out and give his friends a break. "I thought it was really unfair to everybody else on the farm. There was this constant invasion and when they had been turned back, you knew there were these very powerful lenses zooming in on you from miles away and, naturally, it made everybody ill at ease. Some of the stories were very funny—apparently an American journalist approached the garage man in the village with a fan of £20 notes, wanting to know what colour socks I wore!

"Also I was told that hundreds of thousands of pounds were being offered for the story of my life with Princess Margaret. So one afternoon, without telling the others, I leapt into my van and drove across the field to the back-road entrance. Then I looked in my rear-view mirror and saw this string of cars chasing me. I'll never forget—the first was red, the second white and the third blue. I intended seeking refuge at Edith Foxwell's house a few miles away and just before the village they were repairing the bridge. The lights were red so I stopped and as I did all the doors in the pursuing cars flew open and out jumped photographers. So I went through the light and the chase was on again."

As Roddy approached Home Farm, Sherston, where Edith lived, he had managed to put a couple of hundred yards between him and the pack, then to his dismay he saw that the gates were closed and Bert, the Foxwell gardener-cum-handyman, was standing outside them. Pausing only to instruct Bert to stand in the middle of the road, Roddy sped onwards to seek sanctuary at Diane Cilento's, and the last he saw of Bert was with the bumper of the leading car at his knees, gently propelling him into a ditch. Diane was away but Tony Shaffer offered Roddy a drink, and was then asked if he would help draft a statement to be given to the Press Association, which might, he hoped, put an end to the harrassment. The press posse soon ferreted Roddy out and accosted Shaffer as he left for the local pub. "Roddy has prepared a statement," he said breezily to eager ears. "I'm just off to buy him a bottle of scotch—he deserves it."

But when the waiting journalists hammered on the door later for the statement, their clamor was answered by Bob Brown, a young Australian who helped Diane with her acres. Brown told them that Roddy was remaining silent. Then Shaffer appeared and announced: "Roddy is not being allowed to make his statement. He feels he should say something, he doesn't like the situation and he wants to speak. Anyone in his situation would." What Shaffer had helped Roddy compose was mawkish, confused and rather embarrassing, but luckily, before telephoning the Press Association, Roddy had rung Princess Margaret's Private Secretary, Lord Napier and Ettrick, who had taken over in 1973 from Lt. Col. Frederick Barnaby-Atkins, and had been *au fait* with the romance from its inception. Nigel Napier froze as it was read over to him, and ordered Roddy not to issue it under any circumstances. "It was all about how everybody must live off the land and get rid of their deep freezes. Perfectly absurd," says Roddy. "I didn't keep a copy but Tony Shaffer must still have the original, I suppose."

To escape the press again, Roddy set off on foot under cover of darkness, across fields, heading for a rendezvous with Rendall at Home Farm. No torch could be found, and he was guided by another of the young men who helped out at Diane's. By the time they approached Lady Edith's, they had battled over barbed wire, waded through streams and ditches, and fought their way through a pine forest. As his escort turned back, Roddy was about to leap over a wall into the road. From there he could leap over another wall into the Foxwell garden where John Rendall was waiting, having heard his approach. But suddenly it seemed that a car was coming in their direction, and Rendall shouted for Roddy to get down.

"I was crouching when suddenly I heard a noise behind me and was hit very hard from the back—it was a ram which lived in the field. I was totally winded and wanting to go ooohaaah but trying to keep silent, and there was this beast lowering over me with unforgettable yellow eyes. The car stopped just on the other side of the wall and someone—it must have been a pressman—got out, looked around, then drove on. I jumped into John's car and he drove me to Llanvair. I was so nervous I didn't dare come out of the house for days and kept all the curtains drawn, although no one could have had a clue I was there."

On Margaret's advice he tried to formulate another, more conventional statement, and was helped by Richard Court-auld who had arrived at Llanvair. Approved by Kensington Palace and released on March 24, it read: "I am not prepared to comment on any of the events of last week. I much regret any embarrassment caused to Her Majesty The Queen

(165)

and the Royal Family for whom I wish to express the greatest respect, admiration and loyalty. I thank my own family for their confidence and support, and I am very grateful for the help of my friends at the farm who, with myself, share a common interest in restoring a house to its original order and beauty, and in farming land which it is hoped will provide food for our Parsenn Sally restaurant in Bath. Could we please be permitted by the media, who have besieged us, to carry on our work and private lives without further interference."

The media did not permit, especially as stories started to surface in Fleet Street about Margaret's visits to Surrendell, and much was made of a wooden collage with a toy car, a moth, bow tie, marbles, a pen nib, pheasant feather, child's fan and a parchment burned at the edges, which hung above Roddy's bed and was assumed to be a coded message of love. Roddy was accused by the *Daily Express* of having been on the dole, which tainted him as a scrounger off the State, while enjoying the favors of the Queen's sister. Harry spoke up on his younger son's behalf, after the *Daily Mail* carried Roddy's denial of this canard.

"I feel I should point out that this young man is powerless to defend himself against anything that is untrue, published by certain newspapers, such as allegations that he is on the dole. In the light of the overall significance of the attack on him, he cannot contest the allegations of large newspaper groups for the simple reason that court action would merely prolong the period of embarrassment for his friends and family, and the continued harassment by certain sections of the Press who continually telephone even those remotely connected, sit on their doorsteps, and offer large sums of money to everyone including members of the family, for exclusive stories. At the same time I would like to thank friends and many strangers for their kind messages of support, as well as cooperation received from some members of the Press, many of whom are old friends."

Roddy ventured up to London briefly, to see Princess Margaret and entertain her with the excitements that had befallen him. He appeared in Tramp, the Jermyn Street nightclub, wearing a T-shirt bearing the legend "Roddy for PM," before returning to Llanvair where Sarah and Rendall were having a short rest after the dramas at the farm. "By this time the whole thing was playing havoc with my relationship with Sarah. We were trying to live a quiet life and Sarah wasn't able to paint or sculpt and she was getting tetchy," says Rendall. "But it had shaken things up, and it was the beginning of the end for us—I was running out of money. Surrendell had cost me a great deal and I was going through capital while Sarah and Tickner both had incomes."

It seemed to Roddy, who had been told by Margaret that it would be inadvisable for them to be seen together in the immediate future, that his whole world was crashing about his ears: another crisis immediately occurred at Parsenn Sally, which, despite the cash injection of £5,500, was found to be insolvent after the local butcher refused to continue supplying, claiming that he had not been paid for three months. Rendall asked Courtauld, the only man he knew with any business experience, to investigate the books. The answer came back that the concern was indeed in a desperate position, owing several thousand pounds to local traders. "Bath was not the best place to site a restaurant. Despite all its elegance, the people there were not rich—the Jeremy Frys are few and far between," says Rendall. "And because we were all involved in the farm at Surrendell, we had to employ staff to do our work. We were all right in the summer with the tourists, but through the winter it was hard going."

As the holiday in Mustique formally ended Margaret's life

with Tony, so it also caused Roddy to abandon his association with Surrendell. When the coast was clear, he went back to the farm for a few days, cleared up his belongings, and returned to Llanvair. Teeny told a local newspaperman: "He informed his father and me that he was fed up with the commune because he had to do all the work. It really wasn't fair on the boy. His job was to do the garden, but he was often too busy with other things to do it, and they used to grumble, which upset him."

The cameraderie of the commune soon dissolved, and in July, John Rawlins, the patient neighboring farmer, had the telephone cut off after refusing an offer of hay in exchange for a £300 bill, much of it incurred by calls to places like Australia. "There are no ill feelings," he said. "We live and let live. I'm sure I will get the money, but I don't know when." Facing the bankruptcy of Parsenn Sally, which closed with an eventual deficit of £28,118, Tickner remained behind, the only occupant apart from Sarah. "Everyone has gone their own way," he said. "The main trouble, I suppose, is that people have got to earn money. The days when you could just live in the country for nothing have passed by. Roddy came to us after he gave up his job and, like all of us, he was searching for something." Rendall went home to Australia and eventually Sarah sold twenty acres of the land to repay him his initial investment of around £14,000. That closed the chapter on the commune.

During the summer Margaret was a guest at Llanvair, bringing Sarah again, but Dai was excluded from the party. He had achieved a certain notoriety, having become engaged in quick succession to steel heiress Isabel Richli; Tessa Dahl, daughter of writer Roald Dahl; and Orson Welles's daughter Beatrice, and, had jilted them all. The Princess, influenced as always by Roddy in her judgment of his family, had decided he was a bad hat. Harry, who disapproved strongly of Roddy's liaison with Margaret, managed to hide his feelings and was a charming host, inviting local friends to meals to help entertain his guest, and Teeny was on her best behavior. Roddy's future was the main talking-point of the weekend, and in the light of his success with the gardens at the farm, it was agreed that his best hope lay in a horticultural course.

Margaret heard occasionally from Tony, who was dividing his time between the basement flat in Jeremy Fry's Belgravia office and Old House, while looking for a suitable new home in the Kensington area. As the dust settled, they entered into a period of wary friendship. It was while he was at Old House one summer weekend that Tony received one last visit from Jackie Rufus-Isaacs, on the eve of her wedding, locally, to property developer Mark Thomson, son of baronet Sir Ivo Thomson, after an on-off two year romance.

After Tony, she had become involved with Jonathan Aitken, who was then working for Yorkshire Television while waiting to run for Parliament. She said he proposed to her, but she found him a little too serious, and went off with Dominic Elwes, whose elopement in the fifties with teenage heiress Tessa Kennedy had been front-page news for a fortnight, as they dodged the High Court Tipstaff [the official instructed to arrest Elwes], and fled to Cuba to marry. But Elwes, if amusing, was erratic and impecunious, and by 1974, Jackie was in love with financier John Bentley, who had been educated at Harrow and had made a £2 million fortune in the City as a protégé of Jim Slater. He bought a neighboring estate to Staplefield, but sold it when the affair ended and Jackie found love locally with Mark, whose mother lived a few miles away.

Lovers who have been parted, as Margaret discovered with Townsend, tend never to say goodbye, and as she made the final preparations for her marriage, Jackie appeared on

Tony's doorstep escorted by Gavin Hodge, a friend and hair-dresser she had invited to attend to her coiffure. "I'd known her for years as a pal and on the Friday night before the wedding we'd all had a bit too much to drink and Jackie told me she wanted to go up the lane to see Snowdon," says Hodge. "He opened the door and I was shown into a sitting room with a television and one of those new remote control gadgets to amuse myself while they talked. About half an hour later, maybe more, they came back and she looked as if there were tears in her eyes. There was one last peck before I drove her home—we said we were going to the pub when we left—and on the way back she whispered. 'Well, that's the end of that.' "

Apart from the brief flare-up of scandal when Tony's affair with Lucy was revealed by the *Daily Mail*, illustrated with photographs taken in Australia of them on the set, which led to speculation about divorce, Margaret's separation attracted no further comment, and her meetings with Roddy were discreet enough to remain unobserved. He applied successfully for a TOPS restraining grant and wrote off to half a dozen places applying for vacancies for courses starting that September. They all turned him down, and he was beginning to despair when he went to stay for the Perth Ball with Lord Napier's brother, the Hon. Malcolm Napier, whom Roddy had met during his adventures with Dai in southern Africa. Malcolm had built up his own trailer business in Rhodesia.

Just as he was changing for the evening, Malcolm's wife, Lady Mariota, whose brother, the Earl of Mansfield, lived nearby at Scone Palace, brought in a telegram for Roddy. It was from Merrist Wood Agricultural College in Guildford, informing him of an unexpected vacancy when the term started in two day's time. "It was a Saturday night and I was just getting into my white tie and tails when I received the marvellous news. I ripped off my clothes, packed my case, jumped into my car and drove at a million miles an hour back to Llanvair to get my things. A friend in Wales told me of a couple near Guildford with whom he had stayed, and I arranged to be their paying guest. They were the local vicar, Geraint Meirion Jones and his wife, Grace. She lectured at the local university and he had a distinction in agriculture from Cirencester, so they couldn't have been more perfect."

The course was for one year, at the end of which there was a diploma for those who passed a steady series of tests and exams. Ten years after he left public school Roddy was back doing homework at night, rousing himself early to make classes, and after a short time told Margaret that, at last, he felt he had found his vocation in gardening. In some ways his talk reminded the Princess of her father, whose greatest pride was the grounds of Royal Lodge, which had been a wasteland before he patiently transformed it to his own design, doing more than his share, on occasion, of the spadework.

To demonstrate the fervor of his application, Roddy turned down the opportunity to accompany the Princess to Mustique for Colin's fiftieth birthday celebrations at the end of November, even though the host was paying all expenses and, with prescience, had bought a batch of Apex air-fare tickets to minimize the cost to himself. Margaret headed thirty guests from Britain, including Bianca Jagger, Lichfield and his wife Leonora, daughter of the Duke of Westminster. Tennant, whose actual birthday was on December 1, had organized a week-long entertainment, culminating in a Gold Night, when all his guests—others had flown from Venezuela, Mexico, the United States, and Canada—were asked to dress up in a gold theme. Just what he had missed,

Roddy was able to see when he went to Kensington Palace at the start of the Christmas holidays and Margaret showed him the color photographs taken at the beachside bash.

Because Roddy would not interrupt his studies, Margaret cancelled her plans to return to Mustique the following February, probably feeling she had seen enough of the island for the time being, and Les Jolies Eaux was let out profitably instead. The early weeks of 1977 found Roddy diligently applying himself, only occasionally venturing the thirty miles up to London to have supper in front of the television with Margaret and play the baby grand. The piano had been a wedding present from Lady Rosse—in the division of spoils, the Princess kept most of the wedding presents.

"We had these dreadful fortnightly assessments and so it was very necessary to work hard. More often than not we did a lot of outside practical work which was very tiring, and afterwards you only wanted to have a hot bath and get into bed. But I loved the feeling of physical satisfaction and really began to think I was destined for the country," says Roddy, who at weekends would drive the ten miles to Ewhurst, where Johnny and Wendy Kidd lived with their two young children and her two teenage children from an earlier marriage. He helped them with their rambling garden, and one weekend he brought Princess Margaret to stay, a visit that was found out by a gossip column. When Margaret telephoned the Kidds to thank them, she said, with only a slight trace of humor: "We had a lovely time, but what a pity the press got hold of it."

Grace Meirion Jones and her three children became very attached to Roddy, who was enthusiastic about the simple, tasty food she cooked. They would answer the telephone once, sometimes twice a day to calls from the Princess for him. But in his last term, Geraint Meirion Jones was posted to another parish, and Roddy had to move to the Kidds, working in their garden as payment. Rendall had returned from Australia, his finances in better shape, and was obviously at loose ends, once turning up uninvited at the Kidds and disturbing their social arrangements. "Roddy was sweet and marvellous with the kids but hopeless as a guest," says Johnny. "We'd arrange a dinner party for, say, 8:30 P.M. and include Roddy, but then he wouldn't turn up until hours later and say he'd forgotten. One evening when we were just about to eat, his Australian pal turned up and they went off together and talked until he disturbed the children when he left around four or five in the morning."

11

OF THE ROYAL FAMILY, ONLY THE QUEEN
Mother had met Roddy, when Margaret had finally taken
him to Royal Lodge, and they had struck up a chord, but in
the face of her sister's evident disapproval, she was in no
haste to force an introduction there. Prince Philip, she knew,
would never take to Roddy so it was best that their paths
never crossed. The Llewellyn lifestyle was the antithesis of
everything Philip preached and stood for, and while allowances had been made for Tony, there was no hope that
Roddy would ever find favor in that quarter. In time, Margaret hoped that he would meet more of her relations—she
was sure that Prince Charles would be sympathetic, if only
for her sake—but for the moment she was content to keep
him to herself.

As for the public, the waters were tested for the first time
in the summer when Margaret took Roddy to the theater,
along with Norman St. John Stevas, the Tory M.P. and an
old friend of hers, to see Penelope Keith in *Donkey's Years*.
There was no adverse reaction, and when she flew back to
London in September after a stay at Glen with David and
Sarah, Roddy came with her, stepping from the plane just
behind the Princess, grinning winningly and waving for the
waiting cameras. At Glen everyone had remarked on the
new confidence Roddy displayed: it was difficult to reconcile
the bold Roddy, whose personality seemed at times to domi-
nate the Princess's, with the feckless young man who had
appeared four years before.

Displaying Roddy was part of a carefully orchestrated campaign, an attempt to gain public acceptance of their friendship as aboveboard, to wipe away the hole-in-the-wall impression which the Mustique photograph had created. They knew the disparity in their ages would always be commented on, even if they had long forgotten to be aware of the gap, and Margaret wished that her sister's subjects would accept Roddy as her own children had. They had fallen into an easygoing relationship with Roddy and were fiercely loyal if anyone at school criticized their mother's odd attachment to him. In the same spirit, they had become friends with Lucy Lindsay-Hogg who, while she did not actually live at their father's imposing new residence, bought for £85,000 ("with what I regard as my money," says Margaret, "because he had been living off me for so long.") and extensively redesigned at greater cost, spent much of her time there and joined them for school holidays at Old House.

It was a measure of the self-esteem Roddy had acquired from being recognized as the Princess's escort that he felt able to hit back when Robert Lacey, in his best-selling book *Majesty*, misinterpreted the spirit of Surrendell, and Roddy's role in reclaiming the land there, and labelled him a "dropout." He told the *Daily Mail*: "I've never been a dropout and I demand that this man Lacey apologises. He's never met me and doesn't realise that I spent months at the farm turning a jungle into a kitchen garden. And at Merrist Wood I was called a diligent, hard-working student. The reference is very insulting, like all those lies that I was on the dole."

He left Merrist Wood with a coveted National Certificate of Horticulture, which he hung in the bedroom in Walham Grove, and set about incorporating himself with the help of Don Factor, an American friend whom he had met through Rendall. Factor had inherited part of the cosmetics fortune of his father, Max Factor, and decided to settle in England. Jokingly Roddy put up Llewellyn Garden City as a name, but it was registered eventually as Roddy Llewellyn Landscapes Limited and he began touting for commissions, telling the Princess he was willing to take on anything from a small London townhouse garden, even window boxes, upwards.

When Roddy marked his thirtieth birthday, in October 1977, with a weekend party in Wales, Margaret was absent because of the very real threat of the press running amok across the Llanvair lawns, but she had planned a special treat of her own for him two days later at Kensington Palace. The Princess had invited a dozen to a black-tie dinner, including Johnny Nutting, son of the former Tory Minister, and his wife Diane, the Lichfields and Lord Buckhurst, who had been at Aix-en-Provence with Roddy. Later, fifty more mutual friends arrived to celebrate—Margaret led them all in a chorus of "Happy Birthday" while at the piano—and Roddy was quoted as saying: "I didn't enjoy my twenties very much and I am glad to be thirty. I think a lot is going to change—we'll see."

Margaret was in Mustique in November to welcome her sister, who had stopped off on a flag-waving tour with the Concorde to see the island and Les Jolies Eaux for the first time, and Roddy was made to wait in Barbados for the coast to clear before completing the journey to the island from London. It had been conjectured that Roddy would also be in residence, and that the Queen's visit would thus finally give the romance the royal seal of approval, but journalists in search of a scoop were disappointed. They did spy him, however, at the airport as the Queen's flight was about to head home, and a picture was painted, rather unfairly, of Roddy trying to get in on the royal act and draw attention to himself, much as Townsend had done, unwittingly, during the Queen's State Visit to Holland in 1958. She must have read the accounts with a sense of déjà-vu.

"There was no possibility of meeting the Queen because we didn't know each other then. But the press were waiting for a gaffe and it was awful bad timing being caught at the airport at the same time," says Roddy. "The red carpet was out for Concorde and there I was getting on this tiny island hopper. Most unfortunate, but we weren't trying to avoid each other." The incident had a surprising repercussion when a sackful of hate mail from Monarchists, furious at Roddy's apparently seeking to upstage the Queen, was delivered to Llanvair. Teeny and Harry, who had finally been given a knighthood that year for his services to equestrianism, agreed once again that the involvement would end in ruin for Roddy. Both boys looked as if they were heading for the same fate, and Harry said: "I blame it all on their going to live in London. They should have stayed in Wales, near their roots."

Drumming up landscaping business proved hard for Roddy, and when he discussed his future with Margaret, he mentioned off the top of his head, the urge to make a record. She had not laughed and, miraculously, the opportunity presented itself at the end of the year. She urged him to take it. It came through Victor Melik, a leather merchant who had Turkish origins but had lived in France. Melik had arrived in London with money to burn and an ambition to launch himself as a singer under the name Claude Franck. He had become close friends with Dai, and dined out in London with him twice a week. Dai had been entertained at Melik's St. Tropez villa and Melik, in turn, had stayed a weekend at Llanvair. He had become excited about the possibilities of a pink house on one of the Llewellyn hill-farms, which he at first rented, then bought, along with ten acres, on to which he added a tennis court.

Melik had heard Roddy sing and passed the word to an old school friend, Claude Wolff, the husband and manager of Petula Clark. They were not slow to realize that Roddy's connection with the Princess could be exploited commercially, and Wolff suggested to Melik that he bring Roddy out to the French skiing resort of Megève to talk over the possibilities. "I've got a list of things I want to do in life, and one of them actually was to sing a record and Victor, who had sung himself, suggested it. We went out to Megève to meet Wolff who was skiing there with Petula and their family and stayed in a terrible hotel in the main street, which was so noisy that I didn't get a wink of sleep," says Roddy. "We used always to meet up for lunch with Sacha Distel who kept on glaring at me across the table. I asked Petula why on earth he was looking at me like that and she said, 'It's because he is jealous of you.' Imagine that!"

On January 10, it was announced to fanfares that Roddy had signed up with Wolff, who estimated that his earnings could be as high as £250,000. Melik, delighted at his coup, added: "If we can find the right song for him and produce a hit, the sky's the limit. Claude is a marvellous operator. We think Roddy had a very good voice and has a great future. He will sing ballads in the John Denver style. I don't think he is cashing in on his fame through Princess Margaret."

The Princess may have thought otherwise—certainly the rest of her family did when the event received coverage, quite out of proportion to Roddy's merits as a singer, in every newspaper—but she wanted financial security for her "angel" and was content to let him achieve it on her coattails if necessary. Little did she suspect, though, to what extent those around Roddy would use the association and how much it would sully her reputation.

Roddy quickly became public property—Hughie Green promptly issued an invitation for him to appear on his *Op-*

portunity Knocks television talent show before it ended its run in March, and West End estate agents Knight, Frank and Rutley made capital of his gardening talents to boost the sale of a £750,000 penthouse in Grosvenor Square. They put it on the market with the added inducement of a thirty-five foot by twenty-five foot Llewellyn-designed roof garden. Clifford Elson, whose clients included Mike Yarwood, Des O'Connor and Norman Wisdom, became his public relations adviser, and Roddy returned to Megève later in January, with Melik and his girl friend Melinda Long, who was half his forty-three years, to finalize the agreement and plan the next vital steps.

When asked for Princess Margaret's view of the change of direction in his life, Roddy said he had embarked on his new career with her full approval. "I consulted the Princess before taking up the offer to make records and she had no objections. She likes my voice and she likes the idea of my becoming a pop singer. We are always singing together—one of our favourites is 'The Bells Are Ringing.' I am very serious about singing. I'll try to get a bit of gardening done as well, if I can, but my musical career is my first priority. I know I've been quite a fickle character in the past and hopefully I can settle down to singing."

To launch his protégé, Wolff arranged for Roddy to sing a duet with Petula on French television and chose a current Parisian hit, "Venez donc Chez Moi" ("Come around to my place"). Petula said: "Some people think his voice is folksy, but I think it's very romantic. It's great—after all he is Welsh. We have spent a lot of time together and he really is a sweet boy." With Roddy in a dinner jacket and Petula wearing a shimmering strapless chiffon dress, the telerecording was brought forward a day because of a threatened strike. Roddy ruined the first two takes by standing up at the wrong moment. In the third it was discovered that the glass of champagne he was meant to hand to Petula was empty, but the fourth was judged to be perfect, and Roddy, who went off to telephone Princess Margaret with the news of his debut, said: "It went like a dream. I had done my homework like a good boy and they are all thrilled. I don't think I was too bad but I'm not ready for British television yet. I only wish I'd been a little prettier."

Petula claimed that 18 million viewers watched the program and said she was pleased with the end result. "The duet was a fine first-time effort and had a very favourable public reaction—they loved him. His voice is certainly good enough to get him a Number One but everybody needs the right material. You don't get there by voice alone."

Before he set off for Mustique with Princess Margaret on February 25, Roddy had one more ordeal to face: his first day in the recording studios—complete with press photographers—where his producer, Tony Eyers, said he hoped Roddy would sound like Bryan Ferry "with class" and envisaged that the album would be completed in two months. As a bank of flashbulbs illuminated him at the piano, Roddy admitted: "Although I value my privacy, I think I've well and truly blown it this time. Now I have to face up to the consequences."

The day after arriving at Les Jolies Eaux, Roddy took to his bed, complaining of a cold and being run down, and when he showed no signs of improvement a week later, Princess Margaret sent for Charles Manning, an Englishman who'd been a doctor in the West Indies and who had retired to a house on the island. Tests showed that Roddy's hemoglobin count was seriously low, and when Manning learned that his feces were pitch black, he diagnosed hemorrhaging and advised that his patient be taken forthwith to Barbados for proper treatment. He was flown to the £60-a-day Barbados Diagnostic Clinic in Bridgetown, and put in the care of Dr. Ritchie Haines, a Barbadian. Princess Margaret followed two days later to stay with Verna Hull. She was pleased to discover that Johnny and Wendy Kidd were at Holders, and arranged to spend some of her time with them. With a crowd of around 100 waiting outside to cheer her, Margaret arrived at the hospital to spend two hours with Roddy. He looked better after blood transfusions, more cheerful, and, she noted, had cornered the clinic's only color television set.

Verna, who painted proficiently for a hobby, had known Margaret since her first visits to Barbados. Her house on the beach was next door to Claudette Colbert's: she and the former Hollywood movie queen had been very close friends until they became involved in a protracted emotional wrangle, which ended with Verna constructing a high wall between their two properties since which they had not spoken a word to each other.

Roddy suspected that Verna, through a misguided sense of humor, had been behind the jape which had sent him to Mustique and led to his breakdown three years earlier, but when she came to the clinic, he found her sympathetic and friendly. She told a reporter of her guest: "Obviously Princess Margaret is very upset, but she's keeping calm. As a member of the Royal Family, she is very well trained and contained. But they are both nice people and this is a nice story. There is nothing sordid about their relationship and they have nothing to hide."

Alas, the headlines over Margaret's bedside visits and Roddy's disorder lent fuel to the continuing campaign against the Princess by Willie Hamilton, who had found an ally in Dennis Canavan, another Labour MP for a Scottish Constituency—West Stirlingshire—with a flair for self-publicity. "Here she is, going away with her boyfriend to a paradise island while we are being asked to tighten our belts," carped Canavan: "The Princess should be paying her own way in life—the taxpayer shouldn't be subsidizing her luxury trips abroad." In the Commons Hamilton chastized the Labour Government for sanctioning Margaret's Civil List allowance, which had risen to £55,000 a year. He later pointed out that the Elizabeth Garrett Anderson Hospital in Euston was threatened with closure, for lack of funds, and offered his advice: "I suggest that £30,000, or whatever it costs, should be taken from the annuity of the young lady now holidaying in the West Indies. If she thumbs her nose at taxpayers by flying off to Mustique to see this pop-singer chap, she shouldn't expect the workers of the country to pay for it. There would be a marvellous response from the working people if she were told that she could get on with her private life and that the Government couldn't go on supporting her."

As the Republican fusillades were sounding off back home, Margaret had a night out with Oliver Messel. He took her to a theater revue in Bridgetown and when asked about his nephew, replied: "I am very devoted to them both and have known them for many years. Their personal situation does not affect our relationship. We don't often speak of it and we don't want to go into that now—Princess Margaret is very relaxed and enjoying being out. She went backstage in the interval and was most interested."

Roddy was discharged after eight days and driven by Dr. Haines to Verna's to convalesce. Although Margaret was worried that his illness would interfere with his recording plans, she urged him to stay in the sun until he felt completely recovered. Another job awaited him in London, a lucrative commission to promote Bennett, a new club in Battersea, but feeling weak and anemic, he was in no hurry to return and said about his ailment: "I've got something wrong with my tummy—there's a sort of pipe in the upper duodenum which should be U-shaped, like a lavatory, but in fact is slightly corrugated. Whenever I drink brandy, it gives me a burn there and I have to hit myself to ease it. It decided to complain when I arrived in Mustique—very tiresome. I woke up one morning very sick and the retching must have torn something. In all I lost seven pints of blood."

Margaret left him by the pool to fly back, and March 19, the second anniversary of her separation, went unremarked, although it was the legal juncture at which a divorce could be applied for: Tony was in no hurry to remarry and the Princess in no position to. A week later Roddy arrived at Heathrow and, stung by the criticisms from Hamilton and Canavan, felt emboldened to retaliate.

"I would like to see Willie Hamilton or any of the others do all her jobs in the marvellous way that she does. People love the Monarchy and appreciate with their whole hearts the job she does. I shall go on seeing Princess Margaret when and where I want," he said. "Let them all criticize—I don't mind. As far as Mr. Hamilton goes, I feel it a shame that such a capable politician does not direct his abilities to more important matters. I certainly do not believe that Princess Margaret has done anything to give the Royal Family a bad name, as suggested. I am a loyal and obedient servant of the Queen. It's a pity that the only way these MPs can get their names in the newspapers is by attacking women, unjustly, who cannot answer back owing to their very position."

The last word lay with Hamilton who replied with stinging effect. "For anybody to say seriously that Princess Margaret works hard is absurd nonsense. She has had eight public engagements to date this year and that is in three months. In that time she has drawn about £14,000—not bad for eight performances. The Royal Family themselves must be very disturbed by the defence coming from this quarter. I think this is the last thing they would want."

Matters were not helped by erroneous reports that Roddy had invested £50,000 in Bennett—he told the Princess he had not put in a penny—which was due to open in April. His involvement had been a publicity coup for Liz Brewer, a public relations lady who had been hired to launch the club (which had been refurbished at a cost of £150,000) and had roped Roddy in to organize the pots and plants on the patios and attend to the floral decorations, for a weekly retainer. Miss Brewer, who met her future husband, John Rendall, when Roddy brought him along to an early site meeting, was not averse to getting mileage out of the Margaret connection, even though she knew there was no possibility of the Princess's lending herself to any part of the project. When a gossip column suggested that Margaret would attend the opening night, Miss Brewer did not deny it and said: "It's up to Roddy to invite her, but we hope the Princess will be the No. 1 guest at the opening."

On April 5, the *Sun* printed an "exclusive" story with the provocative and eye-catching headline "Give Up Roddy Or Quit," purporting to reveal that the Queen had issued an ultimatum to her sister because she was distressed at all the unfavorable publicity Roddy was causing her. The report added that Margaret had plenty of time to give the matter thought, as she had cancelled a journey to Scotland to attend the annual meetings of two children's charities in Edinburgh." The truth was that Margaret was very ill, but the royal advisers were worried for other good reasons: It had become apparent that the Princess was becoming involved in a series of unseemly publicity stunts, starting with the LP, and it did not really matter whether this was with or without Roddy's complicity. Quite simply, he was bad news. The headlines he trailed in his wake reflected directly to the Queen, tarnishing her image. The story in the *Sun* was a "flier"; Margaret had never discussed with her sister the alternatives of renouncing either Roddy or her allowance—that hurdle had been crossed once before with Townsend and was a closed issue. But there was a solution to the problem: Roddy received instructions from "on high" to leave the country for at least three months, and to give no interviews during that period. "Where can I go?" he wailed to a friend. "I've got no money and yet they expect me to vanish."

On the night of April 13, there was a riot outside Bennett, as local residents and their supporters packed Battersea Square waving banners reading "We Don't Want You" and "Square Deal for Battersea." They objected to the club, whose owners hoped to attract one thousand members to join, paying £50 a year, on the grounds that it would make the working class area fashionable, push up property prices and force out the old inhabitants.

Although Miss Brewer, who had previously launched Wedgie's, a club in the King's Road, had no hand in the demonstration, she was delighted at the coverage it received. Apart from reporters and photographers, there were television cameramen filming the arrival of guests who included Angela Rippon, Terence Stamp, Margaret, Duchess of Argyll, Liberace and Lady Melchett. They had to run the gauntlet of a 250-strong baying crowd. Two days later the licensing Magistrates turned down the club's application for a liquor license, agreeing only to a restaurant extension to 2 A.M. Artist Ernest Rodker, a lecturer at Chelsea Art School, and David Imbert, who had formed BRAG (Battersea Redevelopment Action Group) claimed a victory.

When Roddy discussed his banishment with Margaret, he found her in no mood to fight on his behalf. She was unwell, and unable to shake it off, and continuing to smoke and drink did not improve her condition. She did not even seem interested in his good news—he had signed a long-term recording contract with Phonogram, the company for which Tony Eyers had worked on the Twiggy album, and entered into a management agreement with Claude Wolff, for three years at a basic £1,000 a month. On top of this he was to receive £150 a week from Bennett, ostensibly to look after the greenery. After years of penny-pinching, Roddy's fi-. nances had shown a dramatic improvement. He felt more comfortable now at the prospect of going abroad.

Just as an article appeared in the magazine *Woman's World,* based on an interview given two months before, Roddy was packing his bags to disappear. He was quoted as saying he would never marry, adding: "Sitting with one woman indefinitely is out of the question. I'm far too selfish; I couldn't bear to have a wife who snored or slept with the window open when I wanted it closed or did anything I didn't want her to. And I have no desire to have children. I find it difficult enough getting along in life so I don't see why I should bring another person into the world to suffer it too. I'm a yokel at heart. I don't really like London much, though I must admit I love visiting for two or three days, being terribly naughty and then disappearing again."

At Hearthrow his alias of "Mr. Johnson" was penetrated as he appeared to board a Royal Air Maroc flight to Tangier, a cosmopolitan city on the North African coast, facing Gibraltar. But he was not prepared, he said, to discuss the matter with the airport journalists. "I am very sorry, but you have got the wrong person. I have no comment to make—I am not even going to tell you where I am going or what I am doing." And fingering a jaunty straw hat and carrying two plastic bags containing duty free liquor and cigarettes, he boarded his flight.

With Princess Margaret's health worsening—her doctors were unable to pinpoint the exact problem—and with mounting speculation that the unwise affair was finally over, the press followed Roddy to Tangier in the hope that he would at last spill the beans. There was an offer from an American publication of £150,000 for his story. He had borrowed a villa, staffed with two servants, from Tessa Codrington, a photographer he knew in London, but found little in Tangier to interest him. The reason why he had been told to vanish became clear on May 10, when it was announced that Princess Margaret, after all, was seeking a divorce. Her statement stressed that she had no plans to remarry, and that she intended to lead her royal life as the Queen's sister to the full. It was taken, wrongly, as a renunciation of Roddy. Piqued, he finally broke his silence in Morocco. "I am saying categorically that I will never marry Princess Margaret. Circumstances—personal reasons—would prevent it. I don't consider myself in any way responsible for the divorce. Of course I hope to see her again. One always likes to see one's friends."

Sniffed out at his villa, Roddy fled in the dark of night to York Castle, an old Portuguese fort in the Casbah, which was owned by French philanthropist Yves Vidal, one of the few people Roddy had met and liked in Tangier. Vidal had made a fortune manufacturing furniture and had bought the castle, in 1958, from Lord Rhidian Crichton-Stuart whose father, the 4th Marquess of Bute, owned great estates across the water in Spain near Algeciras. Vidal was organizing a charity ball for one thousand people, to take place in June, in aid of the local childrens' hospital. He enlisted Roddy's aid, inviting him to stay for as long as he liked. After a while, however, Roddy became homesick: "Tangier was a great mistake. I was lonely, miserable and bored. There was nothing to do and I hated all those British 'queens' who live there. When the Press found me I had to escape through the garden of Tessa's villa at midnight, dressed in a djellaba."

On the occasions Roddy had telephoned the Princess, he

learned of no improvement. The cold she had caught on her return from Mustique had worsened into flu and there had been bouts of migraine. The lingering malady had prevented her from witnessing her daughter's confirmation on April 5, when all the Royal Family, and Tony, had turned out at St. George's Chapel, Windsor, to see Sarah, Prince Edward, and James Ogilvy, the son of Princess Alexandra and Angus Ogilvy, received fully into the Church of England. But Margaret had attended the lunch party afterwards at Windsor Castle, where all the childrens' godparents were present, including Anthony Barton with his wife Eva, who had been greeted warmly by the Princess.

12

A WEEK BEFORE THE DIVORCE ANNOUNCE-
ment, Margaret had been admitted to the King Edward VII
hospital for tests. She was treated by Dr. John Batten, the
Queen's physician, and Dr. Nigel Southward, Apothecary to
the Royal Family, for eight days after it was discovered that
she had been suffering from, among lesser ills, gastroenteritis
and alcoholic hepatitis, the only cure for which was to ab-
stain totally from drinking alcohol for a period of up to one
year. During the debilitating weeks of her sickness and recuperation, Margaret found her greatest support came from
her lady-in-waiting, the Hon. Davina Woodhouse, who was
then twenty-three and had been working in Kensington Palace for three years, following a recommendation for the job
by Lady Elizabeth Cavendish, a friend of her parents, Lord
and Lady Terrington. With Roddy away, Davina's was the
nearest shoulder to cry on and, despite her youth, she
offered a surprising amount of comfort for the Princess who,
friends were saying, had suffered a nervous breakdown.

In addition to her paid role as the Princess's social secretary and personal assistant, working five days a week from
10 A.M. to 6 P.M. to help her "boss," as she called her, answer
the mail and organize her private life and shopping, Davina
was happy to take late-night (usually early morning) telephone calls from Margaret, who sought solace in the lonely,
still hours. On occasion they would go out to the cinema,
returning to the Palace to cook themselves bacon and eggs,
clearing up afterwards so as not to offend the cook. In the

wake of the divorce, the Princess received more letters than she had in years, nearly all of them sympathetic to her, from young and old, male and female, and she spent days personally answering every letter, aided by Davina. It was the first step on the road back to recovery, and the second, was the unexpected return of Roddy, who finally ignored his orders.

On the actual day Margaret obtained her "quickie" divorce—the decree was granted in the High Court in just 113 seconds—Roddy contrived to turn up at a Paris nightclub with Petula, Wolff, Eyers, and an attractive fashion designer called Celeste, who obligingly held his hand for the ever-present *paparazzi* photographers. Celeste was one of several women with whom Roddy made sure he was seen in public at this time. His object was to lay a false scent, which would keep newshounds at bay for a while, at the suggestion of Princess Margaret. His most regular companions were Bianca Jagger and Naima Feth-Eddrine, a Moroccan whom he had met at Surrendell when she worked as a waitress at Parsenn Sally. A year younger than Roddy, Naima had gone through a marriage ceremony in August 1976, with Michael Kelly, the youthful director of the Bath Young People's Theatre Company, who used to patronize the restaurant, but there had been a suggestion that the wedding was a ruse to secure the bride the right to British residency.

Margaret would meet Roddy in the privacy of her home or at country weekends with friends like the Nuttings at Chicheley Hall, their stately home near Newport Pagnell, or Bryan Forbes and his actress wife Nanette Newman, longstanding chums of the Princess, whose Virginia Water home was close to Royal Lodge. To the surprise of many friends, who had always been concerned about her drinking, she accepted the no-alcohol edict without rancor. At the beginning some went dry themselves when entertaining her, to keep temptation out of her path, but she soon put an end to the "nonsense" and urged them to carry on as normal as she had the problem under control. "It may be six months, it may be a year, nobody knows," said the Princess. "And I'm feeling so well! I don't miss it at all."

By June Roddy had completed the recording of his album, after sessions in Paris as well as London. To set the publicity in motion, he appeared on Pete Murray's Radio Two *Open House* show, sent love to his Nanny, and told listeners that the final result of his crooning was "very good indeed." A week later he learned he had been included in the will of his uncle Sir Rhys, who had died in Brighton leaving £552,116, and passing the baronetcy on to Harry. There were reports that the brothers stood to inherit £20,000 each, but Dai, paradoxically because he was the elder, received only £3,000. Roddy received £11,500 and a set of platinum and mother-of-pearl buttons and cuff-links to be worn with white tie and tails. About half the fortune went in death duties; the remainder was divided between nineteen nephews and nieces after a few charitable bequests. By coincidence, Tony was also the beneficiary of a will when, in July, Oliver Messel died leaving him his house in Barbados and all the set-and-costume-designs from his long and very distinguished career in the theater.

Distancing herself in the public eye from Roddy, the Princess went to Amalfi in early August to stay at the villa of Mario d'Urso, a merchant banker based in London for a New York company, who had been her host once before. They had met through Mme. Imelda Marcos, wife of the President of the Philippines, who liked to lionize the Princess and shower her with gifts. Mario, despite his hopes to the contrary, was viewed by Margaret with only platonic interest, although she enjoyed his presence at her parties. While she was in Italy, Roddy took up an offer from Petula and Claude to join them in a villa they had rented in St.

Tropez and Melik flew him to the South of France in a chartered executive plane.

He was beginning to discover that the path to success, while paved with influence, was also punctuated by pitfalls, and in London he had become involved in an unseemly squabble with Liz Brewer over his role in Bennett, accusing the club of "exploiting" his name. "All I did was shove a few plants in a few pots, yet the world was made to believe I was a director for publicity purposes. When I came back from Mustique, I discovered that my name had been put all over Bennett's blurb without permission and suddenly letters were popping through people's doors informing them I was the head of the membership committee. I haven't set foot inside the place since the opening."

Miss Brewer told the press a slightly different story. "Originally Roddy was just going to landscape the garden. Later it was agreed that he would pose for photographs and supervise membership and be paid £7,500 a year," she said. "He even told us he would bring Princess Margaret along to the club. All was well until he went to Mustique and became ill."

The air in St. Tropez became no less acrimonious because of Roddy's seeming unwillingness to part with even one franc, ignoring the bill when it was brought to the table at lunches on one of the fashionable beaches, or at dinners overlooking the port, or in neighboring villages, and both Wolff and Melik began to have personal reservations about their "discovery." At the end of the holiday, Melik was less than pleased to find that Roddy had grandly invited two friends to share the flight back, again chartered, and Melik retaliated by sending Roddy a bill which was grudgingly, but eventually, settled.

"The only way I can live in a fairly civilised way is by being fairly mean," Roddy explains, and Dai was taxed about his brother when he next saw Melik. "There was this huge row in St. Tropez over Roddy's meanness and he couldn't understand why. But they'd had him to stay in Megève and then in St. Tropez and not once did Roddy ever offer to pay for a single meal, drink or taxi, and nor did he buy a present, however simple, for Petula's children. He said he hadn't got the money but Wolff and Melik knew exactly what he was being paid by them. After that, they all got this thing about Rods, an absolute mania about how anyone could be so mean."

Princess Margaret spent her forty-eighth birthday at Balmoral, laughing off press inventions that she might marry d'Urso. She then went on to Glen, where she was joined by Roddy. They were favored by good weather, made the usual tour of the Edinburgh Festival, and in the evenings Roddy played and sang some of the twelve songs which Eyers had chosen for the debut album. Their stay was a reaffirmation of the feelings they had discovered for each other five years before, although the first physical urges had been replaced by a cosy companionship beyond the reach of lovers' quarrels. On the last evening there was an extravagant fancy-dress party where guests were entertained by the Princess, who dressed up as Sophie Tucker and did a devastating impression of the Red Hot Momma, while Lady Anne snapped away with her camera, little realizing that the results were destined for wider circulation than her own family album. After the films were developed and printed, she left the negatives in a drawer, where they were chanced upon by her eldest son Charlie, who had become a heroin addict. Colin had stood by him when he had been arrested at Heathrow returning from Thailand with the drug, and Charlie had been saved a jail sentence by joining a rehabilitation program, but that had not worked.

Now Charlie's pusher was threatening to cut off supplies

and, in need of cash, he pocketed the negatives and gave them to a friend, Michael Waters (known to the Tennants and Margaret as "Muddy") to sell to a national newspaper. Waters went to the *Daily Mail*, with which he had done business before, selling them tidbits of information, and convinced senior editors that the film belonged to Charlie. A deal was done for £7,000, and the intimate photographs were then spread across three pages of the *Mail*, to the great horror of Lady Anne who promptly sued for breach of copyright. Charlie, who was only twenty-one, was eventually forgiven, although Tennant disinherited him in favor of his younger son, Henry, to give security to the tenants on the Glen estate.

"Charlie is, in spite of it all, such a star, such a charmer," says his father. "I'm afraid he was the casualty of the rather different social attitudes of my wife and me. She saw him as a naughty boy who should be spanked. I saw him as an unhappy boy who should be psychoanalysed. I took him away from private school against her inclination and sent him to a progressive place. I'm sure now I was wrong. Anne has brought up our twin daughters her own way, and I must say they're perfect, always busy, never bored. If they're not sewing, they're playing hopscotch, if they're not playing hopscotch, they're making those potato things.

"I suppose it is much healthier than Charlie's experiments or Henry's, who is into Transcendental Meditation. I could never find it in my heart to condemn Charlie. I know that if that sort of badness had been available to me when I was younger, I would have jumped at it as well. In my youth one just didn't have to get that far to create an effect. I remember causing outrage for weeks by getting my tailor to make me the suit with no pockets."

Margaret was on a major official tour when she heard about Charlie's chicanery. After flying halfway round the world to represent the Queen at the Independence celebrations of the Ellice Islands, she had to abandon her Pacific tour in Tuvalu after contracting a fever and, with a temperature of 104 degrees, was flown 2,500 miles to Sydney. An acute febrile upper respiratory illness was diagnosed and treated. She then proceeded to the Caribbean to represent her sister at the Independence of Domenica before taking her party, including Davina and Nigel Napier, to Mustique. When she returned, she went round to the Tennants' London home, near Kensington Palace, to receive Charlie's apologies for his treachery, only to discover that he had escaped through a narrow window from the room he had been locked into for safe-keeping!

Ineptly, Charlie made less than £100 from the sale of the negatives, but the incident led to a handsome offer from a woman's magazine to tell his story. Colin helped negotiate a fee of £6,000 and stipulated that the money be sent direct to him to pass on to Charlie, rather than find its way immediately to predatory pushers. Roddy also received a four-figure sum, though less than Charlie's, for a magazine interview which appeared before the launch of his LP. In it he embroidered wildly on his schooldays, claiming that he had been whipped often at Shrewsbury, until blood had poured down his legs, which, he claimed, had done him no lasting harm, and he advocated the return of caning in public schools.

The article brought him opprobrium and a quick rebuttal from Michael Charlesworth, the senior master of Shrewsbury, who said: "It's an absolute fabrication. At the time he was a pupil, we were in the process of abolishing corporal punishment. The only thing used was the cane and in any case the housemaster who was in charge of Llewellyn, Robin Moulsdale, did not approve of corporal punishment and did not beat boys. It is quite out of the question that Roddy

Llewellyn would have been whipped in the manner he describes."

By the autumn, life was moving at a bold pace for Roddy, with a well-controlled publicity campaign. In September he had been a judge of the Miss Great Britain beauty contest at Morecambe, along with Harvey Smith, Harry Worth, snooker champion Ray Reardon, and comedienne Marti Caine. It was "leaked" that he had been invited to appear on the Morecambe and Wise Christmas TV show, an accolade reserved for only the famous, but Eric and Ernie denied that anything had been fixed. Thames TV did admit, however, that Roddy was one of the many "star guests" whose names had been discussed.

Phonogram executive Rick Blaskey said of the record: "We think the album will be a big success and we hope to follow it with a single." An advance copy was given to Radio One disk jockey Tony Blackburn who thought the production excellent and told listeners: "One song. 'Everybody Wants to Find a Bluebird,' could be a big hit for him. He sings it very proficiently and, after all, not having the greatest voice in the business has never held people like Sacha Distel back." Another BBC disk jockey, Jimmy Young, said: "I think the songs are extremely well chosen. Roddy might not have the greatest voice in the world, but the album is bound to sell well. A lot of care and effort obviously went into the production."

A nightclub, Tramp, was chosen for the noon launching of *Roddy* (Phonogram 9109 227) on his birthday, October 9th. Perhaps sensing an unseemly gathering, Sir Harry cried off, citing a "business meeting." Undeterred, Roddy mustered together his mother, sister Anna, Dai and his aunt, Vicky Llewellyn-Palmer, who made a dramatic entrance down the stairs to the basement on the stroke of midday as the discotheque started blaring out the record. Taken to a podium with larger-than-life cutouts of himself and the record, Roddy posed for twenty photographers. When they asked him to vary his attitude by drinking a glass of champagne, he saw his chance to gain revenge for all the telephoto lenses in the past two and a half years, and shook the bottle up, spraying all the cameramen. Later the man from the *Daily Mirror* retaliated by pouring a bottle over Roddy, drenching his blown-dry hair and gray chalk-stripe suit.

Even the *Times* printed a photograph of the event the next morning, getting Roddy's age wrong in the process, and Phonogram was reported to be investing £50,000 on promotion. A spokesman claimed: "If there is anyone who doesn't already know that Roddy Llewellyn has made an album, then they most certainly will between now and Christmas." Alone among the reviewers, David Wigg of the *Daily Express* forecast that the LP would be a winner.

Princess Margaret, who had received an advance copy with an affectionate inscription, thought his performance marvellous, and apparently did not object when he told one interviewer: "Of course I took advantage of the publicity that surrounds my friendship with Princess Margaret. Had I not been Roddy Llewellyn, I don't suppose anyone would have bothered to take an interest in my ambition to make a pop record. But I made perfectly certain I hurt no one in getting my wish." Good publicity degenerated into bad when the *Daily Mirror* alleged that BBC Radio Two producers had been ordered to give Roddy star treatment and play the LP as Album of the Week, following in the grooves of Frank Sinatra and Bing Crosby. Immediately Charles McLelland the Radio Two Controller, ordered it to be dropped, saying: "The record has not been banned but I am not convinced that the whole package is strong enough for

Album of the Week treatment. It is well produced with some lovely arrangements, however, and Roddy has a pleasant voice." It was then replaced by *Bobby Goldsboro's Greatest Hits.*"

In the first two weeks on sale at HMV in Oxford Street, London's biggest record store, it sold just thirteen copies—against 460 of *Grease.* Eyers tried to be optimistic: "It's still too early to judge. We hope it will do well around Christmas." But sales remained slow and without a resounding success to his credit, Roddy's chance of appearing with Morecambe and Wise vanished. He did, however, make an appearance on Spanish television. Eyers dropped plans for a follow-up within weeks, and said: "As for any future records, it is in the lap of the gods—certainly this album is not setting the world on fire. We really should have had it out in June, but Roddy was ill and by the time it came out in October, the publicity had gone on too long."

It is doubtful that Roddy had the dedication to pursue a singing career had the record been a success, and Margaret for one was relieved in some ways that it was over almost before it had begun. Maybe she did not want to share him and, certainly, the time he had to devote to her needs and entertainment would have been curtailed. With failure came a reasonable degree of anonymity. No one sought to draw attention to them when they twice went to the theater before Christmas, with David and Sarah, to see *Evita* and *Under The Greenwood Tree,* and danced the night away at the ball Lichfield gave for the birth .of his son and heir, Viscount Anson, at the Hyde Park Hotel.

Looking back on the episode, Roddy put most of the blame on the content of the album and his producers. "Anthony Eyers chose the record and it was out of my hands. I don't think the tunes were really right and I don't think I came through as strongly as I could have done. I didn't know anything about the record business and I didn't know where to start because there were millions of songs to choose from. In my album there were four standards, which weren't bad at all, and the rest were from here, there and everywhere. It was a very generous deal and Phonogram spent £20,000. I don't think they got any of it back but it was the company, not Claude Wolff, who lost the money. I'm glad I did it, but the whole thing was fairly tense for about nine months, starting when I was thrown into that Paris studio in a dinner jacket at 10 A.M. and then had to mime the words of a French song while all the British photographers went click, click. They all came over to crucify me but then had to admit I could sing—they were longing for me to sound like a toad in labor. It was a terrifying experience without any lessons in production or how to behave. I didn't know how to walk, how to open my mouth, how or when to smile. In retrospect I should have been very angry with Wolff, but then it was very lucrative for me."

It was Tony's turn to take the limelight when it leaked out that he had arranged to marry Lucy at Kensington Register Office on December 15. She had been assisting him that year on his new documentary about a special social services program in Kent, but had remained in her flat. When friends went to dinner parties in the kitchen of his new house in Launceston Place, they were not always sure to find her, and if she was present she did not assume the role of hostess. Nor was there any trace of her touch, only reflections of Tony's love of gadgetry in places like his ground-floor study, which was dominated by a modern steel desk, and had an elaborate video entry system to check out callers.

Lucy had always thought, and medical opinion appeared

to back her up, that she could not have children. Besides she was approaching her fortieth year. The surprise confirmation early in December that she was, at last, pregnant, hastened the marriage. The ceremony was delayed until David and Sarah had their holidays from Bedale's, and the couple gave a small celebratory lunch afterwards in a Knightsbridge restaurant.

The first intimation Margaret says she had of the wedding date was a news report on December 13, which revealed that Tony had taken out a license. She greeted it tight-lipped. "I asked him before I went away if he intended to marry and he didn't say anything. I said if you are, tell the children properly, but in the end he didn't," says Margaret, who told friends she was also furious that he did not even have the common courtesy to alert her. But Tony maintained that he had informed her, at least of his long-term plans, earlier in the autumn. Yet she was obviously hurt and taken by surprise and, in any event, Tony had made no mention of the joyous fact that he was to become a father again. Margaret was spending a weekend with friends in the country when the *Sunday Express* disclosed in March that Lucy was expecting a baby, conjecturing that it was due in September. Visibly upset, the Princess told her host that she knew nothing about it, but when guests arrived for drinks before lunch, she told them, in an effort to save face, that she had known all along.

When the baby was born at midnight on July 17, the press graciously said she was premature. Three months later the infant was christened Frances Armstrong-Jones, with the courtesy title, like her half-sister Sarah, of "Lady." Lucy has a daytime nanny, whose other duties are with Lord Frederick Windsor, the son of Prince and Princess Michael of Kent, and his new sister, but spends as much time as possible with her child. "Lucy is completely besotted with her. She never thought she could have one and it was a marvellous surprise. I don't think there's any question of another," says an old friend of Tony's, "Lucy and Tony are very relaxed in each other's company, but you never see them holding hands or kissing. It's strange when one remembers how Princess Margaret and he were always pawing each other."

13

THE DISASTERS AND MISFORTUNES OF 1978, during which Margaret had suffered the trauma of a divorce, been dogged by illness, and enmeshed in cheap and demeaning publicity stunts, continued into the new year. Again Roddy was the source of discomfiture at a delicate time—when her controversial Civil List allowance was being discussed. It had been raised the previous year by £4,000 to £59,000, and was being increased to £64,000 to reflect inflation, amid all the usual rumblings.

Roddy was arrested in the vicinity of the Palace after an early-morning collision in Knightsbridge with a police car—a chase along Kensington ended when he crashed his Ford Transit into a bollard. With Naima, he had been a guest at a party in Regine's nightclub for Shirley Bassey, to mark her twenty-five years in show business. They had arrived after dinner and sat on a banquette for a couple of hours, drinking champagne. Roddy was driving Naima back to her flat when the incident occurred. She accompanied him to the police station where he was charged after failing a Breathalyzer test, and left with him, when he was released at 5 A.M. Tests showed he had a blood-alcohol level of 148, 80 percent over the legal limit, and a police spokesman said: "After the accident, the van continued and the police car, a general-purpose unmarked red Chrysler Hunter, which had not been badly damaged, pursued it and stopped it in Kensington High Street near Kensington Palace Gardens. The car was unmarked but the crew were wearing uniforms."

It was fortunate that he crashed where he did, for Roddy, perhaps unconsciously and in a panic after hitting a police vehicle when he knew himself to be over the limit, was driving to Kensington Palace, hoping to make the safe refuge of the Princess's property before his pursuers caught up with him (both he and Naima lived in the opposite direction). If he had succeeded, he would certainly have been followed to Margaret's doorstep and apprehended on royal ground, and the resultant headlines would have proved an embarrassment which would have strained, finally, the Royal Family's uneasy tolerance of the friendship. Before collecting his impounded van that afternoon, he called in on the Princess for tea: her attitude toward the escapade was relief that no one had been injured, and curiosity as to how he had been treated by the police. There was no mention of the danger that Roddy had nearly placed her in.

When the case came to court, he was fined £180 and banned from driving for eighteen months, a cruel blow since he depended on the van for his gardening work, to ferry flagstones, soil by the hundred-weight, plants and pots and the tools of his trade. "I wasn't drunk at all, which was so silly," he says. "We'd eaten before with friends and arrived around one o'clock at Regine's. We had some champagne and left when the party ended after three and I was dropping Naima back in Lennox Gardens. I had no idea I had touched another car. I did feel a bump at one stage and thought it was a cat or something, but nothing of any importance, and drove on. Then, suddenly, I found I was being chased by half the police force in London. I ended up a mile later, quite the best way to stop!" Of course this excuse did not tally with the actual events—if he had continued to Naima's, he would have been going away from where he had the accident.

The prominent publication by most of the newspapers of

photographs of Roddy with Naima at the party (she was wearing a slinky off-the-shoulder floral pattern dress) had an unsettling effect on her estranged husband that would culminate in distressing repercussions for the Princess. A few months earlier, when asked about Roddy and his wife, Kelly said: "I've no intention of divorcing her and I don't want Roddy to leave her alone. I haven't seen her for six months but she rings me and writes and sends birthday cards. I consider their relationship quite harmless, but what makes it harmful is that she has been put in the public eye. She's not a princess and she's not used to coping with exposure. Roddy has never been in contact with me on the subject, but I still regard him as a friend of mine. She is totally besotted with his pop-star image and she follows him and his cronies around London on a gay social whirl. When we married, Roddy didn't come inside until halfway through the ceremony. He was carrying a bunch of flowers and clutching a bottle of brandy which had been opened."

The year had begun badly for Roddy who, foolishly, had accepted an invitation to fly to New York to appear on Ned Sherrin's Channel Thirteen television show, *We Interrupt the Year*, in a bid to revive interest in his album and recording career. He sang "There's Something About You" and then had to remain on the set while Sherrin's satirically minded panellists laid into him. "You could dance to that—if one leg was shot off," said one unkindly as Roddy smiled wanly, while another prophesied: "It should shoot up the charts—to about number 160."

Roddy's vicissitudes served only to make Margaret even more protective of him, and friends who were critical were known to be reduced to mumbling incoherency by one of those freezing stares which the Princess and her sister used to express disapproval. She consoled him with the thought that the swimming pool at Les Jolies Eaux had been completed—at her own expense—allowing them to bathe under the 80-degree skies in total privacy during their holiday, which would start in the middle of February. They spent the last weekend in January being entertained by portly Prince Rupert Loewenstein, who was the financial adviser to Mick Jagger and other Rolling Stones, and his wife Josephine at their Wiltshire home near Chippenham in the village of Biddestone.

In the first week of February, Claude Wolff arrived in London as Phonogram took the decision not to re-release *Roddy* and cut their losses on the project. Wolff had taken his client's failure philosophically: "It is disappointing, yes, for Roddy, but for myself, no. I never told him he would be successful. I never told him he would be a star. I thought, still do think, he has a very pleasant voice and it was worth a gamble. After all, he was already a very well known person and it wasn't as though I was going to a record company with an unknown who simply had a pleasant singing voice. I always knew it would be a flop or a success, nothing halfway, because of the person he is."

"I think Roddy would have stood more of a chance if it had been played on Radio Two as Album of the Week. He lacks the dedication to become a singer because he has too many distractions around him. If he truly wants to be a singer, he could do it. If he was prepared to work hard and get together a twenty minute act, he could achieve some success. But this is something Roddy must do. I can't make him. He says he would like to have one more try at a single. Perhaps that will work if the right song can be found. If not, there is no point. He tells me he has some plans for a horticultural business. I don't understand exactly what they are or what it is all about. You see, I don't know anything about flowers."

Claude and Petula had come for the opening of Blazers, a

cabaret club in Windsor, which was to be opened by Douglas Fairbanks, Jr. They took Roddy with them and he presented Petula with an arrangement of flowers when she did a cabaret. He then spent several minutes being besieged by female patrons of all ages asking for his autograph, and wrote a personal message in every one, signing with the élan of an established celebrity.

On February 15, his good humor vanished as he was waylaid, using the name "Mr. Petersen," at Heathrow on his way to board a British Airways jumbo bound for Barbados. "How did they find out?" Roddy snapped at an airport official escorting him to the ramp as photographers blocked his path and, brushing through them like a Hollywood star seeking anonymity, he shouted, "No photographs, please." The following day, Margaret, escorted by Colin Tennant, followed, to her second island holiday in less than four months. She had invited two sets of friends to each spend a week, but the first, José Manuel Stilianopoulos, the Philippine Ambassador to the Court of St. James's, and his Spanish wife Esperanza —called Mike and Petita—had to cancel their stay when Mme. Marcos suddenly decided to descend on London and demanded their presence, leaving Margaret at a loose end for a week until the arrival of the second couple, Reinaldo and Carolina Herrera, from Caracas.

Colin, who had sold out his majority share in the Mustique Company to a Venezuelan and a Canadian who were prepared to provide fresh funding for the final stages of the island's development, was in the process of building a house which looked like the Taj Mahal, in a small secluded valley running down to a beach near which three Malaysian-style huts on stilts had been erected for guests. Tennant stayed in one—each had an air-conditioned double bedroom with a shower and lavatory, and a verandah with a recessed kitchenette—supervising work on the Oliver Messel design which featured a domed roof and Moorish arches. The ceiling of the main room was supported by pillars made to resemble palm trees, surmounted by varnished palm fronds. When shown round, Margaret was especially impressed by the emerald and blue chandeliers, the expanses of Italian marble, and a parapet of green stones brought back from an expedition to China. The stone was specially cut and imported from Barbados, and Colin told her ruefully, that he had made the mistake of paying in advance to secure the order, whereupon the company went bankrupt, so that he had to pay all over again.

The Princess found the island brimming over with congenial company to amuse her until the Herreras arrived for the latter part of her stay. With Colin were author David Pryce-Jones and his wife, Clarissa, whose father, Lord Caccia, had been Ambassador to Washington, and Viscount Moore and his new wife, Alexandra, daughter of Sir Nicholas Henderson, the Ambassador to Paris. The two men were writing and taking photographs for an article on Messel's designs in Latin America and the Caribbean to appear in an American magazine, *Architectural Digest*.

Younger friends, like stockbroker Oliver Baring and his wife, Veronica, had taken villas, and Lady Diana Herbert, the sister of the Earl of Pembroke and Montgomery, was there to act as lady-in-waiting. Virginia Royston and Basil had moved into a new house and when Margaret went to dinner to inspect, she was shown the pointer puppy which had just arrived, with another, by plane from a pet shop in Knightsbridge, Town and Country Dogs. Colin had taken the other one, a bitch, and called her Ruby. There were plans to mate the pair in due course.

Any tourists who had availed themselves of the inspired all-inclusive Mustique holiday package in the hopes of rubbing shoulders with royalty, were disappointed, for, by day, the Princess rarely ventured from the house with its pool which overlooked the bay. She did make an appearance though, after dinner, at the Wednesday night Jump-Up at the Beach Bar, which was now the focal point of a discreet development of shops designed to attract passing yachtsmen to anchor for a few days while they revictualled. Colin would arrive early to ensure that a table was kept free for the Princess's party and would then pace nervously up and down the road outside Basil's to greet her, guaranteeing that she was accorded proper respect from the dancing throng and hangers-on as she passed through to the sitting area at the back, where the Caribbean lapped against the bamboo foundations. "It's very different these days from the old style Jump-Ups," says Tennant. "We import a band from St. Vincent and everyone is welcome, construction workers, staff from the villas, boys from the village and crews off the yachts. It does get rather crowded and there's a lot of drinking, so one must make sure the Princess is comfortable and able to enjoy herself."

There would be a running buffet of suckling pig, lobster, chicken, yams, breadfruit and hearts of palm with wine, rum cocktails, and beer available, as well as all sorts of liquor and, inevitably, some drunken scenes would erupt on the fringes later on, although Margaret, in a long dress, and dancing with either Roddy or Reinaldo, would appear to remain impervious. On one occasion she returned to her table to find an inebriated French skipper, off a boat in the bay, sitting in her place, and when she took a seat nearby, he moved over and attempted to sit on her lap. A few charming words in his own language from Colin and Herrera quickly ended the nuisance. Only when Margaret would signal her intention to leave, and a dozen or so people would stand up to bow or curtsey on her way out, did the realization sink in that the sister of the Queen of far-off Great Britain had been among the swaying revellers.

In the evenings, Margaret and Roddy played Scrabble, stopping to tune in to the wireless for the latest about President Idi Amin, who was on the verge of being toppled by Tanzanian forces friendly to Dr. Milton Obote, the man he had overthrown seven years before. Often the cry of "cheat!" would be heard: once Roddy slipped in a Welsh word, and such was Margaret's competitive spirit that she telephoned Pryce-Jones to check its authenticity before continuing with the game.

On March 1, they went to dine at the Barings and during the evening, Roddy stood up and requested silence, as he and the Princess wanted to sing. It was, he explained, not only St. David's Day, but the twentieth anniversary of the death of the mighty Foxhunter, and they wanted to commemorate the occasion by singing the Welsh National Anthem, which they did with great seriousness and in close harmony while some of the party were barely able to suppress a giggle, but everyone applauded. The night ended with guests vying to tell the cleanest "blue" joke and Margaret offered her favorite about a cocktail-bar piano player, his pet monkey, and a customer into whose drink the animal kept on dipping its genitalia.

The mood was too good to last, and idle minds were determined that Margaret's homecoming would not pass unnoticed. Two days before she was due to return, a telegram arrived at Les Jolies Eaux for Roddy from the *News of the World* seeking his comments on a story supplied to them by Mike Kelly. After failing to sell it to the *Daily Mirror*, which had nevertheless paid him £100 to keep him "sweet," Kelly had struck a deal with the *News of the World*. In return for several thousand pounds, he agreed to state that his marriage to Naima had been arranged so she could stay in Britain, and that he now planned to sue her for divorce, citing Roddy as correspondent. As the jet from Barbados was bringing Margaret and Lady Diana home on a Sunday morning, more than five million copies of the paper were carrying a front-page "exclusive" proclaiming: "I'M CITING RODDY SAYS · BOGUS HUSBAND." Below, in the center of the page, were picked out the quotes: "Spent the wedding night at his commune—And I went home to Mum."

The newspaper, which must have known that Kelly's claims were fraudulent, printed that private detectives had tailed Roddy from October to December 1978 and quoted Kelly's solicitor as saying: "We advised him that he would have to wait until three years from the date of the marriage before petitioning for divorce. The papers will be served on August 10, three years to the date of the wedding. The petition will allege adultery and we will cite Roddy Llewellyn as corespondent."

In fact, Kelly, who said the marriage had never been consummated, was legally entitled to gain a nullity decree on those grounds immediately. The whole story was a sordid put-up job designed to gain maximum effect by timing publication to coincide with the Princess's early morning arrival at Heathrow where, bleary-eyed and in a headscarf, she was met at the plane door by a battery of jostling cameramen anxious to record her obvious discomfort. According to Kelly, Roddy told him after the wedding ceremony that he should have married Naima. "I'm not really divorcing my wife, I'm divorcing Roddy Llewellyn. I was hurt, when, within weeks of our marriage, she went to live at Roddy's flat in London. Now that she has been seen around with him so openly when he is out nightclubbing, I feel Roddy is openly flaunting their relationship in my face. As long as I'm married it would seem to everyone that I'm approving of

Llewellyn's conduct and allowing him to act the way he does because he has money, breeding and privilege. I was conned into believing that Naima and I could have a normal married life. But our marriage has been treated as an immigration dodge to let her stay in Britain to be close to Roddy."

Margaret contacted Roddy, who had planned to stay a few days in Barbados, and he returned immediately to refute the spurious allegations and, four days after they were published, Kelly conceded that his claims were untrue and his solicitors, Messrs. Withy, King and Lee issued a statement: "Following discussions between their solicitors, Mr. Michael Kelly and Mrs. Naima Kelly have reached an agreement for the presentation by Mrs. Kelly of a petition for divorce in August of this year, based on the fact that they will then have lived separate and apart for at least two years. We were instructed to confirm that whilst Mr. Kelly acted at all times in good faith with views honestly held, he now acknowledges that the allegations of adultery by Mrs. Kelly, upon which he was proposing to base the petition for divorce, are untrue."

As the Kelly situation was being settled, at a cost to Naima of £800 in legal fees, which she was not able to meet, the ghost of Parsenn Sally, where Roddy had met her, rose for the final time with a call from outraged creditors for a report to be sent to the Director of Public Prosecutions. The Liquidator, Christopher Barlow, had turned up just £47 to meet trading debts of over £15,000, and it was noted that Roddy, although never listed as a director, owned 833 shares. Wine-merchant Michael Robinson of Sainsbury's said: "The small traders of Bath have been treated very shoddily. The reputation and social connections of these people, especially the connection with Princess Margaret, led us to place much more trust in them than we might otherwise have done."

For Margaret, cut off by her isolated position from public opinion, mainly informed by reading two daily newspapers, the *Times* and *Mail*, and the *Sunday Times*, and protected from most of the printed attacks upon her by local staff and friends who did not wish to trouble her with ill-informed abuse, the "silly" business was just another storm in a teacup and did not diminish Roddy's standing with her one bit, to the chagrin of his detractors. It was, she said, yet another example of him being used by unscrupulous people to drive a wedge between them, and she was not going to fall for it. They had come too far together in the face of disapproval of both families and friends to be turned back and, although it was not ideally the life she would have chosen for herself, it was the one fate had decreed and Roddy was a major part of it.

Roddy is an angel with her and sometimes I think he is the only man to have ever treated Princess Margaret properly," says Colin Tennant. "For instance, they were playing gin rummy one day with Roddy keeping the score. Princess Margaret asked what it was, he passed over the pad, and when she turned the page, there was a message he had written, 'You are looking very beautiful today.' "

When Roddy had met his brother at Heathrow, by chance, two years earlier and found they were both flying across the Atlantic, he had confided after a few drinks that he had not had sex with "anyone" for eight months and, surprisingly for someone who had once set so much store by the physical act, the Princess had found it easy to cope with leading a celibate existence with Roddy, where once her body had ruled her heart. Friends likened her to the great ladies at the court of Louis XIV whose libidos were devoted not to their sex lives, but rather to increasing their sphere of influence.

With Roddy firmly established, Margaret's friends polarized into two camps, those against him and those for. In the former were Jocelyn, whose criticism that Roddy was still making money out of the friendship by selling stories to newspapers and magazines fell on deaf ears, his sister Prue, Sunny, and, most virulent of all, Dominic Elliot. Prue Penn had refused to allow Margaret to bring Roddy to the dance —called the "end of term party"—she gave every August at her Suffolk home, and Margaret had refused to accept, petulantly, in an attempt to force Prue's hand. But in the end she had gone, alone.

The Queen had made it clear that there was no place for Roddy in any of her houses and had met him one Saturday evening on neutral territory at Royal Lodge when, wearing just a shirt and underpants, he had burst in on Nanny Sumner to have a button sewed on, to find her in conversation with the Queen. "Please forgive me, Ma'am, I look so awful," said Roddy, freezing. "Don't worry, I don't look very good myself," she replied and put him at his ease by smiling as she left the room. The next day they were formally introduced by Margaret after church in Windsor.

The pro-Roddy camp included the Willses, the Tennants, the Nevills, Bryan Forbes and Nanette, the Nuttings, the Loewensteins, Norman St. John-Stevas, Lord Weidenfeld and Ned Ryan, who was host to the couple in the country on at least half-a-dozen occasions a year. Regarded as the Princess's "court jester," Ryan escorted her to rock concerts and antique enclaves, and lunched with her in small Chelsea restaurants like Walton's (which was once bombed by the I.R.A.), without her detective in attendance. In 1979, he took over a seven-bedroom house at Ickford, near Oxford, which Anouska had rented. Ryan would employ a cook and a maid for the weekends, and on Fridays, Margaret would arrive, driven in her Ford by her chauffeur, Griffin, with four or five suitcases, which would be unpacked for her. The party would be made up of Roddy, lady-in-waiting Davina and a boyfriend, and Ned with a friend—perhaps Lady Carina Fitzalan Howard, a daughter of the Duke of Norfolk. In the evenings, drinking whisky and Malvern water, Margaret would usually watch television with a supper tray on her lap, eating smoked salmon and scrambled eggs. Breakfast of china tea and a boiled egg would be brought up to her in bed with the newspapers, and by day there would be country walks, invariably expedition "antiquing" in surrounding Cotswold towns and villages in search of silver bargains.

Margaret would always take a nap in the afternoon—she had a bedroom and bathroom to herself, with Roddy down the corridor—and occasionally there would be a dinner party out in the nearby country homes of friends like Jeremy and Rowena Cotton, or drinks before Sunday lunch with Gerald Harford—who had been at Hawtrey's with Roddy—at his home, Little Sodbury Manor. If the Princess had an early engagement on Monday, Griffin would reappear to drive her back to London after tea on Sunday; otherwise the party would break up on Monday mornings. Despite the informality, Roddy would observe the proprieties and call Margaret "Ma'am" in front of the others, while she would address him either as "darling" or "my love." To the others they gave the impression of being very good friends and companions rather than lovers, lapsing from time to time into private jokes and shared memories. Their only display of physical intimacy would be entwined arms on country rambles.

In June, Margaret weekended at Llanvair, with Colin and Anne Tennant as fellow guests, and before her birthday she took Roddy to Spain's Costa del Sol to stay with Mike and Petita Stilianopoulos at their villa in Los Monteros, just outside Marbella. It was the second time they had been there.

"I have a small house surrounded by the grounds of five much larger villas," says the Ambassador. "So we have all the advantages of beautiful gardens without any of the upkeep! And its privacy is ensured."

Margaret returned to Balmoral, with her children, for her forty-ninth birthday and then rejoined Roddy at Glen for their sixth anniversary, which came at a time when his finances were suffering because of his driving ban. Accepting that his recording ambitions could not be resuscitated, he had been concentrating on his landscape business and had landed several commissions, for which he charged between £1,000 and £1,500, to remodel the gardens of London houses. Among his patrons was Lord Buckhurst, who had once briefly "walked out" with the Princess during one of her off-periods with Roddy. The loss of his van made the work uneconomical and Roddy was heard to complain that clients like Lady Buckhurst, the former wife of the Earl of Hopetoun, did not indulge his grandiose plans. He told friends that he was living on just £40 a week. His needs were few, however, and at least two or three times a week he was invited out to parties and dinners organized by public relations firms to launch their clients' products, or given tickets for West End first nights.

On October 12, Margaret began a two week fund-raising tour of America on behalf of the Royal Opera House, which needed £7.8 million to redevelop part of Covent Garden to provide new changing rooms and other urgent facilities. But any hopes of a successful sashay across the States were dashed when a Chicago newspaper columnist, Irv Kupcinet, claimed that the Princess had called the Irish "pigs" during a private dinner party, which was also attended by the city's Mayor, Mrs. Jane Byrne, who had Irish ancestry. In August, Earl Mountbatten, his grandson, and his elder daughter's mother-in-law, had been murdered when the I.R.A. blew up his fishing boat while the family was on holiday in County Sligo, which gave some credibility to the report about Margaret's remark. The Princess, who was not accompanied by a Press Secretary, denied that any such conversation took place, and Nigel Napier attempted without success to smooth the incident over. But in seeking to defuse the situation, Mayor Byrne only served to make it worse by asserting feebly that the Princess had been talking about "Irish jigs."

The explanation was not convincing, and from then on Margaret's progress was blighted by demonstrations from Irish-Americans. In San Francisco, whose Irish population of eighty thousand had been boosted by attendance for a Gaelic games, there were threats to let loose one thousand pigs in her path, and shouts of, "You are a pig" greeted her on her rounds. By the time she reached Los Angeles, at the end of the unhappy tour, a more sinister threat was revealed by the police. Claiming to have uncovered an I.R.A. plot to assassinate the Princess on American soil, Capt. Larry Kramer of the Los Angeles Police Department said: "We've established that the man we are looking for is a high-ranking I.R.A. man. I cannot identify him as the investigation is continuing."

California seemed to be a jinx for Margaret, whose second visit to the West Coast this was in four years. When Hollywood's most eminent producer, Ray Stark, whose wife was the daughter of the legendary Fanny Brice, gave a cocktail party for the Princess, he wheeled out most of the old stars. People like Cary Grant and Gregory Peck were on parade at 6.30 P.M. (Los Angeles is an early town) expecting the Princess's imminent arrival. Unused to Californian punctuality, Margaret did not turn up until a quarter to eight, only to discover that nearly all the celebrities had become restless and stalked off in a pique.

Her efforts raised a derisory $500,000, much of it pledged

even before she left England, and it was with evident relief that Margaret flew to Mustique to be met by Roddy for a fortnight's sunshine. He told her that the Irish population of Fulham had taken their revenge on him by breaking all the pots outside the flat and emptying their contents into his basement area. Apologetic, Margaret explained that there never had been a discussion about either the Irish or the I.R.A. at the dinner, nor had she said anything directly to Mayor Byrne other than the formalities of introduction and farewell. The Princess said she had been the victim of a carefully constructed frame-up in which the worldwide publicity had been orchestrated by someone who had been a guest that evening. The purpose was to discredit the British Monarchy at a crucial point—when funds from Americans for I.R.A. arms were drying up: the "insult" was intended to bring renewed impetus to the flagging I.R.A. drive for funds.

Margaret and Roddy returned to London on Remembrance Sunday, and she watched the moving and simple ceremony at the Cenotaph on television. After laying her wreath, the Queen was driven to Kensington Palace. There were rumors that she had gone to welcome her sister back after an ego-bruising trip, but in fact the Queen went to see bedridden Princess Alice, Countess of Athlone, who lived in the Clock House at the palace and was the last surviving granddaughter of Queen Victoria.

Hopes that further bad publicity might be avoided were thwarted that week when the Princess and Roddy learned that they were implicated in two seamy sets of memoirs, and Margaret, alarmingly, found herself on the sidelines of a sensational murder trial at the Old Bailey. The accused, John Bindon, an East Ender with a criminal record who had turned to acting when given a part in *Poor Cow*, had been twice to Mustique, and had been boasting in Brixton Jail, while on remand waiting trial, that he was an intimate of the

Princess, and had photographs of them together to prove the relationship.

In the winter of 1978, during a fracas at a drinking club in Fulham frequented by gangsters, Bindon had knifed to death an underworld figure called John Darke, and had himself received fearsome wounds in the fight. Fearing mortal reprisals, Bindon had somehow fled to Ireland, where he got himself into the hospital. Afterwards, he had given himself up to the Scotland Yard murder squad, to be charged with Darke's murder. He claimed all along that he had killed in self-defense and, sure of his eventual acquittal, his long-standing girl friend, Vicki Hodge, a sixties model and the daughter of a baronet, began negotiations with the *Daily Mirror* to sell his story, along with a photograph of him with Margaret in Mustique. When Bindon was acquitted, the newspaper offered £40,000, which he readily accepted. The couple hurriedly left Britain for an extended stay in Southern California as the *Mirror* launched the series, devoting much of its front page to a fuzzy picture of Bindon with Margaret in a group in the near background. It was taken on a picnic in Mustique, and an embellished account of Bindon's "close" friendship with the Princess followed. As Vicki—the youngest sister of Wendy Kidd, as it happened—told it, burly Bindon had quickly endeared himself to Margaret with his use of Cockney rhyming slang and fund of risqué stories about his adventures, becoming an integral part of the group.

According to Colin Tennant, the articles were far removed from reality, but Bindon had been in Mustique on the two occasions he claimed. The first time, he had been brought to the island by actress and singer Dana Gillespie, whose bodyguard he had just been on an arduous road tour she had made in America. They had stayed in a villa owned by Dana's aunt, and Bindon had been formally introduced to

Colin, who did not object when he reappeared the following year, 1975, with Vicki, who was estranged from her husband, Ian Heath, son of industrialist Sir Barrie Heath, to stay for a month. "We worked it out that, at most, he had met Princess Margaret on two occasions," says Tennant. "On Mustique we have picnics and invite new arrivals or those who have been around for a while and to whom we haven't spoken and, certainly, Mr. Bindon came to one at which Princess Margaret was present. But he wasn't her guest and I believe he met her briefly, in passing, once more."

Margaret, who pronounced herself "furious" at being misrepresented yet again, had only herself to blame. That Bindon appeared in her company arose from her need to be entertained, even by criminal riffraff. Bindon did have an amusing side and an hour or two of his tales had amused her and added to her fund of gossip. But she firmly maintains that she was always in control of the situation. "As soon as he arrived, my detective recognised him and made sure there was no possibility of an embarrassing situation. Yet there have even been reports of my dancing with the man!"

Most annoyed was Tony, who felt Tennant had been in dereliction of his duty in allowing a potentially explosive situation to develop. The salacious "revelations" caused distress only to David and Sarah, who were teased at school whenever their mother was involved in press reports. "Tony was always very careful to protect the children from gossip. He had such a phobia about them becoming involved and did everything possible to keep them out of the Press," says a friend. As timely consolation, a skiing holiday in Klosters was arranged, to which Lucy brought the baby. It was the second time Lucy had gone abroad with Margaret's son and daughter, and like the previous vacation, when they had drifted in a barge through the French canals with Tony's solicitor, John Humphries, and his family, it was harmonious and happy. David had learned to ski the year before and was busy improving his technique, while Sarah lost her timidity on the slopes and helped with the family chores. "Sunshine holidays with beaches and swimming always bored Tony, which is one reason why he never wanted any part of Mustique," says a friend. "He liked educational holidays which served a purpose."

Meanwhile Margaret and Roddy were bracing themselves to be dragged through the mire again. Dai had been deep in negotiations with the *News of the World* to publish his story and had been closeted in a cheap Paddington hotel for almost a day with one of their reporters, speaking into a tape recorder about his family, Margaret, and his own escapades. This came out during a dinner at Wedgie's, where Dai worked for £200 a week as the "greeter," when Roddy was his guest. "Rods was very jolly at dinner and didn't react to my mentioning the series. The food and drinks were on the house and he kept on saying how well he was being looked after. I told him that if publication went ahead, I would buy him a sunlamp, which he's always wanted."

By Christmas, Dai, who was in severe financial difficulties, had signed a contract for £30,000—a sum which reflected the new revelations about the Princess, for he had sold his "life story" twice before—and was in the process of reading through every page of the final version prepared for printing, and initialling them. "The paper came to me with an offer after they discovered I had some County Court Orders out against me and owed money. I was in a very vulnerable position," says Dai. "I was offered the earth to discuss what they called Roddy's 'sensitive areas,' but I refused. The interviewer kept on trying to get me to talk about homosexuality, and I was told the bigger the disclosure the bigger the fee. As it was, I didn't really know a lot about Roddy's life with Princess Margaret—I had always been kept in the dark."

Roddy was not apprised of the precise content of the series, and seemed good friends with his brother on New Year's Eve when he gave a party at Alexander's, a Chelsea restaurant on the corner of the King's Road and Markham Square (charging his guests £6 a head to help pay for the champagne), and Dai dropped in from his own festivities a few yards across the road at Wedgie's. But a few days later, incensed on learning that at least half the series was being devoted to him and Princess Margaret, he went round to Dai's flat in Harley Street to confront him. "I'm told he is getting £30,000 and all he has offered me is a sun lamp," Roddy said to a friend. "If half of this is about me, he should hand over £15,000—this is the end."

But Roddy (who did not tell Margaret about his attempt to cut himself into his brother's fee), gained no satisfaction, and a week before publication, Dai, who had ceased to take calls from an enraged Roddy, made arrangements to leave the country. "I've written Pa and Roddy notes telling them I've been a naughty boy and asking their forgiveness, but I had to go through with it. The money will pay off all my debts and give me a fresh start—it's as simple as that. If I lose Roddy's friendship, it's the chance I have to take," said Dai, who had booked a package holiday for himself and his girl friend, Vanessa Hubbard, a niece of the Duke of Norfolk, in the Gulf of Aqaba resort of Eilat.

When the first of four installments was published on Sunday, January 20, Sir Harry was the most horrified of all the Llewellyns. He said the family had been "humiliated" and they were all deeply ashamed of Dai's treachery in selling family secrets about Margaret, her visits to Llanvair, and her affair with Roddy. He took issue also with Dai's claim that

(221)

had Margaret not been a Princess, Harry would have disapproved of the relationship. "Nothing could be further from the truth. I do disapprove and think she is quite wrong for Roddy and has ruined him," says Sir Harry. "But one has to be civil and when he invited the Princess to stay, we welcomed her into the house, just like any other girl friend of his, although I have been against this friendship from the beginning."

When Margaret was offered the article by Roddy, she declined to read it. So much, she said, that had been written about her over the years had been rubbish. "I've been misreported and misrepresented since the age of seventeen and I gave up long ago reading about myself," she says.

The second part, promised for January 27, was viewed by Roddy, if not the Princess—who refused to discuss the subject further—with trepidation lest it delved into the "sensitive" areas of Haslam and the suicide attempts. Equally anxious was Lady Jackie, who had been in her country home near Newbury when she read a trailer that said that part two was about "the other woman who went from Snowdon to Roddy." She knew it could refer only to her and suspected that the text would be accompanied by some highly unflattering photographs taken of her in the sixties for a coffee-table book called *Birds of Britain*. Happily married, but with a husband prickly over her past, Lady Jackie went to her solicitor to discuss the possibility of an injunction and to find out what other legal remedies were open to her. She sought out Roddy and asked him to sign a statement that there had never been anything physical between them. "It's absurd of Dai to say I was Roddy's first woman," said Lady Jackie, who had learned that Dai claimed that she had been a girl friend of both brothers. "Roddy isn't like that and it was me, after all, who arranged for him to meet Haslam."

As pressures mounted during the week, Roddy became

jittery and resorted to taking tranquilizers. He told Jackie, who bearded him in his basement, that he did not want to become involved, but her threat of legal action did cause the *News of the World* to tone down Dai's recollection of events. "Jackie came round with Mark and wanted me to swear an affidavit that nothing had happened between us," says Roddy. "I told them I wasn't able to."

The installment did resurrect an apocryphal story about Sir Harry, who, on hearing of Roddy's involvement with the Princess, exclaimed: "Well, at least it makes a change from Italian waiters!"

Midway through the disclosures, Dai flew back to host a function at his club and discovered that the London gossip columns had been universal in their condemnation of his action. The *Daily Express* referred to him as "Judas" and his payment as "thirty thousand pieces of silver." When called by his elder son, Sir Harry told him he could not expect any sympathy from any quarter. "I think David was surprised that he took such a pasting from his friends over the series. His attitude was: today's gossip column is tomorrow's fish and chips, but I warned him all along he was wrong. If you write a load of tripe like that and describe your brother as a pansy, surely you must expect to run into flack? I said, David, you've cooked yourself here. You should get out of England, but of course he took no notice."

Early one morning at Wedgie's, Dai received a telephone call from Roddy, who accused him of a "gross betrayal" and told him that both Princess Margaret and himself hated him. "He sounded as if he was either very drunk or very stoned and he went on and on saying I was the most horrible person in the world and that he loathed my guts," says Dai, who discovered soon afterwards that Vanessa was pregnant. They made plans hastily for a March wedding—as a Roman Catholic Vanessa would not entertain the idea of an abortion—at

Morton Hall near Bury St. Edmund's, the Suffolk home of her parents, Lt. Comdr. Theodore and Lady Miriam Hubbard. Roddy was invited to be an usher, but he refused to even answer the wedding invitation, and three days before the ceremony, he telephoned Morton Hall. "Again it was in the middle of the night and, as before, he sounded drunk, slurred," says Dai. "In a hazy fashion he kept on telling Vanessa's parents that they should not let her marry me. He said I was awful, revolting, that sort of thing. It wasn't a new tack. When we were younger, Roddy used to go round to every member of the family, saying I was behaving irresponsibly, that I had girls coming in, that I was doing this, doing that. And I learned much later that he used to go to my girl friends, beseeching them to leave me because I was such a terrible chap. Apparently he said that to all of them."

For Princess Margaret, Dai's devious actions simply confirmed to her once more what Roddy had always said about his brother's uncaring and selfish attitude. On the few occasions she had met him, she said, she had not been taken in by his enveloping charm and had preferred to believe Roddy's stories of how he had suffered at Dai's hands over the years, being forced to exist in his Corinthian shadow, and made to feel second best. Margaret urged Roddy to have no more to do with him and, in no mood to disagree, he vowed never to speak to his brother again.

"That's the trouble with Roddy, he badmouths Pa and me to Princess Margaret and she is taken in by his side of the story," says Dai. "It's not as if I let Roddy down over the years, I've been protecting him far too long. When Pa discovered all those things about Roddy's life after the first suicide attempt, he was bitterly upset, but I'd known all along about them and kept it a complete secret from Pa. I've never let Roddy down, yet I've hardly known an instance when I've helped him and he hasn't kicked me in the teeth.

Roddy has been dealt the most awful blows with his illnesses and operations, but when we were young, nobody used to care about my needs. They devoted themselves instead to Roddy's.

"When he was being difficult, Pa used to say sarcastically, 'Right, everybody stop, I think Roddy's unhappy. Let's switch off the television and all sit round and say, there, there Roddy.' He's only been an achiever in a suicidal sense —after all he wasn't going to threaten it unless he wanted something and it was, for instance, quite an effective way of getting himself a free flat. With Roddy it's always been, 'Look at me, look at me.' He's never been a part of the set that I have, just hanging round the edges and resenting it. I have no interest in his friends—they are the most awful bunch of hippies and queers and I can't stand them. They sit round all evening talking about each other's neuroses."

In January, which Margaret had arranged to be kept free of engagements, public and otherwise, she underwent plastic surgery for the removal of lesions to her jawline and under her chin. The press claimed that she had undergone a full face-lift and, indeed, when she was photographed next, there was no hint of the double chin which had been threatening her profile for a year or so, and she did look much younger and prettier than she had been for some time. Her appearance was helped by the fact that she had slimmed down— perhaps fifteen pounds—and Roddy told friends there was no question of her having had major cosmetic surgery. "All she had done was to have a few bumps removed which her doctor told her would have become larger if they weren't operated on. No one could call that a face-lift."

As the Princess prepared to "sun-up" with Roddy in Mustique, where a new air-conditioned double bedroom had been added to Les Jolies Eaux for his own comfort, her Civil List allowance was being increased by £10,500 to £82,000, while the total disbursement to the royal family rose from £2,778,400 to £3,317,000 accompanied by the usual furor of protest, focussed on Margaret. During 1979, her official appearances totalled 113, eight less than Princess Anne, while the Queen undertook 325, Prince Philip 243, and Prince Charles 194. "The increase doesn't pay for the stamps," says the Princess. "People don't seem to realise that rises are needed because I employ people who need rises. I don't know why Nigel Napier stays with me, he's paid so little. It must be loyalty, and I'm very grateful."

As Private Secretary, Comptroller and Equerry, Napier, a former Scots Guards major, had been paid less than £10,000 a year, and he had suffered a serious financial reversal when the Lloyd's syndicate of which he was an underwriting member, had collapsed with debts estimated at £21.5 million. For a while it appeared that his personal share of the debacle would be in the region of £120,000, but after litigation between syndicate members and Lloyd's, the obligation was reduced to around £40,000. Apart from Napier's salary, the Princess's Civil List met the wages of her butler, John Leishman, who used to be a footman at Clarence House, Mrs. McIntryre, the housekeeper, ladies' maid Mrs. Greenfield, chauffeur Griffin, a cook and two daily cleaning ladies, as well as her lady-in-waiting—Davina had retired after nearly five years and been succeeded by Lizzie Paget. The household was pretty much the same complement as when she had married Tony, but in those days her staff wages bill had been less than half her £15,000 annual allowance.

The night before they left for the Caribbean, Roddy and his suitcase were collected from Fulham, by the chauffeur, to stay at Kensington Palace. Lord and Lady Buckhurst arrived early the next morning to accompany them to the airport. "You know how it is with Roddy, he tends to disappear and you have to capture him when you can," says the Princess. "But even with the Buckhursts especially there with us at the airport, the only photographs the next day in the press were of Roddy and me. You'd have thought they would have tired of it by now."

While they were away, *Private Eye*, the satirical magazine which had been the first to print an item about the romance and has mercilessly lampooned the couple since, came out with a story that far from being furious with Dai, Roddy was in cahoots with him and had shared the payment from the *News of the World*. It went on to state that the Princess was now enjoying the fruits of these ill-gotten gains by taking a holiday in the West Indies. With this jibe, Roddy's patience with the press snapped, and he issued his first writ for libel, demanding a retraction and apology, and asking for a suitable sum by way of damages. When he had embarked on his singing career, the *Eye*, read by more than one million people in Britain, had produced a cover of a picture with Princess Margaret talking to comedian Frankie Howerd after he had been presented to her at a charity first night. The bubble from his mouth had him asking where the Queen was, to which her bubble replied: "He's at the recording studios!"

Roddy had shown the cover to Margaret and had said to her, somewhat rhetorically, "You've got to laugh, haven't you?" But on this occasion he found no humor in her being implicated in allegedly underhand dealings and deceit. "They've made fun of me for years, called me a poof, printed lie after lie, all, obviously, in the hope that I would take them to court so that I could be questioned about my friendship with Princess Margaret," says Roddy. "There's been so much inaccurate rubbish written about us and this time they went too far suggesting she was enjoying the fruits of dishonesty. People know they can get away with it because Princess Margaret cannot sue."

The magazine eventually admitted their story was a fabrication and apologized to Roddy, paying his costs and £1,000 in damages, and printing an apology. Meanwhile Dai found himself in court over his series. He received writs for libel from Jonathan Aitken and Michael Goodeve-Docker, the former headmaster of Hawtrey's. The M.P. objected to Dai claiming that he had been a guest at a party in Marbella given by a fugitive from British justice, and Goodeve-Docker, who had retired to Suffolk with his wife, took issue with Dai's assertion that beatings were so barbarous at the preparatory school that it could have been prosecuted. He was unable to substantiate either allegation and had to make an apology in open court to each, paying damages and costs in excess of £5,000 from his own pocket, as the *News of the World* maintained they had been misled.

In March, Margaret exchanged the tropic heat of Mustique for the sub-zero temperatures of West Germany. She incurred another bad press there when, on the nineteenth, she arrived in a black Daimler at Barossa Barracks in Hemer to inspect a guard of honor of the 1st Battalion the Royal Highland Fusiliers, also called Princess Margaret's Own Glasgow and Ayrshire Regiment. Apparently stunned by the cold and icy wind as she stepped from the limousine, she failed to respond to the salute and welcome of Lt. Col. John Drummond, and immediately climbed back into her car, leaving a pipe band, which had practiced special tunes, mute, and the guard uninspected. Instead she was driven one hundred yards to the Officer's Mess, where she asked for a gin and tonic to revive her circulation. Two days later she travelled by helicopter to Paderborn, to take the salute at a march past of the 15th/19th Hussars, of which she was also the colonel-in-chief. She managed to do this, but although the weather was slightly less inclement, she did not inspect the guard. It was suggested that she had been suffering from the aftereffects of a migraine, but her office said it had not been aware of any illness.

EPILOGUE

Bad health continued to stalk the Princess on the official sixteen-day tour she undertook of the Far East, beginning on April 23, 1980. The rich fare of the Philippines, and hospitality at the Presidential Malacanan Palace with its rooftop discotheque, where her hostess, Mme. Imelda Marcos, often danced until dawn (explaining that she needed only two hours sleep a night), proved unsettling. Even though all members of royal tours take preventative medical precautions, events on one of her five days in Manila had to be cancelled. The bug resurfaced when she arrived in Kuala Lumpur, after a stop in Singapore, and Margaret was advised to cancel the last stage, which she did, with public regret, as she was only too well aware that she was, yet again, letting down part of her foreign fan club.

While she was away, Roddy attempted to organize some of her closest friends into a committee to plan a special celebration for her milestone fiftieth birthday, after she spent the day itself at Balmoral with her family. He approached the Tennants but soon found out that others were unwilling to involve themselves in his project and, for financial reasons as much as any other, he backed out. "I wanted to give her a party in the autumn in a private London house, but couldn't find one and my idea was taken over by those I call 'the courtiers,' " says Roddy, who concentrated instead on writing a book, with many of his own illustrations, on *Town Gardens* for Lord Weidenfeld. He was paid a £1,000 advance, with a further £1,000 promised on delivery of the sixty-thousand word manuscript, and a final £1,000 on publication. It was published on September 17, 1981.

The apathy towards Roddy's rather thoughtful initiative stemmed from the Queen's attitude. She said she would be unable to attend any function at which Roddy was a cohost: it would have been tantamount to giving the relationship official blessing. This, the Queen had always made clear to her sister, was something she could never do, with the inherent danger of the throne itself being dragged into his antics in the same way Margaret had been in the past. A new committee was formed, with Lord and Lady Rupert Nevill, Jocelyn Stevens, John and Jean Wills, John and Diane Nutting, Sir Geoffrey and Lady Elizabeth Shakerley (Lichfield's sister), Eric and Prue Penn, Ned Ryan, Dominic Elliot, and Lord and Lady Westbury. The only convenient date when all the Royal Family—except the Duke and Duchess of Kent who would be on an official tour of the Antipodes—was available was Tuesday, November 4, and Jocelyn suggested holding the party at the Ritz, the Piccadilly hotel owned by the Trafalgar House Group, of which Express Newspapers was a subsidiary, and he the Deputy Chairman.

The cost was to be divided equally among the fifteen members who would compile the invitation list, and Jocelyn assured them that the hotel would discount the bill because of the tremendous publicity the party would bring. The Royal Family would head the forty who would dine at four tables at the Ritz, and a further one hundred and forty guests of all ages would arrive after 10:30 P.M. to dance at a discotheque, while all drinks, from champagne and wines to liquor and liqueurs, would be served until 3 A.M., with breakfast from 1 A.M.

But during the summer, while Margaret and Roddy spent weekends at another country house Ryan had taken, near Cirencester, there was dissension among the committee over

Roddy. Margaret wanted him at the dinner, while the Queen did not wish him to attend at all, and Dommie Elliot, not Llewellyn's greatest admirer, took the Queen's part much to the fury of Margaret. A friendship of thirty years standing ended in an explosive argument, with the Princess telling Elliot that she did not wish to see him again. He left the committee and declined the invitation when he received it, but the problem remained. Eventually the Queen relented to the extent of allowing that Roddy might come later in the evening. To their mortification, the Tennants, because their friendship with Margaret assured them of an honored place at the feast, were told to feed Roddy. When they arrived around 11 P.M., with Colin in a snappy, velvet-faced dinner jacket, Lady Anne sniffed to a friend: "We feel just like the servants, being invited in after dinner." Snowdon was not asked to the party, although David and Sarah took time off from school to attend in a young group which included Prince Andrew (Prince Edward remained at Gordonstoun).

Roddy was treated politely, but felt shunned, and kept away from members of the Royal Family, while Princess Margaret danced with Lord Rupert and Ryan, between whom she had sat at dinner. He still had not met Prince Philip, had spoken briefly once to Charles at a Kensington Palace dinner party, and knew it would be a false move if he attempted to engage the Queen Mother in conversation (it was his proud boast that he had once waltzed with her) when she was among her own. After a while Roddy made his way to the table, near the dance floor, reserved for the guest of honor, and found the very attractive Begum Aga Khan, whose husband had remained in France, sitting with the Princess. "It was obvious that Roddy was itching to dance with her just to draw attention to himself and it was the very last thing the Begum wanted to do—for one thing she's much taller than he is," says a friend of hers. "But eventually Princess Margaret practically ordered her on to the floor and off she went with Roddy, very reluctantly. It was almost the end of the evening before Roddy had his dance with PM, after the Queen and Prince Philip had gone."

Among Margaret's friends, opinions were divided during the autumn as to how much longer such a sterile relationship would last. All were unanimous that if it was to end, the move would have to be made by the Princess, as Roddy appeared stuck to her as fast as a limpet. Stevens and Ryan felt that it would just fizzle out and openly forecast that it would be all over in months. The signs were there: the couple no longer seemed to invigorate each other, and although there was undeniable affection, it was born of long-term habit. Tennant, who was preparing to welcome them back to Mustique in the middle of February, and entertained Sir John Mills and his wife Mary Hayley Bell on the island over Christmas, argued that there was no reason why they should not remain together, perhaps forever. "They need each other," he explained, noting that neither had shown any inclination to search for another partner.

Certainly Roddy did not appear anxious to alter the status quo. In April, Claude Wolff had terminated their agreement when it still had a year to run, cutting off his last source of income, and the lack of driving license, not due to be restored until January 6, 1981, prevented his seeking an alternative. Weidenfeld's book contract apart, Roddy's income during 1980 had been less than he might have pocketed by joining the dole queue, but his outgoings were mercifully small. For holidays in the sun, weekends in the country, and meals during the week, he relied on Margaret's patronage, augmented by the occasional public relations freebie. Some called his way of life shameless sponging, but others, more charitably, put it down as the price to be paid for companionship.

"I know this age business is funny, but there it is. My conscience is clear and I've kept my pride through it all. In difficult circumstances, I feel I have coped very well," Roddy used to say. "Before I met Princess Margaret, I was never very certain what was going on and seldom formulated my own ideas. I just let life go by. I was characterless, very weak, and now I am strong. If our relationship ended, life for me would rather lose its point. We sing, we dance, we're generally happy and I don't see why things should not continue as they are forever."

For his thirty-third birthday last October, Roddy was given a "free" party at a brash Covent Garden discotheque by its Manchester-born owner, Peter Stringfellow, who, no doubt, anticipated some return in the gossip columns. It would have been unseemly for the Princess to have lent herself to such a commercial occasion (journalists were actually invited by the management to "watch" the festivities), but Roddy asked about twenty friends, who were treated to a buffet dinner with champagne and wines, and during the evening a telephone call came for him from, it was said, Margaret. Among those present was Tania Soskin, a freelance travel writer who had trained as a dress designer with Dior in Paris and had been the co-owner of Tsaritsa, a Belgravia boutique during the seventies. Daughter of the late Paul Soskin, a modestly successful film producer of the Sir Alexander Korda era, and three months Roddy's junior, Tania is darkly pretty, with a good figure and large bosom. Roddy had known her since 1971 when she was living with John Rendall (their affair lasted for nearly four years) in the days before Parsenn Sally. They had met up again during the summer, when she returned to London from Paris and gave a few cocktail parties to reintroduce herself. Roddy has told friends that his love for Tania grew from that birthday night, seven years and a month after he had fallen in love with Margaret at Glen.

No mention of his feelings for Tania was made by him, however, to the Princess, although she was aware that Tania had accompanied him on a trip to Los Angeles, and at the start of the Christmas holidays, she busied herself with David and Sarah. On his return from California, where he was reported to be looking for gardening commissions from Hollywood stars, Roddy took Tania down to Llanvair to meet his parents and away at weekends to stay with old friends like Johnny and Wendy Kidd, who became aware of the new development in his life when he asked for a double bedroom—on previous visits with the Princess it had been separate rooms. On December 29, the *Daily Mail* announced that Roddy had found a new love, and printed a photograph of him dining out with Tania in London. Curiously enough, Margaret did not read the newspaper that day and no one saw fit to bring the item to her attention. She was to remain in total ignorance of the affair for a further seven weeks.

With William and Anne Buckhurst, Margaret and Roddy were driven to Heathrow on February 13 to catch a flight to Barbados en route to Mustique for a three-week stay. Although they were travelling on economy tickets, they were given the lounge above First Class in the bubble of the British Airways 747, next to the cockpit, and were joined by wine-merchant Simon Parker Bowles and his Australian wife, Carolyn, friends of Buckhurst who just happened to be on that flight. The Parker Bowles had been invited to stay in Barbados by Lady Vestey, the estranged wife of the multi-millionaire beef baron, at her rented villa near Sandy Lane. On the flight, Roddy was surly and taciturn and Parker

(235)

Bowles, who did not know him very well, turned to Buckhurst at one point, when Llewellyn was elsewhere, and asked: "Is he always as rude as that?" Buckhurst replied that it was unusual behavior.

Reporting the departure, the *Sun* newspaper ventured that Margaret and Roddy had never looked so happy together and claimed, ludicrously, that the couple had "packed" Valentine cards to put in front of each other at the breakfast table the next morning. In fact there was more than the problem of Tania weighing on Roddy's mind. He had no money with him, and before he left, he had told a friend that his telephone was in danger of being cut off as he could not afford to settle the account, and that other important bills were unpaid. Princess Margaret, who was travelling on to North America for an official visit, had been looking forward to the break: for company there were her houseguests—the Buckhursts were leaving after ten days to be replaced by Reinaldo and Carolina Herrera—and Tennant; Lichfield had lent his gatehouse for the honeymoon of his land agent, Major Rodney Haszard, formerly of the King's Shropshire Light Infantry, and his new wife Serena; the Duke and Duchess of Kent were making a return visit to stay at the villa of Tory Arts Minister Paul Channon, a Guinness heir, and there were other friends like Diana Heimann (daughter of the late Iain Macleod, the Tory politician) and her South African husband, David.

On the second evening, an unusually tense Roddy took Buckhurst for a walk to the gazebo in the garden of Les Jolies Eaux, saying that he had something he wanted to tell him. "I'm in love," said Roddy, to which Buckhurst answered that of course he knew he was, motioning towards the villa and Princess Margaret. "No, no, not her, it's someone else," Roddy shot back, then unburdened himself about Tania. Buckhurst, whose first sight of Llewellyn, fifteen years earlier at Aix, had been of a young man in a hacking jacket and cavalry twill trousers blowing a hunting horn, inquired if the Princess knew, and Roddy answered that he had not told her. Buckhurst advised him to do so as soon as possible. Three more days went by before matters came to a head and Margaret tackled Roddy to find out exactly what was wrong with him, and why his inexplicable brooding behavior was ruining her holiday.

"I forced the story out of him eventually. He told me he was in love and wanted to marry the woman. I had absolutely no idea it had been going on," a visibly shocked Margaret—who said she had been "jarred" by the revelation —told friends like Tennant, following Roddy's confession. For her there was inevitable heartache and sadness but also, she was to remember later, a profound sense of relief. Whenever she had mused over how this particular chapter in her life would end, she had never dreamed that it could close with Roddy leaving her to marry. He had always insisted he was too selfish and set in his ways to settle down and did not want a family, yet here he was talking of having children. For once jealousy did not enter into her emotions, and with a touch of pragmatism, she urged Roddy to propose to Tania as soon as he returned to London, giving him her blessing. "I'm really very happy for him," she said later —"anyway, I couldn't have afforded him much longer!"

When the Buckhursts departed from Barbados, Margaret, who was still in low spirits and gaining no comfort from Roddy's presence, asked them to find Ned Ryan, who had called to say he was on the island but had not left a return number, to tell him to come to Mustique as soon as possible to help cheer her up. "We rang every hotel in Barbados but couldn't find him," says Buckhurst. "It was all right in the end though because he telephoned Princess Margaret independently and then went over for five days." The consensus of opinion was that, all in all, it had been a remarkably tidy ending. There had always been a thought in the back of Margaret's mind that if she had ended the relationship, Roddy might have done something silly, and Colin had some good advice for her. "She had spent so long worrying about Roddy, mothering and looking after him that she had been neglecting her own best interests," says Tennant. "I told her that she should start thinking about herself for a change and be selfish. That appealed to her."

When Margaret returned to London from New York, she gave a small luncheon party at Kensington Palace for Roddy and Tania, inviting the Buckhursts, Ryan, and Lord Rupert Nevill. Roddy sat on the Princess's left. The menu included prawn cocktail, followed by out-of-season pheasant from the deep freeze, and the cheerful occasion—the Princess made Tania feel at ease from the beginning—set her official seal on the engagement, which was announced in the *Times* on April 4.

Margaret told the couple she would be delighted to attend their wedding and, after consulting her engagement book as to her availability, June 27 was chosen. With Ned Ryan agreeing to be best man, Roddy chose his local church of Llanvair Kilgeddin, which holds one hundred and twenty people, with a reception afterwards at Llanvair Grange, as Tania's mother, Minora, had remarried and lived in Cairo. But when the date and venue were changed to July 11, in Marlow, where Tania's uncle, retired solicitor John Davidson, had a home and a nursery garden business, Margaret was forced to cry off, since she was scheduled then to accompany the Royal Ballet on its Fiftieth Anniversary tour to Canada and Washington. Roddy explained the change on the grounds that it had been impossible to organize the event so far from London, and the church at Llanvair really was not big enough for the number of guests they intended to invite. There were rumblings in the press that Sir Harry did not approve of his younger son's choice and had called her "a witch" but this he denies. "Ever since I met Tania last year, when Roddy brought her down to Llanvair after she returned from Paris, I thought her a charming girl. I thoroughly approve of their marriage and think they are both lucky in finding each other," he says. "I was perfectly happy to have the wedding reception here at Llanvair, but Tania's mother, Mrs. Simaika, said that the church had too limited a capacity, it was difficult to arrange a wedding one hundred and fifty miles from London, and she felt it would be much easier from her brother's house at Marlow."

It had been a gracious but misguided move by Margaret to accept the wedding invitation in the first place; her presence there would have given the media a field day, and her advisers had foreseen with alarm the inevitable headlines of "the rejected Princess" beneath her photograph in the Sunday newspapers. "I think it would have been all right," says the Princess, "as I intended to go with a lot of friends." The Queen, naturally, was delighted that circumstances had prevented this one final embarrassment, and hoped that her sister's next "companion" would prove to be more appropriate to her position. Only the Queen Mother showed genuine sadness over the departure of Roddy. She saw how Margaret had been amused by his company, told friends how he had made her laugh, and thought that he had aided her through a difficult period for, Roddy or no Roddy, the separation and divorce from Tony had been inevitable.

On July 6, Margaret flew to Ontario on board a Royal Canadian Air Force 707 with her daughter Sarah, who was making her first official trip. They met up with the Queen Mother, who was ending a six-day visit to the Dominion. In the wake of the fiery greeting accorded Prince Charles on a twenty-four-hour stay in New York—when four thousand screaming pro-I.R.A. demonstrators chanted outside the Metropolitan Opera House and several inside halted a gala performance of the Royal Ballet—the Washington part of the Princess's tour had been cancelled on government advice. While she was away, Roddy and Tania were wed at All Saints, Marlow, with a Welsh choir singing hymns; Margaret sent a solid silver cigarette case engraved with flowers and leaves. When Davina Woodhouse, who had become an extra Lady-in-Waiting, married Earl Alexander of Tunis on July 22, Margaret graced the House of Lords reception which followed a service of blessing (Alexander's first marriage to banana heiress Gussie van Geest had been dissolved).

Another wedding in July, that of her favorite nephew, gave Margaret cause for optimism about her own future. With the new Princess of Wales set to start a family quickly—Charles was thirty-three in November—and demote Margaret further down the line of succession to the throne (she is seventh), Margaret felt that, perhaps, her long-held reservations about remarriage were no longer valid and that the climate of opinion was altering enough to allow her to give the matter serious consideration if the opportunity was to arise. She had become reconciled with Elliot and as, freed of Roddy, she was moving back into a more mature circle, her appetite for official duties increased. She knew the more she put herself about, the greater was the chance of meeting new people and making contact again with lost friends and acquaintances, among whom there might just be the man for her. . . .

"Princess Margaret has begun to feel that, somewhere out there, there is the man for her," says a close friend. "Someone of her own age-group, who is amusing, attractive, rich and with time to share her life, as she will never give up performing royal duties. Since Roddy went, I have heard her mention marriage once or twice. She believes it could be possible for her now."

No doubt both David and Sarah would welcome such an eventuality, having seen the success of their father's second marriage and his happiness following the bitterness of the years leading up to the divorce. But, in rational moments, the Princess says: "I'm back to where I started with Peter but this time I'm divorced. One couldn't get married in this country—look at Prince Michael and Marie-Christine who had to do it in Vienna. Remarriage would be a devil of a trouble and one would not want to be a bind to one's family. But if one did find someone nice. . . ."

After the wedding of Prince Charles and Lady Diana, David and Sarah went to Italy with their father, stepmother Lucy, and half-sister Frances for three weeks to stay in a rented house at Asolo in the Dolomites, and they missed their mother's fifty-first birthday, which she spent at Balmoral. During the summer, Colin Tennant gave a ten-year lease on Glen and its estate to Thomas Renwick, who already ran three of the farms and planned to rent out the facilities to parties of up to twenty-five people, especially during the shooting season. "Mr. Tennant was so tied up with his businesses elsewhere that the house was hardly ever being used," said Renwick. "He was thinking of closing the place down for part of the year, until I came up with a proposal to rent it from him and then sublet it."

The cutting of Colin's links with Glen, where Margaret had first stayed with him during that heady summer of 1954, was another break in the pattern of Margaret's life but before her birthday she, too, was on holiday in Italy accompanied by Colin and Anne who, like all her other old friends, noted that she was at peace with herself and in buoyant spirits, excited at the promise of the future. The past, with its perverse meanderings of fate, seemed to her like a foreign country.

"Princess Margaret wants someone to look after her and she's confident that she will find him," says the close friend. "And this time she says she is going to live happily ever after—just like Princesses are supposed to."